Praise for *Entering Hekate's Garden*

"Cyndi Brannen has taken the seeds of ancient and classical lore and grown something lush, beautiful, new, and extremely beneficial for any modern witch, while also maintaining the historical roots. I greatly enjoy all of Cyndi's works and books, but *Entering Hekate's Garden* is by far my favorite of hers to date. I know it will be a book that I reference often in my personal magickal practice and devotional work."

—Mat Auryn, author of *Psychic Witch:
A Metaphysical Guide to Meditation,
Magick, and Manifestation*

Cyndi Brannen has written a profound, complex, and beautifully rich body of work. For those called by Hekate, the botanical lore and practices in this book serve to deepen a potently transformative and devotional path and practice. I truly believe we are witnessing a sacred download of wisdom and guidance through Cyndi's books."

—Elena Rego, creator and
owner of The Witches Box

"One cannot talk about Hekate without eventually talking about Medea and Circe. One cannot discuss the magic of these witches without talking about plants. For the Greeks, *pharmakeia* was synonymous with magic. In *Entering Hekate's Garden*, Cyndi Brannen manages to provide a cornucopia of plant magic that will be useful for anyone interested in Hekatean magic. I expect to be referencing the recipes and lore for years to come."

—Jason Miller, author of
The Elementsof Spellcrafting

"*Entering Hekate's Garden* initiates the reader into the magickal realm of herbs, medicine, and plant-spirit witchcraft by unveiling knowledge, rites, herbal infusions, recipes, and spells made for the serious witch. Brannen uses Hekate and her daughters Medea and Circe to navigate the occult world of botanicals and mythology. Beautifully written, *Entering Hekate's Garden* is necessary for every witch and student of the craft!"

—Lawren Leo, author of *Horse Magick:*
Spells and Rituals for Self-Empowerment,
Protection, and Prosperity

"Cyndi Brannen's gorgeously written *Entering Hekate's Garden* is not your average herbal. Its clear instructions, straightforward exercises, and incredibly detailed individual plant entries will be a long-time valuable tool for any witch who has already stained their fingers green, as well as those who've not yet stepped one foot into the garden. If you walk the Poison Path, read this. If you're an herbalist, read this. If you think you can't hear the voices of plant spirits, definitely read this. The torches are lit and the gate has been opened. Hekate awaits!"

—Tara-Love Maguire, coauthor of *Besom, Stang,*
and Sword: A Guide to Traditional Witchcraft, the
Six-Fold Path, and the Hidden Landscape

"*Entering Hekate's Garden* removes the veil of separation between the reader and the magical world of plants. Cyndi Brannen generously shares her wisdom about thirty-nine species of plants associated with Hekate. Her deep insights on identification, harvesting, preparation, and spellwork can only be described as masterful. It's sure to inspire anyone interested in deepening their connection with herbalism or modern Hekatean witchcraft."

—Astrea Taylor, author of *Intuitive Witchcraft:*
How to Use Intuition to Elevate Your Craft

Entering
Hekate's Garden

The Magick, Medicine & Mystery
of Plant Spirit Witchcraft

CYNDI BRANNEN

WEISER BOOKS

This edition first published in 2020 by Weiser Books, an imprint of
Red Wheel/Weiser, LLC
With offices at:
65 Parker Street, Suite 7
Newburyport, MA 01950
www.redwheelweiser.com

ISBN: 978-1-57863-722-5
Library of Congress Cataloging-in-Publication Data available upon request.

Cover design by Kathryn Sky-Peck
Interior images by Vlada Young/Shutterstock
Interior by Jane Hagaman
Typeset in Goudy

Printed in Canada
MAR

10 9 8 7 6 5 4 3 2 1

For A and T,

my branches and roots.

Table of Contents

I. *Prolog*—Medea's Truth   1

II. *Nyssa*—The Call   5

III. *Origio*—The Source   11

IV. *Praeparatio*—The Foundation   25

V. *Ratio*—The System   33

VI. *Practica*—The Process   45

VII. *Hieros Pyr*—The Fire   69

VIII. *Gnosis*—The Knowledge   77

IX. *Magikeia*—The Spell   209

X. *Sibylika*—The Prophecy   233

XI. *Agia*—The Sacred   239

XII. *Sophia*—The Wisdom   247

XIII. *Initio*—The Mystery   259

Acknowledgments   267

Sources and Further Reading   269

The Garden of the Goddess beckons.

Hekate is Mother of the Eternal Garden,

   With her first breath she created the Green World and her witches.

   Her daughters are our sisters.

   Eternal Circe and Medea,

And the others.

   They are the witches' great teachers and companions.

   High Priestesses of the Garden.

They offer the keys to their magick, medicine, and mystery.

Will you claim them?

I. PROLOG

Medea's Truth

There are many stories told about us. Few of them are true. You already know that, for you are one of us. This is not a new story for you, but a memory long forgotten, now awakened. The plants of our Mother called out and you answered. Return with me now to her Garden. Sit within her sacred grove and remember.

In the beginning, there was only darkness and light. They bore a child who became our Mother. With her first breath she created the universe, and with her second, her children. She, in her infinite wisdom, made us of her, uniquely crafted so we could summon the spirits of the world she created for our use. Hekate knew that, without challenges to temper our talents, we would quickly become restless, so she created the others so that we might learn from them. Their love and hate taught us the lessons necessary so we could transcend our weaknesses. They were the humans, and we were her witches.

Mother knows best, although we often fail to see this. She created me and my sister, and all the witches, including you, are our descendants. She taught us medicine to heal ourselves and others. This medicine did not merely ease our suffering, but offered us entrance into her mysteries. She desired us to understand pain so that we could experience joy. We acquired power through weakness and hope through despair. Our companions were her *Pharmakoi Kyrios*, the plant masters, whom we wove into our charms and spells. They protected us from the harms of the humans who feared us. We were, and remain, one with her plants.

Our ways were not welcome by those who feared our power. At their hands, we suffered greatly. Through their words, we were reviled. It is now time for you to remember the truth and cast aside their lies. We are rising.

The men created their own gods, forever reminding Mother that she, too, must bear her burdens. These gods, made in the image of men, feared Mother.

They sought to rob us of our rightful inheritance, that of the Green World. Through their so-called civilization, they defiled the natural ways. But you already know this.

When I was young, I thought that I knew everything. I would not listen to Mother. She knew that my willfulness needed to be tempered through experience, so she did not interfere with my foolishness. Most likely, you have already learned this. Mother waits. She welcomes us into her sacred grove when we are ready. There are times when we rush into her Garden without thought. Perhaps you, like me, have denigrated her treasures in order to please a man. This was my failure, or so it would appear if you believe the stories they tell about me. Truth be told, it was my necessary lesson. I had to learn not to give away my power to the unworthy.

Jason came to me, not out of affection, but out of greed. He had heard of my powers, such as they were, when I was young. They are much stronger now. Even in my youth, they were considerable. Jason's gods preyed upon his ambitions. They instructed him on how to seduce me. Lonely as I was, I succumbed easily. Not only did I welcome him into Hekate's Garden, but I put a spell on the guardian of one of the most sacred *pharmakoi*, whom you call oak. This was the Tree of Knowledge, whose branches held the most powerful medicine. The serpent who protected this medicine I put to sleep in the name of my desire. That much of the story is true.

Most of what you've heard has been twisted to make me the villain. This is a lie. Jason was a violent and greedy prince. I was heartbroken after all I had done to earn his affection. You see, I had raised his father from the dead, banished his enemies, and assured his power, only to be cast aside on his whim. What they tell you is that I killed my children. If I were to concern myself with the beliefs of humans, this is the only part of the story that would bother me. Look into your heart, for mine is within yours. You know I didn't murder them. They live on still, as your angels and guides. I merely spared them the burdens of humanity. As for the serpent who guarded the oak, he has pulled my chariot across the Starry Road ever since.

My sister has always been stronger than me. You know her name, for she has returned to your world. Circe has spoken. We all must heed. Yes, I still can have my moments of pettiness when it comes to her. I languished with Jason while she flourished on her island. She would tell you how she suffered at the hands of men—the stories she spins of Odysseus, the web of deception he spun around her until she no longer knew her own name. Her son, too, lives on. I will say this of my sister—her medicine is that of revelation. She didn't turn men into pigs; they had always been so. Same thing for that maiden who was a monster in disguise.

There are those who have spoken ill of Mother over the centuries, the same sort who spun their false myths of me and Circe. They created their false religion to control us, and they sought only to destroy the medicine of the Green World. They tortured and murdered her children. We were forced to protect ourselves. That time has passed.

Now the time has come for you to remember the magick, the medicine, and the mystery. Return to Mother's Garden.

Medea

II. NYSSA

The Call

I enter as Nyssa.
Hesitating.
Stopping to take in the beauty that surrounds me.
There is so much to see,
To feel,
To know.
They speak to me in whispers,
The wind carries their voices to me.
Know us, behold our mysteries.
Seek our mistress,
The Queen of this Garden.
For her spirit lives in each of us,
And you.

If you are feeling called to return to the magick, medicine, and mystery of plant spirit witchcraft—perhaps by Hekate herself or by her daughters, Medea and Circe—or if another force is beckoning you, welcome. Plant spirit witchcraft is the most ancient form, practiced by Hekate's witches before time became linear. Go slowly, easing yourself into it. With study and practice, plant spirit witchcraft in the tradition of Hekate and her eternal witches opens a rich understanding of the deeper world.

Plant spirit witchcraft incorporates the magick, medicine, and mystery of botanicals through the use of their physical properties and their spiritual essence. The magick occurs when we cast our spells evoking their powers; the medicine heals when we utilize their physical and spirit attributes to end dis-ease and dis-order. The mystery manifests when we experience the sacredness of a deep connection to the unseen world, crossing the threshold from our visible, material existence into the spiritual Garden of the Goddess. This book comes with the spirit of reunification of the sacred practice of plant spirit witchcraft. That is to say that I've included the spiritual, physical, and magickal properties of the plants because there is no separation between what is magick, what is medicine, and how we experience the mystery of the Green World.

The Garden of Hekate, the great Mother Goddess from whom all the world flows, is the spiritual home for the practice of *pharmakeia*, the ancient art, craft, and science of plant spirit witchcraft. This practice uses botanicals for corporeal purposes, the crafting of magical formulations, and the art of transcending. It is a holistic art transmitted by Hekate and her witches for our use today. Enter her mysteries with the spirit of beginning—the spirit of the crossroads that we enter when we answer the call of Hekate to return to the practice of holistic plant spirit witchcraft.

Hekate is the Triple Goddess of magick, medicine, and mystery. She is also the Mother of all practitioners of plant spirit witchcraft. One of her daughters, the goddess Circe, is the mistress of plant spirit medicine. The other, Medea, is the mistress of the Poison Path. Together, these three form the Triple Goddesses of our craft. Circe and Medea balance each other and represent the creative and destructive natures of the Green World. Connecting to the Triple Goddesses, and to other deities, botanicals, spirits, and correspondences, is natural for witches. It is unnatural and unhealthy when we deny ourselves these associations. These spirits, forces, energetics, and correspondences are as vital to us as air. As we are born knowing how to breathe, we come into this life hardwired for connection. We are attuned to our souls. The knowledge flows freely within us, and between us and the external world, seen and unseen.

Reclaiming the practice of pharmakeia is a homecoming. We hear it in a whisper from Hekate, discover it in an unexpected key, marvel at it in a spell successfully cast. When we experience the feeling of being in flow, we have attuned ourselves and our souls. We are connecting to the spirits who work in our best interests. Our souls are recovered and our shadows healed, to become trusted companions rather than adversaries. When we begin the dance of the *pharmaka*, we enter into our truth and wholeness, confronting the illusion of separation that comes from the acts and laws of man. When you are ready to destroy this illusion, then you are prepared for pharmakeia.

The Green World has its own laws and masters. The plant spirits are ruled by the cycle of life-death-rebirth. They follow the principles of nature. We become attuned to the verdancy—the synergistic experience of the fiery soul that lives within all creatures throughout the Green World, also known as the *Anima Mundi*.

Pharmakeia is the holistic practice of plant spirit witchcraft that incorporates the corporeal, the magical, and the spiritual. There is no division between the three. Pharmakeia breaks down the illusion of separation and reveals how the verdant world reflects the duality within us. Allopathic medicine, mainstream healthcare, would have us believe that plants treat only the physical self. Yet the truth is that this is a recent development in the practice of pharmakeia. If we open our spirits, minds, and hearts, we can hear the call of the Anima Mundi. Heed Hekate's call to enter her eternal Garden.

This Garden contains all the verdant world. It is the mystical epicenter of the master plant spirits known as the pharmakoi. I've selected thirty-nine of these plant spirits for inclusion in this guide—some that are historically connected with Hekate, as well as others that I've associated through research and gnosis. These include everyday botanicals, from corn to garlic, as well as exotic ones like frankincense and myrrh. You'll find several plants and trees that grow abundantly in North America, like American mandrake (mayapple), birch, and yarrow. Depending on where you live, some of these botanicals are "wild pharmakoi," growing naturally without intervention from humans, while others are cultivated or grown as crops. You'll find a mix of well-established botanicals like mugwort and yarrow, as well as often-overlooked plants like moss and seaweed. It was difficult to narrow the list down to the thirty-nine.

I chose thirty-nine because that number, representing the three-fold nature of the Goddess multiplied by 13, is the number most sacred to witches. Thus, the thirteen sections and thirty-nine monographs are themselves talismans of magick, medicine, and mystery that I share with you now. The monographs were developed using my own Book of Life, the sacred records of my personal practice as a plant spirit witch. They are a combination of standard knowledge and personal gnosis. All the formulations and practices have been well tested by myself and my students. The profile of each pharmakoi is augmented with correspondences that can be used to strengthen the power of the plant— either by choosing similar ones, or by choosing complementary ones that are different yet reflect the overall energy you are summoning.

The Garden of the Goddess is without compare. It is our eternal spiritual home. We are offered the key to its mysteries by Hekate to help us remember what lives within us. In the known mythology, this Garden was the domain of her witches, where they harvested the plants for their ministrations.

These witches, blessed by their queen, practiced the art, craft, and science of pharmakeia. Unlike modern herbalism, which is often divided between the physical, the magical, and the spiritual, ancient pharmakeia took a holistic approach. When I started teaching and writing about this, my readers and students resoundingly agreed that it made so much more sense than the more common practices. This is not a book of clinical herbalism. The practices, rituals, spells, and techniques found here work on the levels of the corporeal, the magical, and the spiritual in varying degrees based on the focus chosen. Pharmakeia is *holistic* plant spirit witchcraft.

If you're new to Hekatean witchcraft, you may not have recognized some of the terms I've already used in this introduction. The vocabulary of pharmakeia is a merging of history, gnosis, and practice. For example, I use "magic" to describe the general forces that conspire with witches, while "magick" describes our intentional use of these forces. I use the labels and terms that the botanicals want, under the guidance of the Triple Goddesses. Often, I've received these transmissions through journeying and ritual, the altered states of consciousness necessary for connecting with the spirits. The use of botanicals for spiritual experiences is central to my personal practice.

Likewise, my use of words inspired by ancient Greek and Latin terms is sometimes a literal translation and sometimes more creative. The use of these words, like the entire book, is a combination of magick, medicine, and mystery. Any discrepancies perceived by the reader may reflect my inspired development of a new word that is rooted in an ancient one.

The properties and correspondences of the botanicals included in this book also reflect both the standard properties and my personal experience over the past two decades. I have adapted traditional wisdom by viewing it through a contemporary lens. The properties and correspondences of any plant spirit are vast and often diverse. I encourage you to delve into the world of herbalism to learn more about the properties and correspondences of the botanicals within these pages.

The thirteen sections of this book represent the *Kleis Maleficarum*—the steps in all pharmakeia practices. After hearing Medea's truth—the backstory that drives our intention—we answer the call of Hekate in the person of her ancient archetype, Nyssa. This is the sacred turning point, the initialization, the very beginning. Our magickal path begins with the *Origio*, the source of the goddesses or other spirits we will involve in our working. Next comes the *Praeparatio*, the foundation on which we will build our practice, followed by the structure, the system, known as *Ratio*. Then we determine the process, the *Practica*. Usually, in botanical witchery, there is some involvement of the

Hieros Pyr—the sacred fire—whether the kind that heats our kettles through the spark of electricity or the more obvious sort created to burn incense that is central to our craft. Then we progress to the selection of the botanicals we will use, drawing on our knowledge, the *Gnosis*. Depending on our focus, we may cast a spell (*Magikeia*), use our psychic skills (*Sibylika*), or perform a ritual (*Agia*). The final ingredient in any working is *Sophia*—the wisdom, the added bit that can't easily be explained. Finally, all workings go through *Initio*, their initiation into the mystery, the wholeness. Our witches' journey cycles through these steps, with many going on concurrently, looping back and forth in the glorious cycle of time that is Hekate's Wheel.

Boldness of spirit is required for all true magic, as are curiosity, creativity, and sovereignty. Truth, above all else, is to be pursued and honored. What is true of the Green World is true also for witches. We, like botanicals, are complex, messy, structured yet impulsive, eternal yet always transforming, sexy, dirty, passionate, kind, combative, unknowable yet familiar, and deeply wired for growth. We are force and form, blessing and bane. Pharmakeia is the art of the soul, the expression of longing, and the desire for reconnection. It is responding to the ardent cries and whispers of the plant spirits for a return to the ancient ways. We must respond to their calls from our modern perspective. The past is long dead; this is a new cycle of growth.

Enter now the Garden of the Goddess; answer the spirits and reclaim your power. I offer you this book as a method for doing so. May you be inspired.

> *This book is blessed with the wisdom of Hekate, Anima Mundi, Witch*
>   *Mother, Mother of All.*
> *Mother of the Eternal Garden.*
> *The powers of her eternal witches, Circe and Medea, and the others are*
>   *woven through every line.*
> *The spirits of her plants long for your touch.*
> *I honor them through sharing this Great Work.*
> *May you be well blessed.*

> *Yours in the magick, medicine, and mystery of Hekate's Garden,*
>   *Cyndi Brannen*

III. ORIGIO

The Source

Remember whose you are.
Hekate's Chosen.
Never broken.
Rising stronger.
Keepers of keys.
Seekers of mystery.
Practitioners of the craft.
Firewalkers.
Torch-bearers.
Flame-throwers.
Shadow-walkers.
Victorious.
Dragon-tamers.
Banishers of the profane,
Binders of the evil,
Blessers of the true.
Speak unto the spirits of my Garden,
Allowing them to fulfill their purpose as your true medicine.

The Mother has spoken.

Enter this book with the spirit of Nyssa—the turning point, the cross-roads, the call, the beginning of a new part of our journey. Absolutely no prior knowledge of herbalism is required to start this adventure. The botanical spirits have led you to this place. They were guided by the Mother. I am often asked how to know if Hekate has called you. My answer is always the same: You are here now. This is the return to your spiritual home in her sacred Garden.

The practice of pharmakeia is inherently that of working with the spirit world. The physical properties of botanicals are only the very beginning of the majesty, magick, and mystery of the pharmakoi. These master plant spirits are archetypal forces that surround us always. They await your attention and touch.

It can be daunting to enter this deeper practice of herbalism. The spirit world may be calling you, as is our Mother, but you may still be bound by the common illusion of separation between the material and the mystical. However you have been called to this moment—welcome.

Hekate is the source of all energy, the sacred fire known as the *Hieros Pyr*. The Garden is her creation and habitation. She holds dominion over the animal, plant, and mineral kingdoms. She is leader of the Horde of all the spirits—those with corporeal form and those purely etheric—who are of the earth. She is the *Regina Pharmakeia*, Queen of Witchcraft of the Green World. Hekate's eternal witches are emissaries and guardians of the visible and unseen Garden. Her daughters guard the sacred magick, medicine, and mystery of the eternal Garden. Medea is the *Regina Venificarum*, Queen of Poison. Circe is the original *pharmaka*, and Medea her dearest student.

The history regarding the relationship between Hekate, Circe, and Medea comes in many different forms. While Medea shared her truth at the beginning of the book, I thought a review of the more commonly known myths would be helpful as you deepen your relationship with the Triple Goddesses.

In one account by the ancient historian Diodorus, Hekate is mother to Circe and Medea. Medea's energy and archetype speak to our shadow selves; Circe summons us to embrace the transformation found by speaking our truth boldly. While the historical record provides external confirmation for what I know in my heart, the way these goddesses are typically presented in works of art and literature is often problematic. Filtered through the lens of the men who originally wrote of them and those who did the translations, these figures are presented as vicious, selfish, and cruel. Modern retellings and translations are seeking to correct this, as have I. I adore the Triple Goddesses of witchcraft. In them, I have found affinity, comfort, support, and great wisdom.

The Awakening

The remembering of the medicine that is pharmakeia will awaken parts of you long hidden. This is a retrieval of your truth. Hekate and her daughters have whispered to you to return home. This period of awakening will be thrilling. You'll be eager to rush into this book, to go deeper into the mysteries, and to take your magick to higher levels. Go gently into Hekate's Garden.

This awakening is a period of great transformation that is often accompanied by intense emotions, new ways of thinking, and radical changes in behavior. If you're a tarot enthusiast, think of it as Tower time, when old ways are cast aside to reveal your deepest truth. Some of the symptoms of such a spiritual upgrade include feeling you're on fire in the heart center, a buzzing of your Third Eye, and intense root activation. That's a polite way of saying your sex drive may change radically. Other symptoms can include physiological ones like headaches and digestive issues. You'll experience vivid dreams and sleep changes. Expect to be awoken in the middle of the night with your body vibrating. Dreams of Hekate, Circe, and Medea may occur. You may even have visions of certain plants previously unknown to you.

Hekate and Her Children

Hekate, as Anima Mundi, the soul of all the world, is the origin of all the forces and spirits. Hekate is not viewed as an embodied favor-granting goddess, but rather as the primal source. From the Anima Mundi flow the seven sacred forces of the Three Worlds and the four elements. These forces are the master forces in which all others, including the spirit of each botanical, are nested. The practice of witchcraft straddles these worlds of form and force, breaking down the illusion of separation. Witchcraft is the use of these forces and spirits in an intentional manner. We use thoughts, actions, and emotions to interact with them in our corporeal and spiritual selves. Their energy creates form out of force, spirits of the characteristics, abilities, and powers.

Like us, the verdant world is both spirit and body, form and force. The botanical world is our materia medica, the essential soul of the earth. It is natural for witches to be deeply, spiritually attuned to it. The verdant world is the primal source of all spirits on earth. It is ruled by the Green Devil, the Moss Queen, and innumerable other spirits of place. They are aspects of the Anima Mundi, the sacred fire force that fuels all creation.

Witchcraft flows from the Anima Mundi, represented by the powers of Hekate and her daughters, Circe and Medea. Together, they are the *Triformis Pharmakeia*, the Triple Goddesses of plant spirit witchcraft. Circe is the original witch, the transmitter of the knowledge of Hekate as Witch Mother, the keeper of the keys of the mysteries. Medea is the original student, learning

the secrets from Circe. The Mother, the Eldest, and the Youngest. Through direct holistic connection to their spirits and through epithetical practice, we strengthen our magick. These Triple Goddesses of pharmakeia will guide us deep into their sacred Garden. Like them, we have a true self and a shadow. The goal of the witch's journey is to learn from the shadow and progress toward authenticity. Practicing pharmakeia is a spiritual path of enlightenment, a journey through darkness, toward our truth.

Hekate—*Regina Maleficarum*

Hekate is the Witch Mother, the Queen of Witches, the *Regina Maleficarum*. Throughout history and before, she is the source of all witches' power. Through secret rites under the moon, in singing songs to her, and in cursing in her name, Circe, Medea, and others across the centuries have turned to their Witch Mother. Hekate is a complex goddess, which is most befitting the true Regina Maleficarum. Her ancient and contemporary witches are as complex as she is, bringing blessing and bane to themselves and others through their witchery.

Hekate, as the three-formed Goddess within herself, is the primal shapeshifter, moving from one form to another, changing her appearance and personality. She is Anima Mundi, soul of the world, who presents herself as whatever archetype is needed by her beholder. She is the guardian for our Under World journey of healing the body and integrating the shadow and soul. She is our guide as we walk the Middle World of everyday life, and she is the mistress of the Starry Road, who was born of the stars and darkness of the Upper World.

Hekate is the benevolent force that fuels the world, driving the universe ever toward expansion. She is the embodiment of the force we understand as the Goddess. She brings death, life, and everything in between. She is primal. All things, no thing. Beyond time and time itself. She is the power that runs through her witches and their practice of pharmakeia.

When Hekate calls, we experience an awakening of the primal divine feminine within. She calls us to return to her sacred Garden to enter the mysteries of plant spirit witchcraft. From her Garden, the power of witchcraft medicine flows. It is feared by those who seek to control the feminine and to guard the secrets for themselves. She is the Anima Mundi that exists beyond the laws of all men, including any religious designation. She is more ancient than time and we have struggled to understand her for millennia.

In recorded history, Hekate was most likely known by other names, as part of a great Mother Goddess. This goddess evolved and traveled into Anatolia

Hekate, Regina Maleficarum

Anima Mundi, Spirit of All.
Queen of Witches.
Hail, Hekate, Chthonia.
Hail, Hekate, Enodia.
Hail, Hekate, Astrodia.

Mother of Mysteries,
Mother of Magick.
Mother of Medicine.
Mother of Witchcraft,
To you I turn.

and other parts of Asia Minor, spreading into what is now Eastern Europe and the Balkans. She became Hekate, adopted by the Greeks as their own, and was later co-opted by the Romans. The earliest records of Hekate, dating back about 3,000 years, tell us that humans understood her as a Mother Goddess, ruling over land, sea, and sky.

Hekate's cult spread throughout the ancient Mediterranean region until the regular practice of venerating her on the Dark Moon was common in certain areas of ancient Greece. Ancient writers and philosophers wrote eloquently of her many powers. Her role as Witch Mother was solidified in many tales and by ancient practitioners. She was *Kleidoukhos*, the Keeper of the Keys of all the universe.

Throughout art and literature, as well as in existing records of practitioners and scribes writing about her ancient followers, Hekate is always associated with witchcraft. While some feared her power, others described a benevolent, yet fierce, goddess of healing. Philosophers described her as Anima Mundi, and practitioners petitioned her for their spells, while the religious venerated her as a mighty goddess.

With the rise of Christianity, the reverence for Hekate and her companions was snuffed out, often with great violence. Her witches hid themselves and her keys. The complete darkness came. Now, the New Moon has come, however. Hekate is rising, calling forth her witches to return to the bounty of her sacred Garden.

We are nourished by Hekate. She is the Garden, the source of our power and all life. She is the fire within each of us that is connected to the spiritual force of the Garden. Our spiritual umbilical cord connects us to her in ways that defy mundane understanding. She is our Mother who sustains us along our journey. We are eternally hers, and each incarnation is part of the cycle of life and death. We walk her Wheel, that serpent of life, the true cord that creates and destroys. At the heart of the Wheel is the Under World, the womb, which lies deep in the heart of her Garden. Like all children, we have our own lessons to learn. No better examples of this can be found than in the stories of her original children, Circe and Medea.

Banishing the Profane

As you awaken to the sacred fire of the pharmaka within you, you'll become aware of the profane in your own life. The Witch Mother desires only to nourish her children, but she offers sacred banishing of what doesn't provide sustenance. The banishing of the profane through Hekate's power is the first act of witchcraft medicine. Through detoxification of the mind, body, spirit, and of others in your space and place, you cleanse yourself of the miasma—the collected spiritual junk that accumulates on us from other people, spirits, and places. This must be removed before any witchcraft can be practiced. The sacred ritual of banishing all that harms is the foundational practice—the *anima sacrum*—of plant spirit witchcraft. Once we remove the harm, we can protect ourselves from future trouble and then bless ourselves and our beloveds through the use of plant spirit medicine and magick.

Khernips Ritual

Khernips is the process of combining the three realms of land, sea, and sky using botanicals, their smoke, and water for purification. This sacred ritual of the transformative power of the three primal forces has been passed down by Hekate's witches for thousands of years. The method of combining the essences of land, sea, and sky using water, plant, and smoke evokes their ancient presence. It is primal, effective, and useful for all situations requiring cleansing.

Ideally, the sacred water used in this ritual is made by combining saltwater with fresh water (rain, snow, ice) from natural sources. You can substitute spring water or purified water with sea salt added to represent saltwater. You'll need a sprig of a dried purifying plant like juniper or thyme (see the *Gnosis* section).

If you are using fresh botanical material, let it dry out for a few days so that it will be easier to burn. I usually have a black candle burning and a chunk of obsidian in the khernips vessel. The obsidian can be used in place of the burning sprig. I also like to use black cloths for washing. The vessel or bowl can be whatever you wish. A small brass bowl works well.

SUPPLIES

- ⚜ Pure water
- ⚜ Sprig of juniper or thyme
- ⚜ Sacred vessel
- ⚜ Lighter

DIRECTIONS

- ⚜ Stand before the prepared water, then light the sprig of thyme with the lighter.
- ⚜ Quickly immerse the sprig in the water before it goes out.
- ⚜ Hold the vessel up to the sky, then down to symbolize the depths of the sea, and finally at your heart center to represent the land.
- ⚜ Wash your hands with the water, then your face.
- ⚜ Cleanse your root (pubic bone), heart center, and Third Eye with three counter-clockwise circles.
- ⚜ Flick off the water when complete. As you are cleansing, release your miasma into the water on your fingers. As you flick it off, feel the release. At each center, say:
  I cleanse myself with sacred water..
- ⚜ Purify any others present, then asperge the space by sprinkling the khernips using your left hand and proclaiming:
  The unwelcome are banished.
- ⚜ Once you're finished asperging, cover the khernips with a black cloth. Dispose of it outside if you can, in the compost or in an area that you and your beloveds don't frequent.

This technique banishes all sorts of harmful spirits from a place or person. Always start with yourself, then move on to others, and finally to the environment. Envision the miasma leaving you and a protective shield forming after it's gone, especially if the concentration of toxins was high. It can be intense work to do the khernips ritual properly and it can be equally profound. This ritual can be performed as often as needed. It will shield you from unwanted spirits as your awakening as a pharmaka occurs.

Circe—*Regina Pharmakeia*

Circe is the original witch, the first of Hekate's children. To her our Mother gave the sacred art of pharmakeia, the use of the spirits of the natural world—plant, animal, and mineral—to weave her magick.

The mythology of Circe tells varied stories, but in all the them she enjoys a mother-daughter relationship with Hekate. In some, she is Hekate's biological daughter; in others, the relationship is more spiritual in nature. Circe's childhood, like many of ours, was not happy. She was a misfit in the family she grew up in. Perhaps this was her earth-school where she learned the lessons necessary to claim her place as the original witch. Circe's human voice was particularly troublesome for her adopted family, and this may be the origin of the tradition that a witch's voice is different from those of others.

According to myth, Circe turned a fair maiden named Scylla into a sea monster because a demigod she fancied had a thing for the nymph. These were some of her earliest forays into transformation magic and truth-revealing sorcery. Circe used her potion of revelation to transform Scylla into the monster she really was. As punishment, she was banished to the island of Aeaea, where her metamorphosis into the original pharmaka truly began.

Alone, abandoned, and beset with problems all around, Circe could have chosen to go about her business meekly. Instead, she taught herself pharmakeia. She tamed the wild beasts on the island, including lions, panthers, and wolves. She took advantage of her isolation to develop her full capabilities. There is much to learn from Circe's period of isolation, not the least of which is the lesson that we experience magick, medicine, and mystery through deeply connecting to the visible Green World around us.

Eventually, visitors showed up on Circe's island, including Jason, Medea, and Odysseus. Circe blessed Jason and Medea along their journey, which would ultimately prove to be disastrous. Her relationship with Odysseus, on the other hand, was incredibly complex. Using her true-self revelatory spell, she trans-

Circe, Regina Pharmakeia

Original Witch,
Sorceress Divine,
Queen of Animals, Plants, and Minerals.
Revealer of Truth,
Spirit Speaker,
Opener of the Ways of the Witch.

formed his men into pigs. In this spell, she relied on moly, which some historians believe to have been garlic, although others identify it with completely different plants. This botanical was given to her by Hermes and used extensively by Circe in her potions, eventually becoming her closest plant helper. Odysseus eventually left Circe with their infant son, and she returned to her solitary ways.

Connecting with Circe

Turn to Circe to connect with your internal eternal witch and to petition her favor in all sorts of magic. Her ancient tools included the wand, the chalice (for those potions), the loom (she is quite a weaver of spells and more), and the blade. Her home and one version of her parentage have her firmly associated with the sun, although her powers were chthonic (related to the Under World). She is thus both an Upper and Under World goddess, yet another way in which she represents opposites. Emotional and intellectual. Base and refined. Circe found her strength through weakness. She was skilled in change, in revealing things exactly as they were, and in accepting the inevitable. Odysseus had to leave no matter how she felt about him.

The original witch's true self was only fully revealed following triumph over trauma. Circe's true self-witchery is unbeatable. Call upon her assistance to reveal your own truth. Hopefully, you won't turn into a pig.

I love to connect with Circe while wildforaging and when I need to work some serious magic, especially for getting to the truth of a matter. One simple technique is to do some phylactery, wearing a charm made of plants associated with her. Call upon Circe when you need to speak your truth. She can also be involved in animal spirit work, as she is strongly associated with animals, both

wild and domestic. In this regard, she controls the beasts, so enter these rituals and journeys with this mindset. Rule over those lions and wolves.

Circe's Protection Paquet

Witchcraft medicine follows the stages of banishing, protection, and healing. Banishing, the cleansing of toxins, is accomplished through the khernips ritual given above. It is the source from which all other pharmakeia flows. Without first cleansing, no subsequent magick will be effective as desired. The following ritual creates a *paquet*, one of the cornerstone methods of the pharmaka that descended from Circe's practices.

The paquet is a botanical charm wrapped in fabric or paper, usually carried on the body. This protection paquet consists of a bay leaf wrapped in black that you keep with you at all times (see Bay Laurel in the *Gnosis* section). To create this amulet, summon Nobilis—the spirit of the bay leaf, a kitchen staple. The pharmakoi are all around us, awaiting our witches' touch. Bay is an excellent example of this. It is fantastic for protection, prophecy, and prosperity. To create the amulet, you will summon Nobilis through the *vox magikeia*, your powerful witch's voice.

SUPPLIES

   ✣ 3 bay leaves

   ✣ Piece of black cloth

   ✣ Black string

   ✣ Piece of paper

DIRECTIONS

   ✣ Cleanse yourself with the khernips ritual.

   ✣ Hold the bay leaves in both hands at your heart center and say:
Fair Nobilis, grant me your protection.
Fair Nobilis, grant me your prophecy.
Fair Nobilis, grant me your prosperity.

   ✣ Now hold the bay leaves over your root, the area around your pubic bone, and recite the incantation again.

   ✣ Hold the leaves over your Third Eye (the center of your forehead) and say:

With these words, I activate your powers now.
With gratitude for your power, Nobilis,
As I speak it, it is so.

☙ Wrap the three leaves in the black cloth. As you wrap the string around your bundle, recite the incantation.

☙ After knotting the tie, recite the incantation one final time.

Your amulet is now ready. You can tie the string so you can wear it, hang it, or keep it in your bag or pocket. You are now well prepared for the return to Hekate's Garden.

Medea—*Regina Venificarum*

Medea was the daughter of Hekate in spirit and, in some versions of their mythology, her biological offspring as well. Medea represents the Poison Path inherent in the practice of Hekatean witchcraft. She weaves her magick through the blessing and bane of toxic potions.

In contrast to the truth she shared with us at the beginning of this book, her mythology paints her as a horrible sorceress. Her grandfather was Helios, the sun itself. She was a daughter-priestess of Hekate. When Jason the Argonaut arrived seeking her help to acquire something he really, really wanted (a throne, which required the acquisition of a golden fleece), Medea killed her own brother to make it happen. Jason then seduced Medea into using her powerful healing abilities to "rebirth" his father in her cauldron (i.e., restore his health). She was persuaded to do the same for his uncle, which ultimately led to the death of his father, the king. Jason and Medea fled the scene. Following a series of complex events, the power-hungry Jason abandoned Medea for another, more politically advantagous woman. Medea—unwelcome in her home island for killing her brother and spurned in Greece, where she was a foreigner—felt backed into a corner. The King of Athens offered her refuge in exchange for curing his sterility.

Medea then went on a murderous rampage, killing her own sons and Jason's new trophy wife (to whom she gave a poisonous crown and dress), and generally wreaking havoc. Finally, she escaped in a chariot pulled by dragons. All of this appears to have been orchestrated by a goddess with a grudge against Jason's uncle. In some versions of her myth, Medea fled to Athens, married the king, and then tried unsuccessfully to poison his son.

Medea, Regina Venificarum

Mistress of Healing and Pain,
Queen of Fire and Passion,
Goddess of the Shadows,
She who commands the cauldron of rebirth
And wields the dragon's chariot,
Sings the poison mysteries to those who listen.

Medea's story can be both an inspiration and a warning to anyone who uses the label "witch"—and even for those who don't. Medea is the mysterious and dangerous "other" that is both alluring and frightening. Moreover, she is the symbol of outlaw witches who refuse to play by the rules. While she has shared her true story with us, the popular view of her as a manipulative evil sorceress remains. Those who fear female power always have, and probably always will, spread lies about us.

Connecting with Medea

Medea as the Regina Venificarum offers many themes for us to incorporate into our own witchery. Medea was a skilled herbal crafter, well-trained by both Circe and her mother, Hekate. One powerful witch, indeed. Like all witches, her magick and medicine were neither good nor bad. She used them many times for healing, including in her rejuvenation spells.

In fact, that cauldron of hers was a highly effective tool, no matter how she used it. Her cauldron flowed from the primal one of Mother Hekate. Claim your own rebirth in the Mother's cauldron. Take a ritual bath using nontoxic fruits from Hekate's Garden, like lavender. Envision being immersed in Medea's cauldron as she rebirths you into your true self, freeing you from your pain. Hekate awaits on the other side.

Cauldron of Rebirth Ritual

Ritual bathing in sacred water (*animarum aqua*) is a profound way to enter the spiritual womb that is symbolized by the cauldron. Into it we climb to have all our miasma dissolved. Emerging from it, we are rebuilt into our truth as one of Hekate's witches. This is the blessing of the Triple Goddesses.

SUPPLIES

- ⚜ Epsom or sea salts (unscented)
- ⚜ Lavender
- ⚜ Rose petals
- ⚜ Olive oil
- ⚜ Candle

DIRECTIONS

- ⚜ Read the poem below to prepare for the journey.
- ⚜ Perform the khernips ritual if your space seems miasmic or if you are feeling tense. Then run the water for your bath.
- ⚜ Add the salt first, sending your intention to be purified of the past and born anew into a sacred pharmaka, a practitioner of plant spirit witchcraft in the tradition of Hekate and her witches. Then add the oil, lavender, and rose petals. While you stir the water, contemplate the power of the Triple Goddesses.
- ⚜ Stand in the water with the candle in your hands. Hold the candle up, saying:
  Medea, bless me as I step into the Cauldron of our Mother.
  Circe, infuse me with your protection.
  Hekate, banish all that blocks and binds me.
- ⚜ Light the candle and place it on the edge of the tub.
- ⚜ Allow your mind to travel to the cauldron, using your breath to create the space for the journey to occur.
- ⚜ Recite the poem to help you enter the trance so you can fully journey to the spiritual cauldron.
- ⚜ As the water surrounds your physical being, feel the spiritual cauldron embrace you.
- ⚜ Allow the process of release to occur, trusting in Hekate and her witches to guide you through the experience. You are free to stop at any time and return to your physical self.
- ⚜ When you return, express gratitude to the Triple Goddesses. Record the experience in your journal.

THE
SOURCE

So deep I ventured into Hekate's cave
That I came upon her cauldron,
From which the moon rises and sets.
Tended by her closest companions,
Will I enter the cauldron?
It was decided when I began this journey.
My path of transformation into
The witch I was born to be.
I slide into the warm potion,
Embraced by the spirits of her garden,
Washing the wounds,
Cleansing my body,
Until at last all that remains
Is my truth.
The hands of Medea and Circe gently pull me from the womb,
While our Regina watches from her throne.
Their magick moves swiftly,
Weaving me back into form
Using my soul thread.
I am reborn from their labors,
My queen anoints me with the red-fire of her torches.
They sear me with power,
And my hands now hold
The keys of magick and mystery,
Wisdom and truth,
Sovereignty,
Peace.
Wholeness.
The power of pharmakeia.
"Enter my Garden, child," the Queen says,
    And I do.

IV. PRAEPARATIO

The Foundation

Separation is an illusion. The sacred fire is found within. That fire is known by many names, but at its essence, it is the same vital force. This force fuels the verdant world and lives with the witch. The key of this fire is the quest for understanding my life's purpose within the mysterious fabric of the universe through the mysteries of pharmakeia.

The pharmaka fills their apothecary with plants both domestic and wild, following the path of Hekate and her eternal witches. We know that the sacred fire of this Green World—the *Mundi Viridis*—is medicine we need to heal ourselves, others, and the world. This dissolution of the illusion of separation is part of our Great Work. Reconnecting to the Green World is a vital part of our development as powerful witches.

Like us, the creatures of the Green World inhabit both the corporeal and the ethereal. We are form and force combined, forever intertwined within ourselves and with each other. The more we delve into the energy of the Green World, the more the wall of separation crumbles. This doesn't require moving to the wilderness. The sacred green fire burns bright all around us. Through the material Green World, we reconnect to our sacred origin point of Hekate's Garden.

Entering the Green World

The key to entering the Green World—the *kleis viridis*—is simply to end the illusion of separation and to enter the world of magic and mystery. This key, which is freely offered, is the same one that reconnects us to our own sacred flame. We can become separated from this truth through life experiences. If you look back on your childhood, were you content to be in nature? Did you find magic there? Has that magic gone missing?

The illusion of separation results from our modern disconnect from the Green World, but it is also symptomatic of being disconnected from the truth that all things are part of us and we are part of them. Witches know this intuitively, but can fall under the illusion of separation through trauma, invalidation, and fear. When the shadow self is dominant, it becomes like a wall that divides us from connection—an unhealthy type of boundary. Pharmakeia is the path of reconnection to this fundamental knowledge. Therefore, whenever a witch says to me that she isn't drawn to "green witchcraft," I know that she is still under the delusion of separation.

All witches inherently practice pharmakeia, unless, of course, they never consume a plant, burn incense, use scented products, or are humbled by nature. The illusion of separation extends to the idea that what works in the spirit world—*ethereality*—is somehow different or separate from how the same thing functions in the material world—*corporeality*. In truth, there is no difference. The dandelion tonic you consume to cleanse and strengthen your body will do the same for your spirit, if you choose to let it.

This reconnection, this blending and merging of ourselves with our souls, is the same for combining the corporeal and etheric properties of plants. Pharmakeia dissolves that separation through the green fire of the Mundi Viridis. It is how we claim the reconnection as our right.

Receiving Messages from Plant Spirits

Botanicals have archetypal characteristics and distinct personalities. They are not verbal themselves, but contain energetic currents that can communicate with us—for example, yarrow is associated with the planet Venus, which speaks of steel-strong love and healing. As humans, our primary methods of perception are through words, images, feelings, and bodily experiences. The spirits communicate with us along these energy currents. The messages are often symbolic and require that we figure out what they mean. Spirits don't follow the same rules of interpersonal contact that operate in the mundane world.

When you perceive a message or image, you must process what it means to you. Botanicals, like all other entities, present in diverse ways based on your traits, needs, and experiences, and their own psychospiritual properties. Botanicals and stones can be conduits through which "greater" entities like deities speak. These spirits provide guidance along your path. How you perceive their messages is influenced by your psychic abilities. These include the "clairs"—clairvoyance, clairaudience, and clairsentience. When an image or message comes through in trance work, it reflects where you are at that moment and represents a complex interaction between your individual characteristics (psychic abilities and experience) and the entity's properties and divinatory spirit guidance.

You may perceive colors, emotions, memories, and more as the plant or stone spirit reaches out to you. During the trance, don't push these sensations away unless they become overwhelming. If this happens, take a deep breath and draw yourself back into your physical body while communicating with the spirit that you are finished speaking with it for now.

Sometimes the spirits don't appear to send messages during trance, but there will be signs in the days following. You may find an unexpected object that relates to your current magickal practice or one that seems entirely random. You may sense a general knowing—a sort of claircognizance—in the days that follow. Pay attention to any unusual thoughts or feelings you may experience.

Meeting Your Pharmakoi Loci

Your *pharmakoi loci*, or plant spirits of place, are the botanical spirits that are closest to you naturally. This can be in the corporeal sense—the plants and trees that comprise your local environment—or in the spiritual sense—the botanical spirits with which you are already entwined. For this exercise, the focus is on master spirits, rather than individual ones. Spending time in your local environment observing the plants and trees with the intention of understanding the master spirits that reside there is where we begin. You don't need to be in a vast wilderness to experience these spirits. Your backyard, a local park, or a natural grouping of botanicals works very well.

Go to a location that calls to you. Get comfortable in that space. Resist the tendency to label the botanicals you see. Your intention is to connect to the master spirits of the place and to experience these spirits as they come forward to you, whether as the Green Devil, the Moss Queen, or any others. You may also encounter lower-order spirits that are attached to a specific location or that reflect certain types of energetic signatures of botanicals. The world is vibrant with wild plant spirits. There are many deities who can be seen as Green Devils, including Herne and Pan. Don't be surprised if they show up in numerous ways as you begin your practice of pharmakeia.

This exercise focuses on the pharmakoi loci, your own spirits of place connected to your chosen location. They will come when you call out with your breath and energy. In fact, they're waiting for you to do so.

DIRECTIONS

- ✣ Breathe in the life force offered by the botanicals around you. If possible, close your eyes or at least soften your gaze.

- ✣ On the outbreath, exhale your life-giving force into them, using slow, steady breaths that release the tension from your body and mind.

- ✣ After three breaths, stretch your energetic roots into the earth below, down through your own root, into your legs, and out through your feet.

- ✣ Take another round of three breaths, deepening your connection with each one. Feel the vibrations and essence of the hidden spirits.

- ✣ While staying connected to the root spirits, turn your attention to your heart center, breathing in the trunks, stems, and leaves of the plants around you. Using the three breaths, connect your heart energy to these parts of the botanicals.

- ✣ Staying connected, stretch your energy up to the branches above, reaching up to the sky, repeating the three-breath cycle.

- ✣ Now fully attuned to the botanicals around you, become still, keeping your breath steady and your awareness on the experience.

- ✣ Allow the vision of the spirits to present naturally however it chooses. Don't resist or impose your preconceptions on this. Commune with them, without giving name to their energies. You will experience them perhaps as corporeal beings, but more often we perceive them as shades, variations in light, swift movements, and unexplained sounds. Like all spirits, these plant spirits come in all shapes and personalities. Some are benevolent, but others not so much. They speak in the language of emotions, so you may feel certain things and even receive their memories.

- ✣ Once you've seen the vision of the master spirit for your chosen location, disconnect from the place, sending out gratitude as you disconnect from root, trunk, and branches.

Meeting Plant Spirits in the Dream World

Meeting plant spirits in your dreams is common after experiencing your pharmakoi loci. This is one way in which we experience the sacred rite of the Green World (the *animarum viridis*) without the restrictions imposed by our waking minds. I've had many students somewhat embarrassedly tell me about erotic dreams of the pharmakoi. This is perfectly natural. After all, the botanical world is just as sexual as ours. Whatever spirits present in your dreams, they may use their emotional language or communicate through more human means, which may include the appearance of written words.

When we encounter plant spirits during our dreams, and during meditation and trance, we often perceive them as embodied beings. Indeed, tales of plant spirits appearing as corporeal creatures are found throughout history and across cultures. These spirits, called *devas* and by other names, are our experience of the daimon of the plants filtered through our human perception. They vary in complexity and power. Sprites are one example of a lower-order green daimon. Seeing the Green Man in the woods is a common experience among witches. One master spirit, sometimes called the Green Devil, represents the synergistic energy of all the verdant spirits combined, whether in general or representing a specific place. The Moss Queen is how I experience the deeper world of botanicals—the dense, heavy energy of root work and bryology (the study of mosses)—while the Green Devil mirrors the above-ground botanicals. The pharmakoi are the spirits of individual botanicals. Certain locations will have Green Devils that manifest mostly as one species that thrives in the local topography. But most master spirits, whether the Green Devil or the Moss Queen, are amalgams of many pharmakoi.

Master spirits and spirits of place can be very similar or quite disparate, depending on a variety of factors. The Moss Queen you meet while exploring the lichen on coastal plains may be the overarching force of the lower reaches of the verdant world, or she may be completely of the place in which she comes to you. Master spirits may show you specific botanicals that they want you to explore. Pay attention to the verdant imagery appearing in your dreams.

Start keeping a record of your dreams, if you don't already do so. This is essential for deepening your understanding of yourself and the spirit world. Scribble notes in your dream journal immediately upon awakening or make a voice recording. Whether or not you follow the messages received through your research, divination, and intuitive practice is entirely up to you. Always keep in mind that what is most important is to do what is right for you.

Soul Medicine

I was unwanted,
And witchcraft was my medicine.
I was left broken,
And witchcraft was my medicine.
I fell into the abyss,
And witchcraft was my medicine.
I walked through the fire,
And witchcraft was my medicine.
I healed,
And witchcraft was my medicine.
I was reborn,
And witchcraft was my medicine.
I stand in my power,
And witchcraft is my medicine.

Holistic Healing

The illusion of separation occurs when we separate magick from medicine. Allopathic healthcare has completely divorced spiritual aspects from practice. It's something I ran into in my career as a health researcher. Only over the past few decades has the role of spirituality been taken seriously within mainstream healthcare, but there's still a long way to go before the sacred green fire is truly embraced yet again in mainstream treatment protocols. As you grow in your practice of pharmakeia, it becomes apparent that there is no separation between applications—botanicals work on the corporeal in conjunction with the spiritual. This is part of your reconnection to the eternal abilities of the witch as a practitioner of "medicine."

Recognizing botanicals for their medicinal properties—as the materia medica that they are—deepens our understanding. All plants are medicine. Witchcraft consists of working with medicine to heal whatever is broken and to create that which is whole. Shallow practice that avoids the true nature of botanicals as medicine prevents successful witchery, leaning more toward wishcraft than witchcraft. The green fire burns bright—intimidating for certain, but holding so much power.

The word "medicine" comes from a Latin root word meaning "remedy" and the "art of healing." To the ancients, medicine was holistic rather than reductionist, as our modern mainstream healthcare system has become. Traditional systems of healing around the world, on the other hand, treat the whole person, including the spirit, when there is dis-ease. This is the path of pharmakeia.

Our society is suffering more and more, with ever-increasing amounts of pharmaceuticals being forced down our throats. While this sort of medicine may at times be necessary, it rarely treats the underlying spiritual ailments that give birth to their corporeal symptoms. Children who may be undergoing an awakening of their psychic abilities are force-fed drugs that may harm them forever. Adults who are in the grip of sadness are denied comfort and given pills instead. While there are many well-intentioned professionals in mainstream healthcare, the mechanism driving the whole system is profit, particularly that of pharmaceutical corporations.

When the patriarchy took hold of medical practice, the prime objective was to silence the healers who refused to conform. The long road from pharmakeia as the holistic practice of herbalism to what we now think of as "pharma" began when medicine was taken away from the healers by men of power. But now, we reclaim the power of pharmakeia as our right. It is our true medicine.

Practicing True Medicine

To banish, to connect, and to protect. To heal. To make ourselves whole. To share our healing with others. These are the skills of the botanical witch. This is our true medicine. It is through reconnection to the pharmakoi that we find our true power. Cleansing and protection through plant spirits are the two basic techniques of pharmakeia.

To understand how the magic of botanicals works, we turn to their origins and properties. Practitioners of pharmakeia seek to understand the underlying forces at work so as to strengthen their practice. Like Circe and Medea and all our witch ancestors, we find our strength in knowledge. Like us, plants are borne of Hekate. As such, we are remarkably similar. We are the soul made into body. The spiritual as corporeal. Our DNA is almost identical to that of plants. Botanicals were the first exhalation of the Mother. We rose from them with her second breath. In the physical sense, we evolved from the Green World and are interdependent with it. The pharmakoi nourish us as we sustain

them. They are the true medicine. Healing is the work of the pharmaka, the practitioner of holistic witchcraft herbalism.

Pharmakeia has been corrupted by profiteers so much that even using this ancient term to describe the practice of witchcraft as medicine is confusing. Contemplate that for a moment. The original definition of the word *pharmakeia* is both "medicine" and "a spell or potion." The original practice of pharmakeia was thus holistic, meaning that there was no separation between spirit and body. How different modern pharmacology would be if this approach had never been abandoned. Our spells and potions are healing. Not only do they reduce suffering; they create abundance. That is true health. The pharmakoi are the plant teachers, the over-spirits of each individual plant. We work with these spirits in their many forms, from imbibing their pure energy to consuming them. Pharmakeia is the medicine of life.

Pharmakeia is the merger of the scientific and the sacred. It is remembering that this is what medicine is, and that witches have always been the stewards of this power. Hekate as Anima Mundi, the World Soul, is infused in all life. Her fire runs through all of creation. Spiritually, this is known through experience. Physiologically, this is found in the carbon that infuses all life. Scientifically, we know that botanicals contain vital nutrients like antioxidants, stimulants, and vitamins in their corporeal selves. The same vital nourishers are found in their etheric beings. When we practice witchcraft as medicine, we summon both the physical properties and the spirits of the plants.

Witchcraft is the medicine that heals the spirit and nourishes the soul for those who walk this crooked path. It's not found in a pill or in a ball of light, but in the pungent scent of herbs, in the wild energy of the natural world, and under the pale moonlight. For centuries, our true medicine has been suppressed by others who sought to silence us. Now the time has come to reclaim it.

V. RATIO

The System

For where there is chaos, there is order,
This is the system of the witch.
May my passion guide me deeper,
With a will strong and true.
Daring greatly,
But with restraint.
Growing in knowledge,
And trusting in myself.
I call to the elements, worlds, and planets
Providing the structure,
And to the plants who render it into life.

Ratio is the organizing system for understanding how the energetic currents, archetypes, and spirits exist and function within botanicals. Knowing what to do with these energies requires knowledge and personal understanding. In this section, I discuss the traditional taxonomical approaches to working with botanicals, including their correspondences and classifications.

Reclaiming the pharmakeia of Hekate's Garden offers a new way of understanding the spirits of the Green World. Hekate rules over the three worlds of sea, land, and sky. These realms represent the three dominant forces of all creation: emotions, actions, and thoughts. Interpreting botanicals through these archetypal currents permits a deeper connection to them as they mirror our own selves. Our intuition and our connection to the wisdom of our spirit guides is as vital to the practice of pharmakeia as structured taxonomies.

Botanicals are spirits with *vibrations* and *essences* that also possess physical properties. Each plant represents a unique archetype that is a combination of these two. These are interpreted using the standard correspondences associated with the botanical. These correspondences are also used to assign the plant to one of two main classifications—the elements and the planets. Knowing these characteristics provides a quick summary of the energies of the plant.

The Doctrine of Signatures by Paracelsus identified the properties of plants as being reflected in their physical appearance. Mandragora lore is an example of this. While this perspective doesn't hold true for many New World plants, it is a good guide to use when following your intuition and wildcrafting.

Archetypes

As we have complex personalities, so do our botanical allies. Archetypes are primordial essences that reside as energetic signatures in all creation. They are the forms of the universe. We know archetypes as the elements, the planets, and the many names given to Mother Hekate. I've based the archetypes included in the plant monographs on ancient epithets, which are titles and characteristics associated with Hekate, Circe, and Medea. Most plants have one overarching archetype that describes their most powerful attributes. As practitioners in Hekate's Garden, we reclaim these archetypes using the ancient epithets of Hekate. They are the connectors between Hekate and the plant spirit representing their sacred attunement. Linked to these archetypes are the elemental and planetary correspondences of each botanical.

Elemental Correspondences

According to Empedocles (c. 450 BCE), the elements combined to create all there is. They are the "roots"—the core properties—of all things. The Greeks' medical classification system, based in the humors, was governed by the elements, and there are other traditional systems that incorporate the elements into the physical and energetic bodies.

Further illustrating the connectivity of all, botanicals are also associated with different elements. A plant of Water will have properties reflecting the Lower Self: vibration (dense) and essence (emotional). Rose is an example. Some botanicals are comprised of more than one dominant element. Bay laurel is associated with Air and Fire. Consider some of the properties of the mighty laurel: abundance, prosperity, protection. This plant gives strong, fierce kindness born of truth. Knowing the qualities of Air (communication, intellect) and Fire (spirit, creation, destruction) gives insight into the powers of laurel.

The characteristics of the four elements are generally given as follows:

- ⚘ *Earth:* Balance, groundedness, intuition, sensing. Earth energy is dark, dense, and still.

- ⚘ *Air:* Thought, mysticism, intellect, travel. Air energy is bright, light, and still.

- ⚘ *Fire:* Actions, will-power, passion, summoning. Fire energy is bright, light, and active.

- ⚘ *Water:* Cleansing, emotions, healing, instinct. Water energy is dark, dense, and active.

Planetary Correspondences

The ancients used the original Sacred Seven, the celestial bodies visible to the naked eye, to categorize plants. Each planet had distinct characteristics, often associated with deities, representing the archetypal forces within us and in the external world. If a plant is governed by Mars, and we know the characteristics of this planet, then we can easily determine that the dominant energies of the botanical would be assertive and powerful. Mars is mistakenly viewed by some as only a warring, angry planet. But Mars is also about courage and strength, which may be aggressive or uplifting. Consider benzoin, that stalwart of creating healthy vibes while fending off harmful spirits. All the planets have complex features.

The signs of the zodiac are associated with plants through their planetary correspondences. Some complex botanicals will have planets and signs that appear contradictory at first glance, but an understanding of basic astrology helps us to know the importance of determining which "house" a planet is in when describing the signs. This applies to botanicals just as it applies to human astrology. Sage is a great case study, as it is a plant of both Jupiter (sovereignty, power, wisdom) and Venus (compassion, love) in Leo. Adding the elemental associations of Air and Earth, a full profile of the complexities of this pharmakoi emerge.

The characteristics of the planets are usually given as:

- ⚘ *Moon:* The moon is ruled by the element of water, signifying the emotional archetype. Sacred to witches, the moon rises and sets from Hekate's cauldron. Lunar energy depends on the cycle—waning for removals, waxing for growth. The Full Moon denotes power and balance. The Dark Moon, the astrological New Moon, is the most sacred night of the cycle.

- *Sun:* The oversoul of the sun is power, sometimes blindingly so. The solar archetype is association with fire, creation, destruction, abundance, authority, health, and illumination.

- *Venus:* This bright morning star has hidden depths associated with secrecy and emotional healing. Its archetype is love. Its characteristics include aesthetics, affection, beauty, creativity, harmony, joy, pleasantness, and openness.

- *Mercury:* This planet denotes all things to do with communication, with a side order of trickery. Its properties include analysis, deception, education, and truth. Mercury is a swift planet.

- *Mars:* This is the planet of courage. Mars is assertive and aggressive; it brings clarity, community, strength, fire, and war.

- *Jupiter:* Jupiter is regal, sovereign, and powerful. It is the archetype of benevolent dictatorship. Its characteristics include kindness, justice, and majesty.

- *Saturn:* This planet is the deep thinker of the Sacred Seven. Its archetype is the detached contemplator, useful for creativity, isolation, insight, and wisdom.

The Three Worlds

The Three Worlds are the spiritual realms over which Hekate has dominion, mirrored in the corporeal vastness of sea, land, and sky. Combined with the elements, they comprise the seven sacred forces and map onto the planetary energies as well. This is a taxonomy that truly expands our connection to botanicals.

I started teaching and writing about this system several years ago. My interest was based partly on my own shamanic training, but was also an expression of Hekatean currents in my thinking, rather than just an extension of what I had learned from other traditions and cultures. It is rooted in the Under World that represents magick, the emotional depths, and the mystery of birth—the dark, wet womb from which we all come and to which we ultimately return (at least our corporeal beings).

This is the realm of sea, connected to the elements of Water and Earth. The Lower Self is our root, the source of our emotions and intuitions. All plants have chthonic (Under World) aspects that we connect with through their roots, but some are more purely of the Under World. Hekate, as *Chthonia*, presides over the botanicals of the Under World, which include many poisons like aconite and several emotional healing herbs like yarrow. These botanicals comprise one of her most ancient aspects, representing her role as guardian. On our bodies, this is our root, the Lower Self, governed by emotions and intuition. The symbol is the wave.

The enodic pharmakoi are the plants of the Middle World. They are primarily concerned with material possessions and problems—including romance, sex, paid work, and property. The Middle World is the active energy of behavior. It is the trunk and stems, which move and grow. It is the Middle Self, expressed through the heart center, where the inner and external worlds meet. Hekate, as *Enodia*, is the guide we meet along the road—Goddess of the Crossroads. Representative botanicals include black cohosh and damiana. This is the Middle Self, the energetic center for actions and interactions with the external world, situated at the heart center. The symbol is the crossroads.

The heights of the Upper World are governed by Hekate Astrodia, the Queen of the Starry Road. Within this realm, thoughts, intellect, and mysticism reside. This is the home of Hekate's Hall, where the ascended plant masters (the Pharmakoi Kyrios) reside. All botanicals have Higher Self consciousness to varying degrees, reflected in their upward-reaching branches. Pharmakoi associated with astral travel, communication, dream work, intellectual pursuits, and mysticism are classified as astrodic. This is the Higher Self, located at the crown. The symbol is the star.

The Seven Sacred Forces

The four elements and Three Worlds combine into the seven sacred forces, also called the *Septem Novum*. The seven wandering stars also reflect these forces. All matter, of which we and botanicals are comprised, consists of combinations of the Septem Novum. These forces are the seven rays of Hekate's crown and are reflected in the Star of Seven. They carry with them the characteristics and laws of witchcraft. They are reflected in the phases of the moon, with the Dark Moon, that which is the most sacred in Hekatean witchcraft, representing the beginning and the end, where wholeness is experienced. The pharmaka seeks this wholeness through the practice of plant spirit witchcraft.

These seven forces are:

- ✤ *Passion* (to feel; *sentire*): Hail to Einalia, Queen of Emotions. Passion is the wet womb from which we emerge, ready to pursue that truth of ours.

- ✤ *Strength* (to will; *velle*): The witches' will, the strength that drives us in the pursuit of wholeness. The sacred fire (Hieros Pyr) that burns within. Tenacity, resilience, and courage are all characteristics of will. It is our fire in the belly, the driving emotions and our intuition.

- ✤ *Sovereignty* (to dare; *audere*): Sovereignty permits us to dare to live our truth, to sever ties that no longer serve. It is honoring our own torchlight and following the trail of Hekate as our torch-bearing guardian.

- ✤ *Power* (to go; *ire*): Agency fuels true connection to the Triple Goddesses and the sacred botanicals. Empowerment gives us the drive to go forward toward our truth.

- ✤ *Discipline* (to be silent; *tacere*): Earth covers Fire and Water and stops Air. It is the meeting of land, sea, and sky. It is our interface with the external world, the protection we need as we pursue wholeness. It is the discipline to keep silent when necessary, to protect what is sacred to us. The creed of the pharmaka is to keep their secrets unless Hekate wills them to be shared.

- ✤ *Awareness* (to know; *credere*): The pharmaka seeks to know the mysteries of Hekate's Garden through learning, practice, and experience. Tempered by discipline, our awareness becomes focused as we enter into this practice.

- ✤ *Integrity* (to believe; *noscere*): As we continue through each crossroads, a new key is offered to unlock the next part of the journey toward wholeness. Integrity is required to keep these keys when the going gets rough. It is in believing that we can accomplish the mission that each key moves us toward wholeness.

These seven forces are associated with the Three Worlds and the four elements. They are reflected in the primary archetypes of the seven visible celestial bodies. Our plant spirit teachers are associated with the Septem Novum in different ways. Think of the various aspects of the Sacred Seven as properties of botanicals. Knowing a plant is a fiery Under World plant of Jupiter paints a very specific profile of its personality.

The seven sacred forces are reflected in the laws of witchcraft as well. Each archetypal force can be evoked through these principles. Think of the moon phases, elements, worlds, planets, and principles as all being woven into a beautiful web in which the seven strands of each of the different aspects all come together to form the Goddesses' crown. This crown is the universe; it is the Garden, and it is ours to claim.

The Sacred Seven Ritual

This ritual is suitable for any evocation of the Sacred Seven within and without. Perform it regularly to stay connected to your power source. *Corpus* here refers to the physical being. In this ritual, the powers of the Sacred Seven are merged with your corporeal self, in addition to activating your slumbering soul powers. Thus, it is truly a ritual that unleashes your power as a practitioner of plant spirit witchcraft. Connecting to these primal forces attunes you to their reflections in the botanicals with which you work. It represents a download of the knowledge of these core archetypes of all the universe, symbolized by Hekate's crown.

This is a rite of the Full Moon, *Luna Splendida*. Prepare the rosemary as an anointing oil by soaking three sprigs of rosemary in a cup of olive oil, beginning three nights prior to the ritual. An offering of rosemary should also be made to the moon.

SUPPLIES

- ⚜ Khernips ritual supplies, using sprigs of rosemary
- ⚜ High-quality organic olive oil
- ⚜ Sacred bowl (silver or white)
- ⚜ Optional: seven white candles, one for each of the Sacred Seven and botanicals of your choosing

ACTIVATION

- ⚜ Stand under the Full Moon, either outside or by an open window. If neither is available to you, direct your mind's eye to the moon above and hold the image firm as you stand before the altar.

- ⚜ Envision a black cord running throughout your being, permeating each cell. This cord contains the emotional Lower Self. Direct this cord down through your root, your legs, then your feet, extending

your roots deep into the earth. You are grounded below. This is your tether that will enable you to invoke the moon without losing yourself in the energy, while connecting you to the lunar energy of the earth, land, and Under World.

⚜ Envision a red cord running throughout your being, permeating each cell. This cord contains the active energy of the Middle Self. Use it to engage with the material world around you. The moon's energy permeates all things on Earth, from the oceans to our biorhythms. Extend this cord out from your heart center to your surroundings, anchoring yourself in them. This keeps you centered during the ritual and allows you to invoke the energy of the moon reflected on the earth.

⚜ Envision a white cord that contains the energy of the Higher Self, the power of mysticism. Feel this force throughout your being, permeating each cell. The center of the Higher Self is the crown. Focus the energy there, unfurling your connection to the Starry Road. This is the final step in your reconnection to the moon and creates a channel through which the wisdom of the Higher Self flows. Now you are grounded, centered, and connected.

⚜ Soak up the lunar energy beneath you through your roots. Feel the power that controls the growth cycle, gravity, and your body's rhythms. Pull in the lunar energy around you, reflected in the moonbeams, the shadows, and the changes in material objects reflected in her glow. Draw down the lunar energy directly from her, down through your connection into your being. Collect this energy at your heart center until it becomes a beautiful sphere of black, red, and white.

⚜ Place your hands over your heart, letting the spirit-moon spill out into them, creating a new sphere. Using your hands, stretch that sphere all around you until you are completely enveloped in the spirit-moon that is a blending of your three selves and the moon. Your hands, heart, and body are now merged with lunar energy.

⚜ Your spirit-moon protects you from all harmful energies while connecting you to the forces illuminated by the moon's energy. Feel the energy of earth, soaked in the moon's power—how the air changes with the moon, the fiery reflection of the sun in the moon, and the watery energy of the moon's influence on the waters of the Earth.

- ☥ Draw these elemental forces into your spirit-moon: green for Earth, yellow for Air, orange for Fire, and blue for Water. Once combined, the spirit-moon is complete, a perfect mirror of the moon above you.

- ☥ Take your oil and direct the lunar energy into it, activating its power.

EVOCATION

- ☥ Raise your arms overhead and extend the offering:

> *Hekate, Mother of the Moon, Regina Maleficarum.*
> *Circe, Daughter of the Moon, Regina Pharmakeia.*
> *Medea, Daughter of the Moon, Regina Venificarum.*
> *You are the Triple Goddesses, reflected in the three phases of the moon.*
> *I stand in your fullness,*
> *Seeking the sacred wholeness you exude*
> *And that which lives within me,*
> *Drawing down the brilliant light of your illumination,*
> *Attuning me to powers of my own medicine which by right are mine.*
> *The Sacred Seven Laws of Witchcraft I claim tonight.*
> *Accept my offering of your sacred oleum.*

SEVEN STATIONS

In this portion of the ritual, you will pass through the seven stations that represent the seven sacred forces:

- ☥ *Station I (sentire):* Take three breaths all the way to the bottom of your feet, anointing them with the oil in between each breath, chanting "*Sentire*" (sen-teer-ay) with each cycle. Once invoked, let this law become fully activated within your corporeal self, then allow your etheric self to be activated, reconnecting to the law. Say:
> *I draw you down into the waters of my emotions,*
> *I awaken my passion.*
> *Sentire!*

- ☥ *Station II (velle):* Take three breaths deep in your root, anointing it with the oil in between each one, chanting "*Velle*" (vel-lay) with each cycle. Once invoked, let this law become fully activated

within your corporeal self, then allow your etheric self to be activated, reconnecting to the law. Say:

I draw in your power deep into my own sacred root.
My will is strong.
Velle!

☙ *Station III (audere):* Take three breaths deep in your heart center, stretching them down into your left wrist, anointing it with the oil in between each one, chanting *"Audere"* (oh-deer-ay) with each cycle. Once invoked, let this law become fully activated within your corporeal self, then allow your etheric self to be activated, reconnecting to the law. Say:

I draw your power into my eternal flame.
I am emboldened and sovereign.
Audere!

☙ *Station IV (ire):* Take three breaths fully into your heart center, anointing it with the oil in between each one, chanting *"Ire"* (eer-ay) with each cycle. Once invoked, let this law become fully activated within your corporeal self, then allow your etheric self to be activated, reconnecting to the law. Say:

I draw you down into my heart center, the juncture of emotion, thought, and action.
I go forward with power.
Ire!

☙ *Station V (tacere):* Take three breaths fully into your throat, anointing it with the oil in between each one, chanting *"Tacere"* (tah-keer-ay) with each cycle. Once invoked, let this law become fully activated within your corporeal self, then allow your etheric self to be activated, reconnecting to the law. Say:

I draw you down into my throat, opening the way to wisdom.
I claim the discipline of silence.
Tacere!

☙ *Station VI (credere):* Take three breaths fully into your heart center, stretching it down into your right wrist and anointing it with the oil in between each one, chanting *"Credere"* (kre-deer-ay) with each cycle. Once invoked, let this law become fully activated within your corporeal self, then allow your etheric self to be activated, reconnecting to the law. Say:

I draw you down into my mind, granting sureness of purpose.
I believe in my power, my fire, and my truth.
Credere!

⚵ *Station VII (noscere):* Take three breaths fully into your crown, anointing it with the oil in between each one, chanting "*Noscere*" (no-seer-ay) with each cycle. Once invoked, let this law become fully activated within your corporeal self, then allow your etheric self to be activated, reconnecting to the law. Say:
I draw you down in my consciousness, becoming fully attuned to my
*   powers.*
I am awareness.
Noscere!

Release

In this portion of the ritual, you will separate from the moon and the seven sacred forces.

⚵ Express gratitude to the Triple Goddesses and their beloved moon.

⚵ Retract the cord that binds you with the moon and the Starry Road. Relax this force within you and return to your regular state of awareness.

⚵ Draw in the cord connecting you to the external world. Relax this force within you and return to your regular state of awareness.

⚵ Pull up the cord linking you to the Under World. Relax this force within you and return to your regular state of awareness.

VI. PRACTICA

The Process

Through my mistresses' powers and my will,
Do I claim you, spirit, for witches' work.
I borrow your essence,
Boundless and intact,
Keeping only what I need and sending extra back.

Pharmakeia is fundamentally about working with botanical forces to further your soul's progression. Witches are both born and made. It is through practice that we step into our truth, walking the crooked path of our Great Work. While following a working has merit, the most valuable rituals and spells will always be those that we adapt for our own unique purposes. Developing skill in analyzing the properties and abilities of botanicals and then applying them in new ways is true magick. Following are some things to consider when preparing to practice plant spirit witchcraft.

The Apothecary

The witches' apothecary is the tool kit of botanicals, supplies, and instruments that we use in our practice of pharmakeia. Having these few simple staples in your apothecary will provide you with everything you need to practice pharmakeia:

- ⚜ Decent-quality olive oil
- ⚜ Minimum 80-proof alcohol
- ⚜ Sea salt

- ⚜ Activated charcoal
- ⚜ Beeswax (and/or paraffin)
- ⚜ Shea butter (or similar, like coconut or lanolin)

A supply of natural spring water for use in infusions, decoctions, and waters is also helpful. Other oils that are good to have on hand are grapeseed, for its rejuvenative properties, and jojoba, for skin soothing. If you are going to be using high heat, I recommend not using olive oil.

Other supplies that are useful to have on hand include:

- ⚜ Glass jars
- ⚜ Stainless-steel pot with lid
- ⚜ Strainer
- ⚜ Heat-proof measuring cups and bowls
- ⚜ Baking sheet
- ⚜ Parchment paper
- ⚜ Gauze
- ⚜ Cheesecloth
- ⚜ Fabric (black and white are the basics; old t-shirts are excellent for use)
- ⚜ Spoon and knife
- ⚜ Candles, candlewicks (keep an assortment of plain white candles on hand)
- ⚜ String
- ⚜ Charcoal disks for burning botanicals and a diffuser for evaporating them
- ⚜ A censer for burning the botanicals (this can be just about any heat-proof vessel)

Animal bones, claws, feathers, and teeth, and colored inks and papers can also be useful.

The Botanicals

In general, living plants can be the most powerful to work with, although dried plants can be just as potent if your witch skills are up to the task. Some plants, like bay laurel, are best worked with dried. It really depends on how you'll be working with the plant. Having your own Hekate's Garden, even in small containers, is an excellent way to build a relationship with these masters.

I recommend removing any herbs or plants being used for magick from their original packaging and storing them in glass containers. Most things are best kept in sealed glass jars out of direct light. Specific plants may vary in their needs. Some arrive full of miasma. Cleanse these by placing them on a bed of salt or by slipping a small piece of black obsidian into their container. Once cleansed, the botanicals will feel lighter, their smell will be brighter, and their energies will be much easier to attune with. When they are in this state, place them in their final container.

The Book of Life

The Book of Life is your record of the holistic journey of plant spirit witchcraft, including both your personal reflections and the knowledge you gain. Pharmakeia is the merger of the spiritual with the practical. It is scientific, which is to say that it is based on observation and experimentation. Keep track of your work like any good scientist.

On the other hand, the spiritual aspects of plant spirit witchcraft require us to contemplate how our thoughts, feelings, and actions are involved in the work we do. The practitioner is the most powerful part of this path, and our records are sacred. Taking notes as you work through your practice and developing your own monographs like those in the *Gnosis* section will help you evaluate your formulations and practices. In general, record the moon phase and other astrological considerations whenever you do any pharmakeia. When planning your workings, study these factors as well. Also record your personal state of being when planning and then evaluating your practice.

Ethics and Precautions

Given that all plants are medicine, it's their application that determines whether they are used holistically or within the restriction of separation. Discussions of botanicals inevitably lead to their "physiological" applications. I've provided the physical healing properties of the botanicals included in the monographs to give you a fuller understanding of the medicine offered. However, this knowledge can be problematic when we begin to prescribe for others, because there can be real risks associated with consuming botanicals. Allergies, medications, tolerance, and other factors are all involved in how anyone responds to any medical treatment. It is natural for us to want to share our knowledge with others, but we must do so with caution. In general, the rule to follow is to provide support to others only when asked. This is especially true when it comes to making botanical recommendations. If you do provide advice, always add the caveat that consuming a botanical comes with risk. Be knowledgeable about those risks.

Preparing formulations for others is absolutely part of pharmakeia. When doing so, consider who'll be receiving your healing. Considering their age, abilities, sensitivities, and other characteristics will help you connect to their energetic needs and yield a better product. Don't put yourself at risk when sharing your products. Always add a disclaimer specific to the botanicals used and general indications about consuming botanicals. Practicing pharmakeia requires discernment, intuition, and knowledge of systems. We develop a deep understanding through our observations, our experiments, and our learning. And we synthesize all of this knowledge in our sacred records.

Plant Spirit Possession

Possession by plant spirits is a very real risk when you go too deep before you are ready. This a form of shadow bypassing. The shadow self calls upon us to learn all the magick right away. The shadow is not patient, nor does it want to know the true power that comes from knowing the basics. Plant spirit magick requires being ethical to yourself, going slowly, and learning the plant spirits. Don't take the bypass.

Properties and Correspondences

Understanding the properties and correspondences of botanicals is the heart of pharmakeia. The more we understand the characteristics of a botanical, the more we can direct it for our use. Whenever we work with a botanical, we are summoning forth a piece of a whole that exists purely in the etheric/spirit worlds, plus the physiological properties of the plant. The corporeal plant is the unified representation of the spirit and the physical chemical properties. Each piece of the plant contains the whole. Using the piece in no way depletes the whole spirit, unless that is the intention of the working. The material representation connects us to the spirit, which is released through the botanical. Plant spirit witchcraft is holistic; we work with the plant spirits for physical, spiritual, and magickal purposes.

Understanding the difference between properties and correspondences within plant spirit witchcraft helps you to discern between what is inherently part of the botanical and how these attributes correspond to other energetic objects and spirits. Botanicals can be worked with as pure spirits, teachers, and allies on their own, or they can be incorporated into workings as correspondences. We often work with their standard properties, but it is important not to downplay the role of using our intuition and being responsive to what any individual botanical presents to us. Knowledge of the standard properties guides us in what plants to choose and how to approach them. Properties are the standard attributes of a botanical.

Correspondences, on the other hand, are spirits that are summoned and directed or invoked into us as part of any witchery. We use correspondences in our rituals and spells. Our altars are created using them. We can wear them and decorate our homes using them. Understanding the standard correspondences of botanicals further deepens our understanding of their properties. The common correspondences, in addition to the elements and planets, include zodiac signs, colors, stones, and animals. Generally, the spirit of any one of these can be evoked to add depth to a working. Combining colors with a botanical and associating this with an archetype render a very potent ritual or spell.

In the *Gnosis* section, you'll find these properties divided into spiritual, physiological, and witchcraft categories, along with the dominant applications of each plant. Keep in mind that botanicals interact with us differently, so while these major traits are well evidenced, your individual experience may vary. The correspondences of animal, color, stone, and metal can help deepen your understanding of the botanical so that you can use substitutions. Knowing these can provide inspiration for your rituals and spells.

Using Properties and Correspondences

Opening up to a pharmakoi is the first step in working with one. The next is to attune yourself or your intention to the botanical. This works based on the energetic signature of a specific correspondence becoming aligned with your purpose or your personal vibration. All plants have a vibrational essence that is a mix of their archetypal energy plus unique features including characteristics and experience. This is where the standard properties of a botanical can vary greatly. For example, you may start to work with a botanical based on the standard properties, but then find your specific example is nothing like the established qualities.

There are some botanicals that we naturally avoid or that even repulse us. This can be caused by a variety of factors, including previous experience with that spirit (in this life and previous ones), a physiological aversion (like an allergy), or resistance by the spirit to us. Sometimes this can be shadow energy, so it's best to try to connect with your chosen correspondence a few times before giving up. It may be that your energy signature and that of the pharmakoi simply don't connect, just as we don't get along with all people. I've included a monograph on agrimony, although this is a botanical that I find extremely difficult to attune to. But I also find that it works as expected when I do use it. Plant spirit witchcraft is part art, part science, part intuition, and part experience.

Once we are attuned to a botanical, we create synchrony within our working by merging its spirit with the task at hand. This is accomplished through our connection to the spirit, using our will to direct the correspondence as we intend it to be used. Incantations are most helpful in focusing our instructions, as is envisioning the process of synchrony.

Layering Correspondences

Layering of correspondences in any working strengthens the power of our rituals, spells, and altars. This is the process of *synergetics*—creating a unified whole much greater than the sum of its individual parts. Layering is usually done in a number that corresponds to the intention of the working.

We can layer correspondences and properties to ensure the success of any working. Although using a solitary botanical can be highly effective, the minimum number for a power spell is three, the number most sacred to Hekatean witchcraft. In the *Gnosis* section, you'll find the classical correspondences with the planets and elements; these reflect the oversoul of the botanical.

A plant of Jupiter is regal, while a botanical of Fire can be aggressive. These oversouls combine with the unique aspect of each pharmakoi to create an archetype reflective of Hekatean aspects.

Choose a number of layers that corresponds to your intention. Colors make fantastic foundations from which to build your ritual, spell, or altar. The color's vibrational essence and psychospiritual properties will boost the power. Combining these foundational correspondences also adds strength. More complex spirits like animals, botanicals, and stones can provide a good second layer. Finally, the third layer can be Hekatean epithets, her companions, or other deities and complex spirits.

Making Substitutions

I encourage you to swap out botanicals with others or substitute a stone or animal spirit in a spell. The more your workings are your personal creations, the more potent they will be for you. There are two ways to go about making substitutions: adapt the ritual or spell to what's available, or adapt what's available to the working. You can make substitutions by first determining the properties your working requires, then considering whether any of the botanicals you have on hand contain these properties. If not, consider whether you can identify non-botanical replacements with similar correspondences, like crystals or even colors. Be creative and stay ready to accept what spontaneously appears. The pharmakoi have a way of dropping into our laps the things they think we should be using.

You may want to verify that these experiences and signs are legitimate, however. Seeking confirmation of correspondences is easily done by consulting the standard interpretations given here and by using other sources, like *The Master Book of Herbalism* or *Llewellyn's Complete Book of Correspondences*. Ultimately, you must make the decision based on your knowledge, your intuition, and these established norms. Not every decision must fit within the norms, however. Sometimes, pure intuition is the best approach.

To determine a substitution for a botanical, research its properties, the part used, the associated elements, and the ruling planets. Then cross-reference these features with other plants, stones, animals, spirits, deities, etc. to identify your choice. Divination, intuition, and spirit communication are often involved in this process. In general, the corporeals—animal, plant, and mineral—are easily interchanged. Swapping a botanical for an angel can be more challenging, however, because the energetic order these occupy can be differ-

ent. Substituting lower-order correspondences like certain sprites and daimons can also be tricky. You could end up with a "flat" spell. Remember that you want three layers or more in a spell or ritual to ensure success. Corporeals are typically middle order, although this varies.

Working with Wild Plant Spirits

While all pharmakoi are wild to a certain extent, some have become more amenable to the witch's touch. Plant spirits have archetypal properties, energies, and uses. However, they also have individual personalities. And there are subtle variations among different varieties of a species. Experiencing wildcrafted botanicals and their more cultivated counterparts deepens our practice, both through increasing our apothecary and by strengthening our understanding of energies and spirits.

There is a distinction in energetic signatures between botanicals grown as crops and those that naturally thrive. The wild pharmakoi are the spirits that live—and die—without human intervention. Wear gloves when handling unknown or potentially poisonous botanicals. Take only a small sample of unknown plants. There are web-based apps to help identify the ones who call out to you. Even if you are not using an app, however, taking pictures of the plants is helpful.

Summon the spirit of Circe to guide you prior to setting out on your wildcrafting quest. You can also petition Hekate to share her bounty and show you the plant guides you need for your working. Wildcrafting can be done to meet new spirits or to create an apothecary of local botanicals. It can also be strategically focused on a specific working. If the latter is the case, write your intention for the spell or ritual in advance, petitioning Circe to guide you to the plant spirits needed. Or you can use a more structured approach by researching the local flora before you set out to find certain specimens.

If you're collecting roots, make sure you have a very sharp knife and pointed spade in your kit. Take only the root needed, leaving the rest intact. Some plants, like American mandrake, live in colonies so that their root systems can be incredibly interconnected. Be mindful when harvesting these roots so you don't disturb the entire network. Dock, yellow and otherwise, is great for root work since they are stand-alone plants that germinate easily and don't mind sharing a bit of their "heart" with you.

Harvesting from trees, including pieces of bark, seeds (pods, cones), resin (sap), and leaves, is an excellent form of wildcrafting. Always endeavor to use naturally discarded bits of botanicals by foraging around the forest floor. Whenever you approach a plant spirit to collect a bit of its substance, give thanks to that spirit.

Botanical Formulations

Practitioners of plant spirit witchcraft have many options for formulating botanicals for use. The simplest method is to place the chosen plants in a bowl, then summon their properties to your working. A bowl of bay leaves on a bed of salt is an excellent example. Burning botanicals releases their psychospiritual properties directly into the air, as do the vapors released by gentle heating and the steam from boiling. Burning a sprig of sage to cleanse, enclose, and protect a space is an example of this. But ingesting botanicals is the heart of pharmakeia. It is through consuming botanicals that we can truly blend with the pharmakoi, gaining gnosis and entering trance. A mugwort infusion made by mixing about 1 tsp of the plant with a cup of boiled water and steeping it for a minimum of ten minutes will give an immediate boost to psychic abilities. Consume this over longer periods of time to reconnect and strengthen your Third Eye.

All pharmakeia can pose risk. Be cautious of unknown plants. Do not consume, inhale, or apply any botanical unless you are certain that it is safe for you. Botanicals are prepared to release their properties and spirits. Choose the preparation method that makes sense for your working. For example, a gently crafted concentrated oil for anointing your corporeal/spirit bodies during ritual will result in a more steady and sustained release than a rapidly boiled decoction, which can be much more energetically explosive. Of course, these are generalizations. All pharmakeia is a complex interaction between the practitioner, the individual botanicals being used, their master spirits, and the focus.

General amounts for preparations vary based on these factors as well. Pharmakeia is an art and a science; it requires patience and experimentation. A general rule is to begin with 1 tsp of a botanical to 1 cup of water or other fixative. Then test your results and adjust accordingly. Both fresh and dried botanicals can be used. Use approximately three times as much fresh plant as you would a dried plant.

Botanicals, like us, exist in both the world of form and the world of force. Clinical herbalists, like those who practice homeopathic medicine, work only with the physiological properties of plants. Holistic herbalists work with the plant properties and the spiritual nature of the botanical. Pharmakeia is the

practice of holistic plant spirit witchcraft, meaning that the spiritual and physical properties are used as medicine for both the corporeal and the spiritual self, and for the magickal applications. These different applications are not seen as separate, but interrelated; what is good for the body is invariably good for the soul. Tell your botanicals the manner in which you will be working with them. The preparations for botanicals are the same regardless of their specific application. A tincture of yarrow made to soothe aching muscles can equally be applied to a spell to heal a wounded relationship.

Keep in mind that your unique needs interact with any formulation, so that you may be sensitive to one specific botanical, or an application. You may need more or less than what's recommended. Like all of witchcraft, pharmakeia relies on our intuition as much as standard knowledge. In the *Gnosis* section, I've listed the common contraindications of each plant, but it is entirely possible that you'll have a sensitivity to a botanical, although this is quite rare. Go easy when consuming botanicals if you are new to this. Stick to the gentler ones, like our dear allies yarrow, lavender, mint, and dandelion. Work your way up to the more challenging ones, like mugwort, skullcap, and agrimony. It is not necessary to consume botanicals to activate their psychospiritual properties, however. Anointing with them, inhaling their smoke, and sometimes just being in their presence is sufficient. For example, being in the presence of a bowl of myrrh resin chunks gives me a wicked headache even if I am not engaging in mystical activities.

Using Botanicals in Their Natural State

Most botanicals can be worked with in their natural state, whether fresh or dried. Resins—like myrrh, frankincense, and my beloved benzoin—are wonderful to have in their pure state, whether open in a bowl or by adding a few drops of their essential oil to a candle or even a piece of fabric.

A general rule is to use about three times as much when using a fresh botanical, because dried plants are much more concentrated. Fresh plants have a great deal of water in them as well, so this needs to be considered when making a formulation. You can hang botanicals to dry or gently remove their waters in a low-heat oven, placing them on parchment paper to avoid interaction with the metals of the baking sheets.

This is particularly important when making oils or oil-based products, because the water released from a fresh plant may dilute the oil base, causing the mixture to fail to set firmly—for instance, with an ointment. It is generally better to use fresh plants to make an oil, and then use that oil in the ointment, thereby removing the excess water through the staged process. Oils are great formulations for anointing the body or sacred objects. They are also good for placing in a diffuser or a melting apparatus.

The properties of botanicals are generally released through an inductive process. These processes include using heat, cold, the properties of a fixative, or time. However, it is also entirely possible to use botanicals without this sort of processing. Some botanicals, like bay and lavender, readily release their power as soon as we tell them it's show time. Arrange bay leaves in a bowl in the heart of your home, speaking your intention to them, and watch the abundance grow. Arrangements of fresh botanicals are amazing spells in themselves. Carefully choose your plant allies to correspond to your intention, or go wildharvesting for what you need, opening up to the botanicals that want to be part of your working.

Terroir

The local environment, known as terroir, can have a strong influence on individual specimens. I have two sources of wild juniper that are allies to me. One is a variety that grows along the granite cliff tops along the open ocean; the other grows in the bog on my property. Both have the same archetypal powers, but the one from the cliffs tends to be much more potent, being empowered with much more swift energy from the salt and wind. My bog juniper is slower and steadier. Note the environment where you harvest your plants and consider how that may interact with their standard properties.

Solid-Based Formulations

One technique for activating botanicals is to use a solid as a fixative—for instance, salt, charcoal, soil, or sand. The botanical blends with these substances in a way similar to the way it does in any other formulary. The environment from which the soil or sand comes should also be considered. Oceanic sand will have a very different composition from that of earth retrieved from deep in the forest. Salt serves as an all-purpose purifier that is an excellent base for more hearty botanicals that aren't prone to rapid decomposition. Bay, juniper, and

pine are all examples of this. Place these on top of a bowl filled with salt. If you want to banish, placing a delicate poisonous pretty like a foxglove blossom on a bed of soil with the name of the person being exiled works quite well.

Water-Based Formulations

Water has chemical properties that hasten the release of botanical properties. Vitamins, iron, and other agents interact with the plant to yield an activated liquid. Generally, heat is also applied to quicken the release and synergy process, although cold formulations can be very effective as well. I recommend that you use natural water instead of highly treated water. If you are going to consume the water-based mixture, make sure that the water source is safe to drink.

These are the amounts generally recommended when using dried botanicals for water-based preparations:

- ⚘ *Weak*: ¼ tsp to 1 cup water. Steep five minutes.
- ⚘ *Moderate*: ½ tsp to 1 cup water. Steep ten minutes.
- ⚘ *Strong*: 1 tsp to 1 cup water. Steep twenty minutes.

Adjust the amounts and times based on your needs. Blends of three botanicals work well with this process. If using more than three, reduce the amounts of each a bit.

Heated Infusions

The easiest method for preparing botanicals for consumption is by infusing them. Infusions work quickly on the body, making them ideal for imbibing.

To make an infusion, pour boiled water over the botanical, and then allow the botanicals, the water, and the heat to combine into an activated product. This is known as steeping. Commonly known as tisanes or teas, infusions usually have the botanical matter strained from them, either by using a tea ball or a specially designed pot with an insert to hold the herbs, or by straining them after steeping.

You can make this process easier by purchasing herbs in "tea bags" or by making your own. Homemade ready-to-use blends of botanicals are amazing witchy gifts that are so easy to make.

Supplies

- Stainless-steel or silicone strainer with a cover or a teapot with insert

Directions

- Fill the strainer or insert with your botanicals and pour freshly boiled water over them.
- Let the mixture steep.
- Remove the botanical matter.
- Sweeten if desired.

Alternative

- Place your botanicals in an insert or ball.
- Place the ball in a clear glass jar with lid.
- Let steep in direct sunlight for six hours.

You can drink the mixture warm or let it cool. Botanicals that make excellent infusions include rose, sage, skullcap, yarrow, damiana, dittany, juniper berries, agrimony, dandelion (leaf), fennel, lavender, mint, mugwort, saffron, and vervain. Infusions are quick and simple, making them the ideal form for tonics. A morning tonic to get your energy flowing for the day ahead can include dandelion, yarrow, and energizing ginger. In the evening, unwind with juniper berries, lavender, and yarrow.

Because infusions have no preservatives, they are best used within a few days. You can refrigerate them to prolong their use or freeze them as ice cubes. Infusions can also be added to other drinks like smoothies and cocktails, or poured into the tub for a ritual bath. Use them as a skin tonic for cleansing and purifying, or soak a section of cloth in the infusion and use it as a poultice on a specific area. (A mugwort patch is great for activating the Third Eye.) They can also serve as the base liquid for witch jars. Just add a written incantation or sigil, plus extra botanicals and a corresponding stone.

Cold Infusions

Cold infusions are prepared by allowing botanicals to dissolve into water. This is accomplished by blending, mashing, or using another activator like the moon. Fresh herbs, fruit, and vegetables work well in cold infusions. Basil and thyme are excellent in cold infusions with fruit. Pure pomegranate juice concentrate added to cool water then steeped under the light of the Full Moon is an amazing tonic that connects to your inner Goddess. Use about 1 part juice to 2 parts water, then add a sprig of fresh thyme.

Decoctions

Heated infusions are created by boiling water and pouring it over the botanical. The opposite is true with decoctions. To make a decoction, first add the plants to the water and then boil the mixture for a period of time. This process works best for roots like black cohosh or dandelion, or barks like birch. Garlic is also best decocted if you need to use it in a base of water.

DIRECTIONS

- ☿ Place botanicals in the bottom of a stainless-steel pot and pour in the desired amount of water.
- ☿ Cover and bring to a boil.
- ☿ Reduce the heat to a gentle boil for the required time, then let rest until warm.
- ☿ Remove the botanical matter using a strainer and pour the decoction into a glass jar or mug.

You can drink it warm or let it cool and refrigerate it for later use.

Power Cleanse Potion

My favorite decoction is a garlic banisher that eases cold symptoms and can also be used for removal witchery:

INGREDIENTS

4 cups spring water

6 cloves freshly peeled garlic

1 dandelion root

Yarrow

Pinch of cayenne powder

DIRECTIONS

- ⚜ Mix the botanicals with water and let boil for about twenty minutes.
- ⚜ Remove all the botanicals by straining.
- ⚜ Let cool for about ten minutes.
- ⚜ Add honey and lemon to taste if you're drinking it

For a removal spell, use your spoon to write the name of whatever (whoever) is being banished into the decoction, speaking your intention as you spell it out. Then pour the mixture down the toilet and flush it away.

Decoctions can also act as a great base for making activated papers and fabrics. Saffron, blueberry, blackberry, pomegranate, and raspberries can be added to your brew for an added touch of magick. Once the decoction is set, but not too cool, gently submerge pieces of unwaxed parchment paper (this won't break down as easily as regular paper) or fabric in it until the color adheres. Let dry and then use for your witchery.

Sugar Syrups

Sometimes we need to sweeten the magick. Sugar syrups are excellent for attraction spells of all kinds, especially indulgences, romance, and generally spoiling ourselves. You can create a quick sweet spell using a simple syrup in a witch jar with the name of your indulgence written on a scrap of paper and placed within. Swirl it around while the sugar does the trick.

INGREDIENTS

1 cup white sugar

1 cup water

3 sprigs fresh botanical (about ¼ cup chopped)

DIRECTIONS

- ⚜ Bring the ingredients to a boil.
- ⚜ Stir until the sugar dissolves, about one minute.
- ⚜ Simmer another minute.
- ⚜ Pour into a glass bowl and let the potion steep for about ten minutes.
- ⚜ Strain off the botanical while pouring into a wide-mouthed glass container.

- ✣ Allow the mixture to cool to room temperature.
- ✣ Store in an airtight glass container in the refrigerator for up to a month.

The nectar recipe included later in the rosemary monograph will have you feeling just fine.

Oil-Based Formulations

Oils last longer than water-based preparations. They are superior for applying to the skin and for use on sacred objects. They can also be used to anoint the body to activate the sacred self and attune to the external world of spirits, or to vivify and cleanse sacred objects like candles, tools, statues, and stones. They are useful for bewitching poppets, talismans, and other types of charms and can be added to ritual baths. They can be used in magickal cooking and as ingredients in magickal creams, ointments, and balms.

The general procedure for making an infused oil is to combine botanicals with a fixative like coconut, jojoba, grapeseed, or olive oil. Coconut-oil butter is a fantastic base for creams, while fractionated coconut oil is great for oils used for skin tonics. Shea butter is incredibly nourishing, long-lasting, and neutral, rendering it the ideal base for ointments and balms. Jojoba is excellent for more intense work, especially for healing and thickening the skin. Grapeseed is rejuvenative and turns back the clock, reducing signs of aging. Olive oil is the all-purpose fixative for oils, its only limitation being that it will fragment in high heat.

Olive oil, shea butter, and beeswax pastilles (tiny pellets) are the three basics that can be used for almost all oil-based formulations. Soy pellets or paraffin can be substituted for beeswax, which is used to enhance the solidity of ointments and balms, and for making candles. Essential oils are fabulous for use in plant spirit witchcraft. They do have their drawbacks, however. In particular, some are not suitable for consumption. If you are using essential oils, ensure that yours are safe to consume. They can also be harmful when applied directly to the skin, so it's best to dilute them in a fixative oil.

Many fresh botanicals can be quickly incorporated into a liquid oil base like avocado or olive oil. Just fill a glass jar about $2/3$ full of the botanicals and then pour the oil over them. Let the mixture blend for about a week, shaking it daily. For dried botanicals, fill the jar about $1/3$ full, then add the oil. Let them blend for at least a week. You can strain off the botanicals to halt their decomposition or let them remain.

Oleum Maleficarum

The *oleum maleficarum* is your personal power oil that is used for anointing yourself during rituals and for application on your sacred objects. This oil uses warmth to expel the botanical's psychospiritual-physical properties gently into the fixative. Because it is most sacred to Hekate, I recommend using high-quality organic olive oil. A gentle diffusion made through an extended period of warmth captures the botanical properties without activating them all at once. This leads to a long-lasting, slow-release formulary that will keep for at least three months.

This oil incorporates the sovereign power of purple by including a small amethyst in the oil and covering the jar with a piece of purple fabric. It also incorporates a "moly," the botanical that speaks loudest to you and is most attuned to you as a witch. This practice is inherited from Circe and Medea. The oil takes one full day to prepare. Start in the morning. Gather your ingredients. If you can, harvest them yourself.

Holy Moly

It's curious that historians have tried to determine exactly what moly was to Circe and Medea and other ancient pharmaka. The problem is that they are looking for one plant. Moly is not a species. Rather, it describes the closest plant ally to a witch. Mugwort is my moly.

Supplies

- ✤ Clean 750 ml jar (1 quart) with lid
- ✤ Pot with lid (small enough that there isn't a lot of air space between the 3 cups of oil and the lid)
- ✤ Mortar and pestle
- ✤ Wooden spoon for stirring
- ✤ Knife for chopping if using fresh ingredients
- ✤ Cheesecloth or fine mesh strainer (for removing ingredients)

- ⚘ Small bottle for carrying the oil once prepared
- ⚘ Purple cloth and string for covering the oil
- ⚘ Small amethyst chunk

INGREDIENTS

2 cups high-quality organic olive oil

Bay, mugwort, and sage (the Pharmakoi Kyrios)

1 botanical from each of the worlds (use the monographs to determine these)

Your personal "moly"

DIRECTIONS

- ⚘ After you assemble your ingredients, write an incantation or simply speak to them what your oil will be and how you are asking them for help.
- ⚘ If you are using dried botanicals, grind them thoroughly with a pestle and mortar first, working in a clockwise manner.
- ⚘ Chop fresh botanicals so they will fit in the pot.
- ⚘ Gently heat the oil until it is warm to the touch. Don't let it get hot or boil. That will result in it burning off, destroying its ability to absorb the plant matter.
- ⚘ Gently combine the herbs with the warm oil and cover.
- ⚘ Leave the heat on a very low setting, maintaining a warm-to-the-touch temperature. I recommend leaving the heat on for intervals of five minutes, then covering the pot with a cloth and removing from the heat.

Although there shouldn't be any actual steam, the oil will give off heat, resulting in some vapor that may escape if the pot isn't well wrapped. Repeat this process for twelve hours. The constant warmth will permit the slow release of the botanicals' properties. Recite the incantation you wrote each time you warm it. At bedtime, wrap the oil well for the night, reciting the incantation again as you put your oil down for the night.

In the morning, strain off the botanicals and pour into the jar. You can reserve a bit to test on your skin for sensitivity and to "get to know" it while the jar of oil sets. Add the amethyst, then seal the jar. Pour a few drops of wax from your work candle onto the center of the lid, then place the cloth over it and tie it around the rim of the jar. As you tie, recite your incantation one last time. Place the oil on a windowsill for a minimum of three days.

ANOINTING WITH YOUR PERSONAL POWER OIL

To stand fully in your power, use this technique. Proper preparation—i.e., purification using the khernips ritual and ritual bathing—should be followed before the anointing.

- ⚜ Anoint your feet, saying:
  Sentire, to feel.
  My feelings are sovereign and reflect my truest self.
  Confidence is mine.

- ⚜ Raise your right arm and anoint your crown, saying:
  Credere, to believe.
  My mind is sovereign and reflects my truest self.
  Integrity is mine.

- ⚜ Bring your hands to your heart center and envision the top of the pyramid. Anoint your solar plexus, saying:
  Ire, to go.
  My actions are sovereign and reflect my truest self.
  Power is mine.

- ⚜ Using your left hand, anoint your chest, saying:
  Tacere, to be silent.
  Discipline is mine.

- ⚜ Using your left hand, anoint the area under your navel, saying:
  Velle, to will.
  Strength is mine.

- ⚜ Anoint your left wrist, saying:
  Audere, to dare.
  Freedom is mine.

- ⚜ Anoint your right wrist, saying:
  Noscere, to know.
  Awareness is mine.

☥ Feel the oil activating the associated energy center. Take your time at each point, letting messages come through. When finished, return to your physical being gently, wiggling your toes and fingers. Rise slowly.

Anoint yourself with the oil on the seven points for the next few days and whenever you are expecting a tricky situation. You can also use it to restore your sovereignty after a rough day. You can use this oil to prepare altar tools and other objects of great personal power as well.

Ointments, Creams, and Balms

Ointments are preparations made of a solid oil, like shea or coconut butter, with a small amount of a wax added to solidify the product. Ointments are designed to be used sparingly, while creams are for more liberal usage. Medea's Flying Ointment in the oak monograph is a good example.

You can add infused and essential oils to this mixture according to need, but the basic ingredients for making an ointment are:

¾ cup oil butter

¼ cup pellets

1 tsp infused olive oil or 9 to 12 drops essential oil

The more infused oil you add, the creamier the product will be; the more beeswax you add, the more solid the product becomes. Experiment with the ratios to find the ideal one for what you are making.

Creams are generally only the solid oil butter plus infused and essential oils. Balms, often used on the lips, heels, and elbows, have a higher ratio of pellets, about 2 to 1.

There are two methods that I recommend for preparing creams, ointments, and balms. The first is the traditional *bain-marie* technique, in which the oil butter and pellets are melted over boiling water; the second is what I call the "easy-bake" method, which works with heat-proof containers like small aluminum tins.

BAIN-MARIE METHOD

☥ Combine your oil butter and pellets (if appropriate) in a heat-proof glass bowl or measuring cup. You can also use a double boiler—one pot that fits into a second.

- Place the mixture in a stainless-steel pot half full of water.
- Bring the water to a boil.
- Gently break down the ingredients with a wooden spoon while the water boils. Stir until completely melted.
- Add the infused and essential oils, if appropriate.
- Pour into containers.

Easy-Bake Method

- Line a baking sheet with parchment paper.
- Heat the oven to 300 degrees.
- Arrange the oil butter and beeswax pellets (if appropriate) in small tins using the ratios recommended for your product.
- Place in the oven for about ten minutes, or until the ingredients are melted.
- Add infused and essential oils as desired.

Alcohol-Based Formulations

Alcohol-based preparations activate the botanical spirits through the release brought about by the chemical properties of the alcohol. Keep a high-proof vodka in your apothecary for making just about any tincture. Ramp up your pharmakeia by using spirits made from botanicals appropriate for your spell. Need to banish? Use gin made with juniper. Want to create a divine cocktail for unleashing your inner Goddess? Try diktamo made from dittany, or my other favorite, the mysterious Aperol, which is apparently made using super-secret sorcery.

Most alcohol-based formulations take the form of tinctures, which are liquid extracts of botanicals that are taken directly under the tongue or used as a basis for spells. Usually they are distilled in alcohol, but they can be made using apple-cider vinegar or food-grade glycerin for those wishing to avoid alcohol. Another way to avoid the small amount of alcohol is to infuse the tincture in a warm beverage like hot water mixed with honey.

The major benefit of tinctures is that only a small amount is required, usually ½ to 1 tsp. They are taken using an eyedropper. The other advantage is that they work more quickly when applied under the tongue. A simple tincture of mugwort is a staple in the apothecary, used to enhance psychic powers, calm an overbusy mind, and generally soothe the soul. Almost any alcohol that is 80 proof or above can be used as the base for a tincture.

A glycerite is a tincture made using a base of 3 parts glycerin to 1 part pure water. True tinctures and glycerites are stored in a cool, dark cupboard while the vinegar-based formulations must be kept in the refrigerator. Alcohol tinctures can last for several years; glycerol tinctures last around six months.

Tinctures are easy to consume and are used for a variety of medicinal purposes, from soothing distress to activating psychic powers. You can also use them to anoint sacred objects that won't be harmed by the alcohol, or in witch jars to activate the spell quickly.

INGREDIENTS

As with all pharmakeia, these are recommendations. The pharmaka is an experimenter, adjusting the amounts and processes based on the existing practices, intuition, and personal experience.

> About 1 part fresh botanicals to 3 parts liquid or 1 part dried botanicals to 6 parts liquid. For example, ¼ cup fresh to ¾ cup liquid or 3 tbsp dried to 1 cup liquid.

DIRECTIONS

- ⚕ Place the botanicals in a clean jar, then add the liquid. I generally pour just enough boiled water over the botanicals to loosen them up, speeding up the distillation process.
- ⚕ Cover the jar.
- ⚕ Shake gently daily. The tincture will be ready for use after about four to six weeks for alcohol-based, shorter for glycerites and vinegars. Test by dropping a small amount under the tongue.
- ⚕ Strain off the botanicals, gently pressing down on the plant matter to release the most concentrated tincture.
- ⚕ Store in a dark glass bottle with an eyedropper top for convenience.

Vinegar-Based Formulations

Vinegars introduce acidity into our pharmakeia. They burn away the superfluous in the botanicals and do the same within the body and in witchery. Vinegars work the same way as a tincture, but have the added benefits of being safe for children and those who don't consume alcohol. For the latter group, vinegars are much cheaper than making a glycerite. An additional benefit is that vinegars can be added to food to deepen their botanical powers.

For the apothecary, having apple-cider and white vinegar on hand is essential. Apple-cider vinegar with the "mother" (the bacterial culture) is optimal because of its many health benefits. Like using spring water compared with chemically treated tap water, white vinegar also works well, but often has a lot of the health benefits removed through processing. White vinegar's clear color is useful for preparations that benefit from this. The Double "B" Banisher in the basil monograph is an example of a vinegar extract used in a spell, while the Triple Goddess Salad incorporates vinegar into a magickal recipe (see pages 97 and 163).

A vinegar extract can be made following the same process as a tincture. A heated extract can be made following the process for making an infused oil.

The Magick of Oxymels

Oxymels are preparations combining vinegar and honey that were popular with ancient Hekateans. The honey hides the taste of bitters, while the vinegar works the spirits of the botanical. You can swap out the honey for maple syrup.

There is something about making an oxymel that enlivens an ancient part of me, and the whole experience is more spiritual for me than making any other formulation. I love their versatility. Make one with yarrow for a handy heal-all to add to hot water for an instant infusion. Or make one with dandelion to pour over roasted sweet potatoes to maximize sustained energy.

The general formula for an oxymel is to mix equal parts of vinegar, honey, and dried botanical. Place the botanical in the jar, add the honey, and top with the vinegar. Shake vigorously and continue to do so every day for about two weeks. The agrimony oxymel in the *Gnosis* section is great for walking in the dream time (see page 86).

VII. HIEROS PYR

The Fire

Hail, Hekate, Hieros Pyr.
She who is the sacred witch-fire.
Hail to Circe and Medea,
Original, eternal Daughters of Fire.
Hail to the Hieros Pyr,
The sacred witch-fire.
Hail to the ash, smoke, and flame,
And to the plants that render same.
Through your sacred smoke, I am cleansed.
Through your bright flame, I banish all that harms.
Through your alchemical ash, I am transformed.
Hail to Hekate, Hieros Pyr.
Hail to the plant spirits who render your fire.
Hail to smoke, ash, and flame,
Whose powers I now claim.

The *Hieros Pyr*, the sacred fire of pharmakeia, allows practitioners to access the hidden properties of botanicals through ash, smoke, and flame. Hieros Pyr is a practice, a journey, and a reflection of the sacred fire within the witch. The fire dance ritual activates your own flames and connects you to the sacred fire of the Green World.

Many witches experience the sacred fire through the statues, representations, and other icons that symbolize their favored spirits and deities. Techniques for preparing, vivifying, and maintaining these objects are presented below. In order to stand fully in the power of the forces, spirits, and deities we celebrate through our iconography, we often engage in rituals. The sacred fire is frequently part of these rituals, but there are many other ways to incorporate pharmakeia into rites and ceremonies. Honoring deities, spirits, and the dead is inherent to practicing pharmakeia. In the section on poppy, you'll learn how to cross the veil to connect by crafting and applying one of my most beloved oils and rituals (see page 171).

I love a great ritual almost as much as I adore a well-woven spell. So below, we'll talk about spellcrafting, including sympathetic magick, candle witchery, and more. The psychic powers of the pharmakeia are revealed in the section on divination, including incorporating botanical spirits into readings, using botanicals for the practice of cleromantica ("throwing the bones"), and interpreting signs and omens from the pharmakoi.

The dance of fire and earth, eternal and ever-changing, is rendered through the application of flame to botanicals. As witches, we work with the sacred fire in our spells, from candle magick to concocting potions in our cauldrons. That cauldron for me is often a stainless-steel pot on top of my electric range, as described in the monograph for pomegranate. Fire is also found in the botanicals used in witchery and in the spirits we evoke. Dragon energy has long been connected to Hekate and her eternal witches. Medea is most fond of dragons. The phoenix is another spirit of the sacred fire.

The three parts of the sacred fire are activated when we burn botanicals of all sorts and in candle magick. Fire, of course, is a spirit itself. However, it often contains others, some we invite and some who just show up on their own. The plant spirits we use in incense and fire can be evoked by calling forth the specific properties you wish to have as allies in your working—oak for sovereignty, birch for binding, basil for initiation, mugwort for divination, skullcap for clarity.

Incense

The basic technique for burning botanicals as incense is simply to place a small amount on a source of fire. Incense, strictly speaking, refers to a formulated botanical powder, although loose blends of botanicals used for burning are also commonly called incense and this is how I refer to any botanical used in ritual. Commercial incense blends are usually combustible, meaning that they contain enough burnable material (like paper or wood) to make them burn easily.

For activating the sacred fire of botanicals, the traditional method is to ignite a charcoal block and then place the blend on top. This will yield longer-lasting smoke than merely setting the blend alight. Some botanicals have a fast combustion rate, meaning they will burn off quickly, while others are more sustained.

Any botanical can be used as incense, from grabbing a bit of basil from the spice rack to elaborate formulations like the Hekate's Cauldron incense. Plants are transformed into materia medica by the directions we give them through words, emotions, and touch. Every time you touch a plant for pharmakeia, it becomes sacred medicine through your intentions. This is the difference between clinical herbalism and plant spirit witchcraft. When we activate the sacred pharmakoi through fire, the time taken to share our intentions through the vibration of our thoughts, words, feelings, and touch brings the spirits to life.

Resins like benzoin, frankincense, and myrrh melt as they burn. They make an excellent base for incense because of their natural stickiness. Benzoin, in particular, is a wonderful addition to almost any incense. It has a fabulous vanilla smell that is soothing yet energizing. In addition, its spiritual qualities are amenable to just about any ritual or spell. Frankincense is fabulous for all empowering workings, and myrrh is ideal for mystical work. Gum arabic can be substituted as a neutral adhesive.

Several tools are indispensible if you will be making your own incense. They include:

- ☥ Mortar and pestle, preferably made of dense stone like granite or volcanic rock. I recommend that you have one for consumable blends and one for poisons.
- ☥ Glass jars with lids
- ☥ Labels and markers
- ☥ Charcoal blocks
- ☥ A censer (heat-proof bowl or plate) or incense burner
- ☥ Sand for placing under the charcoal block (optional)

Preparing Incense

To combine botanicals into an incense, use a method that is aligned to the energies that you'll be utilizing in the plants. For removal purposes, from relieving cold symptoms to magickal banishings, macerate them enough to release their compounds using counter-clockwise circles with the pestle, the

opposite for attraction workings like drawing healing in or manifesting spells. Seven good turns should work with amenable botanicals like lavender, mugwort, thyme, and vervain. More challenging ones, like most of the poisons, require a more intricate preparation process—for example, foxglove or mandragora.

Seeds like pomegranate and poppy require more vigorous pounding with the pestle. Roots like black cohosh and dandelion also take more time to release. You will feel this as you grind the botanicals if you attune to them while doing the work. An energetic ripple will be released, sometimes like a sigh and sometimes like a roar. As you grind, the botanicals will break down into smaller pieces and their oils will be released. Stage the addition of botanicals when grinding so that the more self-contained plants go in first.

Macerating botanicals in a mortar until they have released their properties and been broken down into smaller pieces is usually enough, but you may want to make a true incense by reducing the botanicals to powder. This is best accomplished using a coffee mill or spice grinder. Investing in a high-quality electric grinder is one of the wisest decisions a pharmaka can make. I have loved the many I've had over the past twenty years. I say "many," because I've yet to meet one that doesn't eventually yield to the demands I place on it. Seeds, especially very tough ones like milk thistle and flax, wear out the motor.

Here are some general rules for preparing incense:

⚘ Hold your hands over the botanicals, allowing the vibration of your intention to soak into them.

⚘ As a general ratio, use $^1/_3$ adhesive, $^1/_3$ highly combustible botanical, $^1/_3$ other *materia*. My no-fail formula is $^1/_3$ benzoin, $^1/_3$ mugwort, and $^1/_3$ ingredient specific to the working.

⚘ Use resin ground to a powder to help the botanicals in your incense adhere to each other so they will work in a synergistic way. Add these first.

⚘ Ensure that your botanicals are very dry. Aster, birch bark, garlic skin, mugwort, juniper, rosemary, pine cones, and sage are some of the botanicals that burn very well.

⚘ For a slow-release incense, use seeds like poppy and berries like juniper. Other botanicals like lavender are also slow to ignite.

- To make pellets or cones, use powders and gum arabic and then form the mixture into shapes. Pack tightly and let set for a week before use.

- Adding oils and tinctures can increase the flammability of the incense, which may or may not be desirable.

Once your incense is prepared, store the herbs in a sealed glass jar. If you have an extra piece of obsidian on hand (in addition to the one in the grounding exercise further on in this lesson) you can cleanse it in a salt bag or under the Full Moon and then slip it in with the incense. The shared properties will mingle quite nicely.

Burning Incense

Use charcoal blocks or disks to provide the steady fire necessary for sustained burning of botanicals. They can be broken into smaller pieces for shorter periods of burning.

Place a bit of the loose incense on the censer, then add the charcoal and ignite it with a wand lighter until little sparkles or whiteness start to appear. Add a bit more of the incense. A bed of sand, small pebbles, or another heat barrier can be added underneath the charcoal.

Save the ash for use in spells and for anointing.

The Hidden Powers of Smoke

Smoke alters the chemical structure of the air in the material world, opening up the doors to the world of spirit. Inhaled smoke, of course, alters our state of consciousness. The plant spirits released in smoke indicate the type of smoke magick you will perform, so choose them wisely. Your individual energy signature and that of the plant will interact. This means that the smoke of some plant spirits will naturally attune to you and others will be repulsive. I never use palo santo, sandalwood, or patchouli in any of my smoke witchery. Damiana, on the other hand, is a plant spirit soul mate to me, always reliably opening the way and bringing healing to my weary soul.

If it isn't possible to burn botanicals, place them in a small amount of olive oil and gently heat the mixture to release their vapor. An electric or candle diffuser is a staple of the apothecary for use when releasing smoke isn't the best option. The vapor released works in the same corporeal-spiritual way as the smoke. Heating them in a small pot on the stove also works. Steam can be used as a replacement for sacred smoke as well. Boil the incense in a small amount of water to release the steam.

Black Smoke Jar of Secrets

This jar can be used to contain things best hidden by capturing smoke, either from a black flame or a suitable incense that protects and binds the contents—mugwort and skullcap, for example. Write what you wish to hide on black paper and insert it in the black jar, along with a candle or incense. Light the candle or incense and let the jar fill with smoke. Quickly cap, then seal with black fabric and wax. This is suitable for things you may wish to release at some point rather than banish.

Hieros Pyr Incense

Basil, skullcap, and mugwort comprise this incense. Basil is traditionally an herb consumed by initiates as they learn the mysteries, so chosen because it calms the mind while releasing our fire. Mugwort is evoked for protection, psychic awareness, and wisdom. Skullcap is a supreme binder. A skullcap spell is almost impossible to break. This incense thus calls forth the characteristics of learning, clarity, and success, in addition to binding the incense together.

INGREDIENTS

½ cup benzoin

¼ cup dried basil

¼ cup dried skullcap

½ cup dried mugwort

This incense is excellent as a fumigator and an activator, and as a connector for trance and rituals. It is evocative of Hekate's sacred fires, both within and without.

Magickal and Medicinal Bundles

Bundles contain several sprigs, flowers, or leaves of botanicals that are well-suited to burning without any assistance. Aster, juniper, rosemary, sage, and thyme all work well in bundles or burned on their own, as in the khernips ritual. Add larger blossoms, petals, and leaves to a base of sprigs of bay leaves, foxglove leaves, rose petals, or small dandelion stems to create your own unique bundle. Bundles are an amazing way to combine plant spirits without adding a base or needing charcoal.

Bundles are made with fresh botanicals and then dried. Bundles four to six inches in length work well. Cut your sprigs a bit longer so you can trim them down when the bundle is finished.

DIRECTIONS

- ⚘ Using a piece of parchment as a base, arrange your botanicals to your satisfaction.

- ⚘ Beginning at the bottom, tie a narrow length of cotton or hemp string that's about five times the length of your bundle. Tie this tightly.

- ⚘ Hold the base you've just created in one hand and wrap the string tightly around the bundle, leaving space between each wrapping.

- ⚘ When you reach the top of the bundle, wrap back down to the base, crossing the first wrapping.

- ⚘ Tie tightly at the base, making a small loop for hanging.

- ⚘ Hang to dry for several days.

- ⚘ Save any scraps for use in other preparations, using the parchment to funnel them into a storage jar.

- ⚘ Loosely wrap the bundle in parchment to store it.

- ⚘ Light the end of the bundle and use it as a wand to summon and stir the powers of the botanicals. Place on a censer for continued activation.

Alchemical Ash

Ash is the pure essence of the plant spirit. High temperatures are required to reduce botanicals down to fine ash, using a special container directly in a fire or even a blow torch. Or you can use the method outlined below. Save the remains from your incense—the combination of botanicals and charcoal ash—to use for anointing yourself and sacred objects. Anointing with ash is a primal technique for making a deep connection to Hekate and our witch ancestors. Another use for ash is to activate sigils, tracing it along the shape while reciting your incantation.

If you have access to a very hot-burning fire—in your backyard pit or fireplace, for example—you can make ash using a small heat-proof covered cast-iron or stainless-steel container. Place the botanicals inside and let them burn off in the flames for several hours. This yields a pure white or gray ash that is the essence of the botanical. Use this in tinctures for enhanced power.

A quick method for making a small amount of sacred ash that I often use when the presence of charcoal isn't problematic is to make a small oven out of heavy aluminum foil around a censer. Burn the botanicals on a block of charcoal, leaving only a small opening in the top of the foil tent. I've used both the spagyrical approach in the high heat of a fire and this easier method with similar results. The charcoal residue may make it unsafe to consume unless you use food-grade blocks, but it can be used for anointing the body.

VIII. GNOSIS

The Knowledge

What is knowledge, you ask?
It is not the words on the page,
Nor is it found within the great teachings.
Without the use of these works,
There is no knowledge.
You, child, know this.
Go boldly deep into learning all you can,
Then render it into life,
Through your rites and spells.
This is knowledge.

The Mother

The thirty-nine monographs included in this section reflect a variety of botanicals, from the deadly poison aconite to commonplace corn and the wild spirits of seaweed and American mandrake. Some, like mugwort, are more commonly associated with plant spirit witchcraft, while others, like black cohosh, are more known for their physiological healing than their magickal applications. These monographs are drawn from my personal Book of Life. They are a combination of history, lore, properties, correspondences, and applications. All the formulas, rituals, spells, and other creations have been well-tested by myself and by my students.

I've divided the properties of each botanical into three types: spiritual, physiological, and magickal. Think of these as corresponding to mystery, medicine, and magick. However, there is no separation between these three; what benefits the spirit soothes the body, and our witchcraft does both. In general, the properties are organized with the most primary listed first. This is typically the most accessible property of the botanical. The order of the properties is similar to the way we reveal our own personalities to others. There are some that almost everyone who has met us will know, while some are reserved for our intimate relationships.

I've included the traditional correspondences of botanicals, like the elements and the planets. Use these to help you understand the energies of the plant. The Sacred Seven activation ritual at the end of the *Ratio* section embedded these forces within you. When reading about a plant, consider the experiences of the worlds, the elements, and the planets you had during the ritual. If you already have an established connection with a stone or animal associated with a botanical, contemplate how they are reflected in its properties.

Three Worlds, Three Energies

Botanicals that are associated with the Under World have dense energy and are strongly connected to magick, the waning moon, and emotions. They are often the poison that heals. Upper World botanicals are attuned to higher vibrations and usually associated with the intellect, psychic abilities, and the mysteries. Those that primarily reflect the Middle World are typically balanced in their essential energy signature and are associated with action, the interface between the internal and external, and the material world.

The archetypes given below are based on modern interpretations of ancient titles (known as epithets) associated with Hekate. These words bring with them much power. They invoke our deep knowledge, so that we understand what they mean in a most primal way. When working with a plant, address it using the archetypal title or your own variant of the epithet. It is a type of honorific, a title bestowed on a respected teacher. I've included the English translation of the ancient epithets along with their modern interpretation.

. Use the properties to guide you in developing your own magick and medicine; use the correspondences to deepen your workings. Adding an animal spirit by including an image or charm to a witch bottle augments its power. Including a stone in a ritual bath, for example, can enhance the corresponding botanicals you use in the water. A rose quartz and a piece of black obsidian in (or around) a tub infused with rose water will banish, protect, and bless you with great *agape*, the universal love. Adding the colors black and pink to the bath, perhaps through your towel choices, can further boost the experience. This is an example of the layering technique described earlier.

These thirty-nine botanicals are the plant spirit teachers that speak most strongly to me and are deeply symbolic of our Goddess. May you be inspired, not only to use them, but to create your own.

Aconite

We begin our journey with the most frightening of all the pharmakoi—*aconitum*, the Queen of Poisons. This is Medea's preferred botanical—hence, their shared moniker as Regina Maleficarum. It seems fitting to begin by discussing a plant that is so deadly that she stands alone in Hekate's Garden.

To Hekate's witches, aconite brings comfort, reducing stress and easing a troubled mind. Having an aconite plant in your garden will help you be true to yourself, while banishing doubt and shame. It is truly the poison that heals.

Aconite, the most prized plant of the Garden, teaches the lesson of Hekate—that without death there is no life. As Hekate taught Medea and Circe to use this plant, which was created from the drool of Cerberus himself, she uses it to teach us that poison is often required for healing. Today, aconitine is used in homeopathy to treat acute distress characterized by very high fever and unbearable pain. It is also used as a sedative and a numbing agent, and in Traditional Chinese Medicine and Ayurveda, as well as in some areas around the Mediterranean and Eastern Europe.

Always handle aconite wearing gloves, preferably rubber or silicone, to avoid poisoning. Speaking from experience, aconite's poison works quickly through skin contact, resulting in a tingling sensation, nausea, and a sharpness of acuity mixed with a sort of fugue. Aconite is sometimes included in commercial "flying potions," salves that may lead to trance states. My personal sovereignty oil contains a small amount of aconite, blended with gentler botanicals. Aconite demands respect, and it is in this way, in addition to its consciousness-altering properties, that I evoke her presence within me.

Aconite is quite particular about her environment and will let herself wither to dust if she is not well-pleased. She's the queen, after all. I have grown aconite inside, but she disliked it and I now let her reign over my poison garden. Curiously, some species of caterpillar feed on aconite, which surprised me when I found that my plants were being consumed. It may have been caterpillars, or it may have been my familiar, the goblin LeRoy.

Caveat Aconitum

The name "aconite" itself refers to a spear, referencing the use of the poison on the tips of weapons. However, with this botanical, the use of a spear is entirely unnecessary. A few drops of an aconite tincture can be deadly by itself. Aconite should always be handled with the utmost care, avoiding skin contact and in an airy space.

There are many species of aconite, but my aconite is *Aconitum napellus*, with beautiful purple helmets for blossoms. All species of the plant are deadly. Other names for aconite include auld wife's huid, blue rocket, devil's helmet, friar's cap, leopard's bane, monkshood, mousebane, wolf's bane, leopard's bane, and women's bane.

Properties and Correspondences

- *Latin name:* There are over one hundred species, but the most common is *Aconitum napellus*

- *Genus:* Aconitum

- *Classification:* Plant

- *Spiritual properties:* Removing anxiety and fear, calming, journeying to emotional depths.

- *Physiological properties:* Relief of intense acute attacks of anxiety, fear, cardiac troubles, and fever. May be useful for inflammation.

- *Magickal properties:* Aconite is the poison that heals quickly and intensely. Best used for situations that are acute, such as calming panic or instant removals.

- *Part used:* All

- *Planetary correspondences:* Saturn

- ✣ *Elemental correspondences*: Water
- ✣ *Archetype*: Thanategos (Death Bringer)
- ✣ *World*: Under
- ✣ *Zodiac*: Virgo
- ✣ *Color*: Violet
- ✣ *Stone*: Howlite (purple or white)
- ✣ *Animal*: Serpent

Indications

Deadly poison. Not to be consumed or applied to the skin without expert guidance. Keep away from the curious, including children, pets, and familiars.

Formulations

- ✣ Aconite can be purchased dried, in homeopathic tablets, as seeds, or as live plants. The seeds are also deadly, so use with care. The homeopathic tablets should not be assumed to be safe to ingest, but can be used in witchcraft. Commercial preparations of aconite, often referred to as monkshood, are typically very diluted.

- ✣ The plant is difficult to germinate and finicky about where she grows. Aconite can be challenging, but when she decides that she likes a spot, she will flourish.

- ✣ When working with any poison, follow safety protocols: wear gloves, avoid unintentional skin contact, and be in a well-ventilated area.

- ✣ Aconite works well in oils and tinctures. Any part of the plant will work well in these formulations. Use only a tiny amount—for example, 1 small leaf, 3 seeds, or 3 homeopathic tablets per cup of alcohol (for example, vodka) or oil.

- ✣ Consider using a botanical oracle card representing aconite when beginning to work with this botanical.

Pharmakeia

Aconite is an unparalleled teacher for those able to study her mysteries. To me, aconite is the truth of Hekatean witchcraft. It is not for the timid—it is dangerous, but beneficial—but may guide us to our own truths. Aconite is the milk of our Mother, nourishing and calming. However, I urge caution in rushing to work with this Queen of Poisons. She demands respect and resists eagerness.

If you want to experience the deep medicine of this botanical, proceed with caution. Start with a very weak oil. The effects of aconite will vary based on your constitution. I am not recommending using aconite in this way, however. Aconite is one of my personal pharmakoi, my greatest teacher. I've been building a relationship with this Queen of Poisons for years. My approach is to use a very small amount of a leaf in my personal sovereignty oil, and to anoint my inner wrists with a tiny amount, just until I feel the tingle. It took several trials for me to determine my reaction. Be wary of commercial products. Ask loads of questions about the concentration of the plant and ask if they've used true aconite and not a substitute.

I highly recommend deeply connecting to the medicine of aconite using the Magick, Medicine, and Mystery ritual later in the book (see page 242). It is a most favored plant master teacher. Place a representation of this Queen on your altar next to Hekate and ask her to bless your relationship with her favored pharmakoi. Note that Medea often comes through when working with her blessed aconite.

Banishing Anxiety Talisman

This talisman can be worn around the neck to reduce anxiety and is especially useful for stopping panic attacks.

Supplies

- ☩ 3 aconite seeds
- ☩ Small key
- ☩ Small glass vial with topper with a hole you can run a cord through
- ☩ Purple cord

Directions

- ☩ Suspend the key on a length of purple cord long enough for you to tie around your neck.
- ☩ Wearing gloves, count out the seeds on a piece of parchment paper. Place the vial on the paper.

- Using tweezers, place the seeds in the vial while reciting:

  With seed of one, anxiety is gone,
  With seed of two, my emotions are true,
  With seed of three, fear leaves me.

- Recite this again as you place the stopper on the vial, then again as you tie it around your neck.

Recite the incantation whenever you need to activate the calming power of your charm. Use caution regarding letting the seeds directly touch the skin.

Emergency Spell for Paralyzing an Enemy

Use this spell when you need an enemy to be stopped immediately. Perform it outside in a secluded area. This spell is as effective as it is simple. It needs to be kept in a place where its paralyzing power can't spread. That is why it is buried in an isolated location.

SUPPLIES

- Aconite tincture (see above)
- Image or written name of an enemy
- Black fabric
- Black cord
- Rock (yes, just a plain old rock big enough to cover the paquet you'll be making)

DIRECTIONS

- Write the name of the enemy on a piece of paper in black ink, then place the paper on a small piece of black fabric.
- Add drops of the tincture to cover the enemy's name or image, while reciting:

  I paralyze (enemy's name) now, no more shall you harm (person being
  protected).

- Wrap the paper in the black fabric and tie it into a paquet with the cord.

- Take the paquet to its resting spot and dig a small hole.

- ☙ Place the paquet in its place.
- ☙ Put the rock on top of the paquet, reciting:
  This spell is set in stone, and can only be broken by me alone.
- ☙ Cover the spell with soil.

To the Goddess

The depths of the Mother,
The brown-black soil
Beneath my feet,
That feeds my soul,
And steals my pain away.
Hail, Hekate,
Mother, Sister, Witch.
Emotional Warrior,
Bone Dancer,
Truth Revealer.
The hidden depths of the garden lie within me.
You are the poison that heals,
The bane that blesses.
The bareness of truth revealed.
This is my power I claim through the gentle embrace of your poisons.

Agrimony

Agrimony was discovered in ancient times by Mithridates Eupator, King of Pontus in northern Turkey. It is sometimes confused with a different plant used by the ancient Greeks to heal eye troubles. Eupator discovered the plant's use as a general tonic. Unsurprisingly, agrimony was known as a heal-all and is recorded as such in the account of Hekate's Garden in *The Argonautica*. Other names for the plant include cocklebur and stickwort. Its genus name refers to about a dozen different species, all with similar properties. The Eupatoria variety is the one usually available for purchase.

This pharmakoi grows wild in its many varieties in many areas of North America and Europe. Look for the tall stalks with their clusters of small yellow flowers.

Agrimony is associated with eternal sleep in folklore and is sometimes known as the herb of Sleeping Beauty. The plant's effects are enduring and it's very difficult to undo any working involving agrimony. Ancient, enduring, and eternal, its archetype is the *Ambrotos* (Eternal One) who both tempts and taunts the witch.

Agrimony is useful for uncrossings involving communication troubles within and without. Consider that the dream world exists as is, and it is up to us to be able to understand what we learn there. Agrimony uncrosses the tangles we can experience in interpreting dreams and relaxes the conscious mind so that we can enter deep, restorative sleep. In a comparable way, agrimony can uncross internal energies, restoring the dominance of the soul over the shadow. She can undo the forces of psychic attacks, toxic people, and other sorts of external curses flung at us. Agrimony is not a boomerang; the uncrossed energy is merely released into the universe to settle where it is needed, so I don't recommend it for banishings.

One of the most useful attributes of agrimony in daily spiritual work is to uncross your mental focus from one of lack to one of plenty, making this a great companion for gratitude work.

Properties and Correspondences

⚥ *Latin name*: Agrimonia eupatoria

⚥ *Genus*: Agrimonia

⚥ *Classification*: Herb

⚥ *Spiritual properties*: Repelling harmful energies, dream journeying, expressing gratitude, general healing, psychic healing.

⚥ *Physiological properties*: Traditionally seen as a heal-all, agrimony is known to soothe a cough and sore throat, cleanse the liver, and cure insomnia and nightmares. Also good as an astringent and for healing wounds.

⚥ *Magickal properties*: Counter-magick, curse-breaking, dream work, good luck, repelling harmful energies.

⚥ *Part used*: Leaves, stem

⚥ *Planetary correspondences*: Jupiter, Mercury

- ✣ *Elemental correspondences*: Air
- ✣ *Archetype*: Ambrotos (Eternal One)
- ✣ *World*: Upper
- ✣ *Zodiac*: Cancer
- ✣ *Color*: Yellow
- ✣ *Stone*: Honey calcite
- ✣ *Animal*: Dragonfly

Indications

Generally safe to consume.

Formulations

- ✣ Agrimony is amenable to any sort of formulary, from a quick infusion to use as an ingredient in incense.
- ✣ I've found that the sometimes-too-sharp edge of agrimony mellows, while its ability as an uncrosser, from negative self-talk to removing psychic vampires, gets amplified in slow-release formulations.
- ✣ The smell is mildly peachy, with a bit of woodsy undertones. However, the taste is slightly bitter, so a bit of sweetener may be in order.

Pharmakeia

An agrimony paquet is excellent when placed under the bed to prevent nightmares. Use an agrimony decoction in your floor wash, and to rinse your hair when you are your own worst enemy.

Agrimony Oxymel

Agrimony's constitution is dry and cool, and making an uncooked oxymel (Latin for "acid and honey") works in a complementary way with this natural vibe.

Use this oxymel internally to uncross yourself, for quelling negative self-talk, and for helping to understand the messages of the spirit world. It can also improve sleep quality and give access to dream-world medicine. One spoonful before retiring should work, but this can be increased to two. For an added sleep tonic, dissolve the oxymel in a cup of chamomile tea.

To use this mixture for uncrossing spells, hold a spoonful in your mouth, concentrate on your intention, and then spit it out on an image of the trouble. Always dispose of the image.

Ingredients

¼ cup agrimony

¼ cup apple-cider vinegar

¼ cup honey

1-cup glass container with lid. You don't want much air in the container.

Directions

☙ Place the agrimony, then the honey, and finally the vinegar in the jar.

☙ Shake vigorously.

☙ Shake every day for two weeks, then it will be ready for use.

☙ Keep in a cool, dark place.

American Mandrake and Mandragora

A proud member of Hekate's Garden since antiquity, mandrake has long been associated with magick in Europe. Perhaps there is no other plant as strongly associated with magick as the mandrake. From the Bible to *Harry Potter*, the magical properties of mandrake are the subject of lore and fiction.

The forked root of European mandrake bears some resemblance to the legs of a man. Combined with the entheogenic properties of the plant, the personality of this plant has given rise to a great deal of lore. It was said to grow only beneath the gallows and, when torn from the earth by its root, to utter a murderous shriek.

European mandrake is incredibly difficult to purchase and more challenging to grow. The vast majority of mandrake sold in North America is of the native variety (*Podophyllum peltatum*). The chopped roots should be sold in double-thick brown paper bags to keep out light and to prevent seepage of the oils of the root. Reputable retailers will label American mandrake as such or as mayapple. If you purchase the cut root, it should have an intense earthy smell.

The European varieties (mandragora) are considered nightshades, while American mandrake is a member of *berberidaceae* (as is blue cohosh). Not all nightshades are entheogens, but many have consciousness-altering properties—for instance, tobacco. American mandrake was most likely so named because its root structure can resemble a person. The First Nations peoples also reportedly had similar lore and uses for this plant. Both are proud members of the Poison Path. As such, they should be approached with great caution.

American mandrake can be found in forests across eastern North America. The plant, like the European mandrake, is very slow to mature. Some colonies of the plant can be over 100 years old. Since the root is used in witchcraft, take only what you need if wildharvesting and always wear gloves. The active component in mayapple is *podophyllin*. Ingesting American mandrake as an entheogen should be approached with caution.

Other names for the plant include duck's foot, hog apple, Satan's apple, raccoon berry, wild lemon mandragora, manroot, circeium, gallows, herb of Circe, ladykins, womandrake (female roots), and sorcerer's root.

In general, mandrake is a complex spirit. Since it is a loner who tends to take up a lot of spiritual room, adding correspondences can be challenging, except in spells where mandrake has been convinced to be a team player.

Properties and Correspondences

- ⚜ *Name and genus*: Three completely unrelated types of plants comprise the many faces of mandrake. To the previously mentioned American and European varieties, a third contender from Britain can be added. English mandrake, the white bryony, *Bryonia dioica*, is a hedgerow plant of southeast England that has a large multi-lobed taproot similar to European mandrake.

- ⚜ *Parts used*: The root is generally used in witchcraft. The fruit of the American mandrake can be used in a variety of ways, since it is safe to consume. This plant has been used as a substitute for mandragora for centuries because of the root similarity, although the properties of the two plants are somewhat different. White bryony roots were carved into elaborate talismans and sold for ridiculous prices. The roots have been substituted for mandragora in other ways, including for use as bitters.

- ⚜ *General properties*: Fertility, secrecy, trance, revelation, increasing potency of any working, sympathetic witchcraft. Prevents harmful spirits from entering.

- *Spiritual properties*: Courage, discipline, increase of spiritual energy, power, protection, trance, sleep, visions. Mandragora is a powerful entheogen.

- *Physiological properties*: Very strong purgative and emetic. Poisonous. Treatment for warts (American). Damaging to the eyes.

- *Magickal properties*: Attracting spirits, banishing, curse-breaking, divination, defensive magick, honoring witchcraft.

- *Planetary correspondences*: Mercury, Saturn, Moon

- *Elemental correspondences*: Fire (primary), Earth, Air (secondary)

- *Archetype*: Borborophorba (Eater of Filth)

- *Stone*: Onyx

- *Zodiac*: Gemini

- *Color*: Black

- *World*: Under

- *Animal*: Bat

Indications

Poisonous. Avoid contact with the eyes.

Formulations

The following guidelines are for use with American mandrake. Avoid getting this botanical into your eyes.

- The cut root of American mandrake can easily be made into a tincture. Use about 1 tbsp root in $^1/_3$ cup of 80-proof vodka or other strong clear liquor. Let steep for one lunar cycle, gently shaking daily. This tincture is excellent for anointing magickal tools. Use as a base for witch jars, especially in banishings.

- Effective as a moon water. Mix ¼ cup of cut root and 2 cups of pure water in a clear glass container. Charge during the appropriate moon phase for a minimum of three nights. Seal and wrap in black fabric until the mixture is ready to use.

- American mandrake's intense, slow-burning energy is well-suited to use in charms. The spirit of mandrake is generally amenable as

an addition to any spell, if it speaks to you. Mandrake is a willful deva, so be confident in your directions.

- ☥ Mandrake can be burned on its own. Sometimes it doesn't get along with other botanicals, so mixing into a blend can be difficult. It does blend well, however, with benzoin. Avoid breathing in large amounts of the smoke and avoid getting it in your eyes.

- ☥ Circe used mandrake in her philter for transforming men into pigs, demonstrating this root's power of revelation. Use the tincture applied to an image of the person of interest to reveal their truth.

- ☥ Use mandrake moon water or diluted tincture in a spray bottle to asperge household thresholds and keep away all evil.

- ☥ Mandrake is excellent for sympathetic magick. Make a guardian poppet by stuffing it with mandrake, or tie American mandrake roots in a bundle. Attune the poppet by adding symbols of that which will be protected. This botanical is especially good for protecting magickal objects, tools, symbols, and such things.

Pharmakeia

Plant spirit work is perhaps the most powerful form of mandrake magick. Using an intact root or whole plant is the easiest for communication. Chopped root can be re-bound into a whole spirit within a witch bag or poppet. My mandragora poppet is a potent source of magick that watches over my spellcraft.

Mandrake in a bag beside the bed will facilitate dream work. Mandrake under the bed ensures passion and fertility. Powdered mandrake root is used to enhance fertility and prosperity charms. Spend time connecting with the magick of this botanical. It is a most powerful spirit that will deepen your practice.

Mandrake Servitor

This poppet is made by stuffing black fabric with the chopped root of either American mandrake or mandragora. This creates a servitor spirit that is made purely from the *deva* (archetypal soul) of the plant. Thus it is a bit of captured essence from the master spirit of the plant. The servitor will abide with you and assist in watching over your apothecary. I keep mine, Mr. Philip Mandragora, in an antique cupboard alongside my botanicals, formulations, and supplies. He is a companion as well as a guardian, watching over my most treasured magickal objects. He resides with them, keeping them safe and charged. I talk to him regularly. It's very difficult for me to have a living plant in my environment, so using the cut root to animate a spirit works very well for me.

Mandrake is a most willful plant that needs strict management, but it is most useful as a spirit to watch over witchery. Once you've established a relationship with the plant, explain to the spirit how you will be working with it. Mandragora responds well to specific instructions. Be mindful that the spirit may have strong medicine for you.

SUPPLIES

- ⚜ Small amount of cut mandragora
- ⚜ Black bag for the mandragora
- ⚜ Darning needle and thread
- ⚜ Burlap fabric
- ⚜ Natural twine
- ⚜ Scraps of black fabric for stuffing the poppet

DIRECTIONS

- ⚜ Sew a small doll out of the burlap, leaving one side of the body open.
- ⚜ Stuff the head, legs, and arms with the fabric scraps.
- ⚜ Place the mandragora in the black bag and insert into the body, then sew up the opening.
- ⚜ Activate the poppet by speaking it to life, explaining what its role will be.
- ⚜ Nourish the poppet by keeping it with your botanicals and place it beside you when practicing your pharmakeia.

Aster

Hail to *Pharmakoi Asteria*, Mother of the Mother. Aster is the epitome of loving-kindness, but she isn't directly associated with Hekate's mother, Asteria, in popular mythology. What remains in the written record is a tale of a different, but similarly named, Goddess, Astraea, who was associated with innocence. She ascended to the Starry Road, where she became the constellation Virgo.

Back on Earth, Zeus flooded the planet to cleanse it of corruption, killing everyone except two people who were stranded on the top of Mount Parnassus. Astraea was deeply saddened by the plight of humanity. As her tears fell to Earth, they created the very first asters. To this day, the spirit of aster is that of compassion and love.

Asteria, Hekate's mother, was, to the ancients, the stars themselves, so that this version of the story, while different, suggests a close association between Asteria and Astraea. Consider Astraea to be an adopted daughter of the Mother of the Mother, Hekate's sister.

Given this complex mythological association, it's not surprising that the beautiful aster is so evocative of Hekate's more tender aspects. We can also be reminded that kindness can help us navigate the complexities of relationships.

Aster is a combination of emotional depths and earthiness, often growing in damp places. Asters, either white or purple, are abundant in the month of September in most of North America and Europe. If you can't pick some in the wild (they love roadsides), purchase a few commercial stems. They are slightly fragrant and very lovely to have fresh. They also dry wonderfully and can be included in bundles.

Aster is also known as the herb of Venus, and she makes an excellent addition to spells for everlasting love, from maternal to romantic. The root has been used for centuries in Traditional Chinese Medicine. In North America, many of the indigenous peoples used the various species for medicine, including using the root to ease congestion, for smudging, and for bringing love. Its use as a febrifuge (a medicine used to combat fever) demonstrates its properties of moist cooling. Aster is the soothing touch that heals body, mind, and spirit.

There are hundreds of varieties of this flower, from the small clustered blossoms of the New England aster (*Aster novae-angliae*) that grows all around my property, to the large China aster (*Callistephus*) that is often grown in gardens and sold as cut flowers.

Properties and Correspondences

- ⚨ *Latin name*: Aster
- ⚨ *Genus*: Aster
- ⚨ *Classification*: Flower
- ⚨ *Spiritual properties*: Calming, compassion, de-stressing, kindness, unconditional love, nurturing, truth.

- ☙ *Physiological properties*: May have use in reducing fever and inflammation, as well as soothing digestive complaints.

- ☙ *Magickal propertes*: Blessings, offerings, revealing love, encouraging kindness.

- ☙ *Part used*: Flowers

- ☙ *Planetary correspondences*: Venus

- ☙ *Elemental correspondences*: Water, Earth

- ☙ *Archetype*: Pantrophos (Nurturer)

- ☙ *World*: Under

- ☙ *Zodiac*: Virgo, Sagittarius

- ☙ *Color*: Purple, white, pink

- ☙ *Stone*: Rhodochrosite

- ☙ *Animal*: Cow

Indications

Generally safe for adults and children to consume the flowers and the leaves. Also safe for cats and dogs.

Formulations

- ☙ Foraging for wild asters is an excellent ritual for connecting with the primal loving force of the universe. When harvesting the wildflowers, ensure that the plant is dry and cut about four inches from the ground. Wash these flowers, and then add to salads. They are mildly bitter.

- ☙ To dry, hang upside down in a cool, dark place. The dried flowers will be beautifully white and fluffy. They make an excellent addition to bundles or can be crumbled easily to add to incense blends. They have a mild, woodsy scent that layers well with sage and wormwood.

- ☙ Aster can be consumed in an infusion. Three blossoms in a cup of boiled water is a good strength to benefit from its calming power.

Pharmakeia

Add asters to any working where you want to let love reign. I always include them in my personal sovereignty oil. They are a huge part of my autumnal offerings as well. Aster is very wise as the primal source of love energy. Asters are the stars that fell from heaven and bore witness to the rebirth of humanity, so they are beautiful allies for emotional work and rituals of renewal. They also will ease a troubled mind and heart, offering reconnection to our trust in ourselves and the universe.

Aster's Blessing Bath Bombs

There's no better way to experience the warm embrace of aster than through a ritual bath using these bubbling bombs. These bombs will prepare you for beautiful, healing dreams.

In these bombs, bergamot and bitter orange are added to the aster. Bergamot brings focus, dream work, openness, optimism, and sleep to the blend. It is associated with Mercury, the moon, and Venus, and is ruled by Air. Bitter orange, also known as neroli, provides confidence, joy, and protection because it is a solar plant associated with Fire. Bergamot is of the Upper World; neroli of the Middle. With all four elements and the Three Worlds represented in the blend, it is a complete spiritual experience. Both are strong allies for healing work in the Dream Time.

SUPPLIES

- ✣ Petals from about a dozen wild aster blossoms (about 1 tbsp), plus a few intact blossoms
- ✣ Bergamot essential oil
- ✣ Neroli essential oil
- ✣ 2 tsp olive oil
- ✣ ½ cup cream of tartar
- ✣ 1 cup baking soda
- ✣ 3 tbsp Epsom salts
- ✣ Water in a spray bottle
- ✣ Mixing bowl
- ✣ Spoon

♣ Silicone or other type of mold. I like to use those small condiment cups with lids to make these easy to store and give as gifts.

Directions

♣ Mix the dry ingredients together well.

♣ Add the aster and 5 to 7 drops of the essential oils. Blend well.

♣ Mix in the olive oil. The mixture should feel "sandy" and slightly sticky.

♣ Take a small amount and squeeze it into a ball in your hand. If it doesn't cling together at all, spray the entire mixture with a spritz of the water, then try again. Repeat if necessary.

♣ If the mixture gets too moist, you'll hear the bubbling reaction start to occur. Simply remove the extra moisture by squeezing the mixture in a cloth or paper towel.

♣ Place one of the intact blossoms at the bottom of your mold if you like. Then pack the mixture on top.

♣ Let dry for twenty-four hours in the mold, then remove and let stand for another twenty-four hours before using.

Basil

Basil is traditionally associated with death, burial, and initiation. In the ancient Mediterranean region, basil was known as an herb of mourning and was likely used in embalming. To the ancient Greeks, basil was known as *basilikon phuton*, the King of Herbs. It may have been used in death rites to banish the spirit from the present, thereby protecting the living and helping the departed transition. Basil banishes through fire energy, burning away what is no longer desired.

Basil most likely originated in India, where it has always played a role in the traditional medicine of Ayurveda, as well as in Traditional Chinese Medicine. Because of its association with removing what no longer serves, it is traditionally an herb of initiation, consumed by initiates as they learn the mysteries. It was chosen for this role because it not only banishes the ignorant former self, but also calms the mind while releasing our fire. Basil is such a complex herb that Culpeper himself urged restraint in using it for medicine.

There are many varieties of basil, from the sweet variety that is most popular in cooking, to others including Thai, holy, and lemon. There are some variations in characteristics. Those given below relate to common sweet basil.

Properties and Correspondences

- ❧ *Latin name*: Ocimum basilicum
- ❧ *Genus*: Ocimum
- ❧ *Classification*: Herb
- ❧ *Spiritual properties*: Afterlife, banishing, grief, initiation, loss.
- ❧ *Physiological properties*: Antioxidant, antiviral, antimicrobial. Taken as part of daily tonic to increase internal heat. Lowers blood pressure.
- ❧ *Magickal properties*: Banishing, confidence, courage, initiation, power, rebirth, release.
- ❧ *Part used*: Leaves
- ❧ *Planetary correspondences*: Mars, Venus
- ❧ *Elemental correspondences*: Fire
- ❧ *Archetype*: Basileia (Empress)
- ❧ *World*: Middle
- ❧ *Zodiac*: Aries, Scorpio
- ❧ *Color*: Red
- ❧ *Stone*: Garnet
- ❧ *Animal*: Ram

Indications

Generally safe in small doses for animals, children, and adults. Those with low blood pressure should use with caution. Basil connects to dragon energy and activates your inner serpent.

Formulations

Basil can be used in the full spectrum of formulary. The essential oil can be purchased and fresh basil is widely available. It is a difficult yet rewarding kitchen herb to grow. Carry fresh basil to be more assertive, fierce, and to help speak your truth.

Serve as part of the meal to ensure that all those present accelerate their personal fire.

Pharmakeia

Basil is a fiery pharmakoi. It burns away and does so with alacrity. Keep that in mind when working with it. Basil is associated with death and destruction, and as such is an excellent tool for banishing in addition to initiation and deathwalking.

Ruled by Mars, basil brings courage. It is also renowned for deathwalking, given the easy transition and fear-removal side of this amazing plant. Remember to let basil know how you wish him to perform.

Double "B" Banisher

This is one of my favorite spells. I make extra of the enchanted paper and store it wrapped in black fabric so I have it on standby for quick banishings. The paper remains neutral until activated with sigils. Create your sigil by decomposing the letters in the name of the person or thing you are banishing, and then crafting them into a unified form. Banishing is a serious business. Make sure you truly want to remove whatever it is before proceeding. I like this spell for removing obstacles, but it also works for people and places.

Blackberry gets along very well with basil because they merge their prickly sides. Both are associated with Venus, but blackberry has her in Aries. Both were used as treatments for poisons, so you can view this banisher as an anti-venom to whatever is toxic in your life. Always remember that botanicals have multiple properties, so be sure to let them know what energies you'll be using. Concentrate on blackberry's power for banishing and basil's death notes while sitting with them. Write an incantation for reciting while you brew the potion.

On its own, use the spell to banish during the waning moon. Add to a spell of attraction (e.g., growth, prosperity) to remove obstacles during the Full Moon. Potent colors for this spell are black and deep purple.

SUPPLIES

- ⚜ Medium-sized stainless-steel pot with lid
- ⚜ Witch's spoon (wooden)

- ✤ Fine mesh strainer
- ✤ Parchment paper
- ✤ Black permanent marker
- ✤ Scissors
- ✤ Knife
- ✤ Funnel
- ✤ Glass bottle with lid

INGREDIENTS

½ pint blackberries

2 cups white vinegar

½ cup fresh basil or 1 tbsp dried

DIRECTIONS

Be sure that all stirring and other activities are done counter-clockwise.

- ✤ Gently warm the white vinegar in the pot on low-to-medium heat until it is slightly hot to the touch.
- ✤ Once warmed, add the blackberries and basil. Reduce heat to low and simmer covered, stirring frequently for fifteen minutes.
- ✤ Allow to cool to room temperature.
- ✤ While the mixture cools, cut the parchment paper into strips about four inches by six inches. Make a few extra.
- ✤ Once the potion has cooled, gently immerse the paper in it, making sure it's completely covered. Do each strip individually, letting each one rest for at least ten minutes.
- ✤ Remove the strips and place them on a towel that you don't mind staining. Let dry. You can hasten the process with a blow-dryer on low or cool. Be mindful not to get the paper on other surfaces, as it will stain.
- ✤ Strain and funnel the remaining potion into a glass bottle.
- ✤ Once the paper has dried, design a sigil representing whatever you want to banish. When you are happy with it, transfer it onto one of the banishing strips.

⚜ Place the banishing strip near whatever you want gone. If this isn't possible, use an image or write the words associated with it on a card and then bind it to the parchment. Place it under Hekate's statue, asking her to release it into the world.

This mixture is safe to consume, so you can use it as a dressing for a salad that you serve to your enemy.

Bay Laurel

Bay leaves are a common kitchen-witch ingredient in spells. This humble herb—probably in your cupboard—has been associated with Hekate since ancient times. Bay laurel's history goes back even farther than this example from the 2nd century BCE. Bay has long been associated with attracting benefits, from love to finances. The latter use of bay has become quite common in contemporary witchcraft, with many a simple spell proclaiming that money can be manifested through burning a single leaf or carrying one in your wallet.

Bay was a religious herb chewed by the priestesses at Delphi while they proclaimed their visions. Wreaths and other objects made out of bay laurel were both status symbols and recognition of achievement in the ancient world of Hekate.

Properties and Correspondences

⚜ *Latin name*: *Laurus nobilis*

⚜ *Genus*: *Laurus*

⚜ *Classification*: Tree, herb

⚜ *Spiritual properties*: Kindness, protection of the home, love, prosperity, visions.

⚜ *Physiological properties*: Healing bruises, astringent, emetic.

⚜ *Magickal properties*: Attraction, manifestation, psychic development.

⚜ *Part used*: Leaves, stems

⚜ *Planetary correspondences*: Sun

⚜ *Elemental correspondences*: Air, Fire

⚜ *Archetype*: Enodia (Road)

⚜ *World*: Middle

- ♣ *Zodiac*: Leo
- ♣ *Color*: Green
- ♣ *Stone*: Aventurine
- ♣ *Animal*: Horse

Indications

Avoid ingesting large amounts, although it is generally safe otherwise. Bay has mild narcotic properties.

Formulations

- ♣ Bay tincture is great for physical, spiritual, and magickal work. Place several leaves in a cup of 80-proof alcohol. Seal well and keep in cool, dark place. Shake daily. It will be ready for use after a few days. Test the mixture on the inside of your wrist for skin sensitivity.
- ♣ Bay can also be used in magickal oils and purchased as a commercial oil.
- ♣ Bay can work in an infusion, but let it rest a bit longer than usual, since the leaves are quite tough.
- ♣ Burn bay on its own for a simple attraction spell.
- ♣ Use a burning bay leaf in the khernips ritual.
- ♣ To add to incense, chop the plant (using fingers or scissors) into small pieces, then pound with pestle/rock/etc. to release its properties.

Pharmakeia

A dish of salt with a bay leaf in it will purify the home. Add peppercorns to keep the energy warm. Bay leaves in a talisman by the main entrance keep out harmful energies and uninvited spirits of all kinds. The popular practice of writing your intention on a bay leaf can be successful, as long as you summon the spirit of bay and choose the color of ink carefully. One of the most amazing attributes of bay magick and medicine is that this plant spirit is amenable to use in so many ways.

Bay Blessing Bowl

A blessing bowl is a spell that is contained within one vessel. Fill the bottom of a bowl with salt, sand, or soil. Then arrange bay leaves around the perimeter. In the middle of the leaves, add an image, charm, or even a stone that represents what you are blessing. Bay can also be used without the talisman (image, charm) to bless the home and everyone in it.

Benzoin

Benzoin is a rather wondrous balsam resin with myriad magickal and mundane uses. Because it is gentler than myrrh and frankincense, it is an excellent "gateway" resin for those new to working with these plant spirits.

Burn benzoin incense, diffuse the essential oil, or asperge a benzoin tincture to cleanse spaces before sacred rites. Use the tincture throughout your home to make it into your sanctuary.

The spirit of benzoin is much like that of the King of Cups in the tarot—steady, sure, and wise. It is celestial, but not overbearing, although the resin is associated with the element of Fire and the planet Mars. Benzoin is not a wild ride through the cosmos, but it will gladly support you through one. It is especially useful for clearing the mind of clutter and is often used as a base for a blended incense, tinctures, and oils. A real team player in the plant spirit world, benzoin brings together, creates wholeness, and makes a perfect binding agent. It is a comfort during most forms of ecstatic witchcraft, because it eases transition into the spirit realm and aids in shamanic journeys.

Guardian of the Crossroads

Ruled by Mars and associated with Fire, Earth, and Water, benzoin is a complex but unassuming spirit. Benzoin derives from the sap of the benzoin styrax tree native to India, Thailand, and other parts of southern Asia. It is a pathological product, since the tree is wounded in order for it to bleed the sap, which hardens into the resin. It is widely used as a sacred incense in India, where it is known as loban and is excellent for burning during sacred rites.

Other names for benzoin include Benjamin, benzoin gum, styrax, loban (although this is a general name used in India for all frankincense-like resins as well), snowbells, and storax (not to be confused with the resin of the witch hazel tree that goes by the same name).

Properties and Correspondences

- ⚜ *Latin name*: Styrax benzoin
- ⚜ *Genus*: Styrax
- ⚜ *Classification*: Resin
- ⚜ *Spiritual properties*: Cleansing the spirit, opening the way to astral realms, facilitating journeying and ecstatic witchery. Burn while contemplating personal balance.
- ⚜ *Physiological properties*: Regular inhalation of benzoin reduces distress. Added to steam, it clears congestion. In a tincture, it is an excellent treatment for wounds.
- ⚜ *Magickal properties*: Add as a binder to any working, from incense to witch bottles. Use for purification, astral travel, and spiritual journeying.
- ⚜ *Parts used*: Balsam resin
- ⚜ *Planetary correspondences*: Mars
- ⚜ *Elemental correspondences*: Fire
- ⚜ *Archetype*: Tetraoditis (Guardian of the Crossroads)
- ⚜ *World*: Middle
- ⚜ *Zodiac*: Aries, Virgo
- ⚜ *Color*: Brown, gold
- ⚜ *Stone*: Brown tourmaline
- ⚜ *Animal*: Peacock

Indications

Generally safe in small amounts.

Formulations

⚜ Benzoin can be purchased in chunks of the resin (grind it in mortar and pestle), pre-ground, and in essential oils and tinctures. It is easy to grind, so don't waste your money on fancy preparations. Grinding it yourself will yield much more powerful results and the smell is amazing. Look for medium-brown chunks with bits of white.

⚜ The pleasant scent and clean smoke of benzoin render it an excellent spirit released as smoke. It is easy to burn on a charcoal disk, and great to burn before and during a social gathering.

⚜ Benzoin has great powers as a fixative, slowing the dispersion of other botanicals into the air, whether as part of incense, blended oils, or candles.

⚜ In Traditional Chinese Medicine, benzoin resin is used to clear stagnation and to eliminate congestion.

⚜ Benzoin is commercially used in food products, cosmetics, veterinary medicine, and scented candles. It contains vanillin and is used as flavoring in alcoholic and nonalcoholic beverages, baked goods, chewing gum, frozen dairy, gelatins, puddings, and soft candy.

⚜ Friar's balsam, also known as benzoin tincture, is widely used in medical procedures and for treating wounds. Pure benzoin will burn to a fine white ash and dissolve in a tincture.

Pharmakeia

Diffuse benzoin oil to calm restless spirits, including your own and other humans. It calms children well and it is usually safe for them to be exposed to the smoke or vapor. Add chips to candles to release the spirit into the flame.

Benzoin tinctures can be purchased easily or made from about 1 tbsp ground benzoin to $1/3$ cup ethanol. Anoint the Third Eye with a tincture or oil twenty minutes prior to journeying. Use as offering to most spirits and deities.

Benzoin Tarot Booster

One of benzoin's most wonderful abilities is to open the door calmly to a deeper understanding of the mysteries. Benzoin burned during tarot readings will amplify your psychic skills without a great deal of fuss. If you've ever had a headache after doing an intense reading, benzoin would most likely have pre-

vented it. Keeping a bit of benzoin in with your cards will clarify and amplify their power. Benzoin advances our understanding of the more challenging Major Arcana, deepens our appreciation of the earthy understanding of Pentacles, adds insight to the watery emotional depths of Cups, calms the fire of Wands, and simmers down the flights of Swords.

Birch

Birch, the Lady of the Woods, offers herself for our witchery in so many ways, from banishing besoms, to creating magickal fires, to healing tonics. Her bark gives us a medium on which we can write our spells. She is one of my favorite trees in Hekate's Garden. Birch offers quiet, undemanding, and remarkable strength. As tenacious as they come, it makes a remarkable binder. Using the bark as a base for a sigil will ensure that it is enduring and powerful.

Birch offers sustained emotional healing, increases stability, and is particularly helpful when working on your sovereignty. It has supporting properties that further augment our sovereignty work: focus, freedom, protection, purification, rebirth, self-work, well-being, and wisdom. Burning the dried bark is a terrific way to cleanse a space prior to a working.

Birch is a master plant teacher in many traditions and cultures, from the Celts to the aboriginal tribes of North America. Traditionally, besoms made of birch branches were used for banishing. Fires made of birch also banish harm while binding blessings to us. Its branches are excellent for wands and stangs.

Birch is kind, yet regal. Always composed, she shares her secrets with witches who commune with her. Honor birch through a simple ritual to connect with her power under the light of the Full Moon.

Properties and Correspondences

- ⚲ *Latin name*: *Betula alba* (white birch), *pendula* (silver), or *lenta* (black or sweet) are common varieties
- ⚲ *Genus*: *Betula*
- ⚲ *Classification*: Tree
- ⚲ *Spiritual properties*: Growth, emotional healing, purpose, wisdom.
- ⚲ *Physiological properties*: The parts of the birch have different qualities. In addition, the various species of birch have specific uses that go beyond its general healing abilities. Birch leaves have powerful

pain-relieving powers. The bark is an antiseptic and treatment for skin irritations.

- ❧ *Magickal properties*: Awareness, banishing, binding, determination, emotional healing, stability, sovereignty.

- ❧ *Part used*: Wood, buds, leaves, bark, sap

- ❧ *Planetary correspondences*: Venus, Moon

- ❧ *Elemental correspondences*: Water

- ❧ *Archetype*: Despoina (Lady)

- ❧ *World*: Under

- ❧ *Zodiac*: Capricorn

- ❧ *Color*: Black, silver

- ❧ *Stone*: Labradorite

- ❧ *Animal*: Wolf

Indications

Birch leaves and bark are generally safe to consume in small amounts. It should not be used by those allergic to aspirin, since birch contains salicylate.

Formulations

- ❧ Tradition dictates that birch bark must only be gathered from fallen trees or from that which the tree has naturally released, or else the wrath of the pharmakoi Despoina will find you. The leaves and buds are safe to pick.

- ❧ Birch-leaf tea is excellent as a tonic when doing deep emotional work, and as an anti-inflammatory. The connection between emotional wounds and physical pain lies in the roots of the source, which is often early-childhood trauma. Birch works on these roots, untangling the dis-ease underlying the symptoms experienced. Birch-leaf tea can be purchased, but it is very simple to make by covering fresh leaves with water, bringing the mixture to a boil, and then letting it steep for ten minutes. Cover the leaves with about two inches extra water. Sweeten with honey to tame the bitter taste.

Pharmakeia

Birch branches will banish all harm. Steep the branches in boiling water and put about two cups of the mixture in a spray bottle with ¼ cup white vinegar to make a banishing spray. Birch bark is excellent for all power workings, especially sovereignty. Drink a birch tea for standing in your power. The buds are amazing for new projects. Craft a talisman using the buds and attach charms symbolic of your project to banish barriers and bind success.

Birch Power Sigil

Create a power sigil using birch bark. Birch is a supreme binder. When harvesting birch in the wild, look around the base of the tree for shed pieces. Use your astrological signs, the letters in your name, and other symbols important to you to construct your own power sigil. Activate the sigil with frankincense oil. Use it to attune objects like a computer or car to your own energy, and as a boost when you are feeling drained.

Black Cohosh

Black cohosh is a uniquely North American wildflower whose roots are prized for their power to restore feminine energy. Prized by many indigenous peoples for its power to treat menstrual troubles and ease childbirth, it has also been used for a variety of health complaints, from snakebite to helping babies sleep.

This plant is a most willing ally in connecting to the feminine divine. As one of my personal favorites, I have a Circe poppet stuffed with this botanical that draws me closer to her when I weave my spells. Black cohosh simulates estrogen, making it a powerful boost for physiologically low levels of this hormone, but take note that this also makes it unsuitable for use by anyone not wishing to interfere with their natural cycle.

Also known as bugbane, fair candle, and black snakeroot, black cohosh is not to be confused with the blue variety. It is an excellent banisher and a traditional part of hoodoo root work.

Properties and Correspondences

- ⚷ *Latin name*: Actaea racemosa

- ⚷ *Genus*: Actaea

- ⚷ *Classification*: Plant

- *Spiritual properties*: Balance, calm, courage, love, lust, strength.

- *Physiological properties*: Antidepressant, emmenagogue, soothes PMS, soothes menopause, inflammation, works like estrogen, increases serotonin.

- *Magickal properties*: Attraction spells, banishings, communication with the divine, protection, revelations, visions.

- *Part used*: Root

- *Planetary correspondences*: Mars, Moon

- *Elemental correspondences*: Fire

- *Archetype*: Erannos (Lovely One)

- *World*: Middle

- *Zodiac*: Scorpio

- *Color*: White

- *Stone*: Moonstone

- *Animal*: Panther

Indications

This plant is generally safe for up to one year's use in healthy adults. Beyond that, liver damage may occur. It is not for use by those on antidepressants, those sensitive to birth-control pills, or during pregnancy, and should not be used by animals or children.

Formulations

- A more resistant root, black cohosh should be steeped a bit longer than the average leaf infusion, about ten minutes. It has a slightly bitter taste, so a bit of honey may be in order. Use about ¼ tsp per cup of boiled water.

- This botanical is excellent to have on hand as a tincture, made with about 1 tsp of plant material to ½ cup of alcohol.

- Keep a small paquet of the root with your feminine products, clothes, and personal belongings to keep them connected to the feminine divine.

Pharmakeia

This pharmakoi, whose epithet is the Lovely One, is a stealthy mistress whose power is belied by her charm. Black cohosh is an excellent spirit to connect with to understand your own feminine side, as well as to open the way to our Triple Goddesses.

Goddess Poppet

The goal of this poppet is to bind yourself to your chosen Goddess. This is useful for forging a strong relationship between the two of you and is most suited for establishing an enduring relationship. It allows the owner of the poppet to access the Goddess energy to evoke and invoke. Keep in mind that the Goddess herself is not meant to be bound, but a portion of her force is contained. I have a Circe poppet that lets me access her powers of pharmakos and explore her other powers.

SUPPLIES

⚜ Piece of black t-shirt fabric (excellent from an old one) about 10 inches by 10 inches

⚜ String

⚜ About 1 cup of black cohosh. You can add other botanicals like mugwort and pennyroyal.

⚜ Small piece of obsidian for the head

⚜ Small piece of moonstone for the heart

⚜ Symbols of your chosen Goddess

⚜ Paper and pen

⚜ Scissors

⚜ Fabric markers for decorating

DIRECTIONS

⚜ Choose a Goddess to whom you are confident you want to be bound.

⚜ Decide if this poppet will be a constant companion or for use only on specific occasions. My Circe poppet is used to evoke and invoke whenever I am doing witchcraft. Otherwise, she is at rest. Don't abuse your poppet.

- ❧ Write a short petition to your Goddess and roll it into a scroll to stuff inside the poppet.

- ❧ Place the obsidian in the center of the fabric. Wrap a piece of string around it, tying it off to create the head.

- ❧ Spread the fabric back over the head, like an open flower.

- ❧ Fill in the space created with your botanicals, the moonstone, and the scroll.

- ❧ Ease the fabric down, wrapping it around the botanicals and shaping it into a body.

- ❧ Tucking in any loose pieces, tie off the body of the poppet, leaving the remaining fabric as her skirt.

- ❧ Add charms and decorate.

- ❧ As you create the poppet, summon the Goddess's energy into it using a taglock—a binding spell or tether that traps energy onto a target using a symbolic representation—symbols, etc. and then pour your own energy into the effigy, saying:

  I summon _____ into this poppet, taking only what I need. Your powers of _____ are now within my control. I merge my own _____ with yours, entwining them within this poppet.

- ❧ Envision the poppet becoming enchanted with the energy of your Goddess.

- ❧ Spend time getting to know your poppet once you've activated her. You may receive messages directly from your Goddess or an emissary may come forward.

- ❧ Disconnect yourself from the poppet when finished by expressing gratitude and saying farewell.

Treat your poppet as you do any other spirit. Use it as an icon and a portal to connect with your Goddess. Give her offerings and pray to her.

Cinnamon

Cinnamon was a prized ritual and dietary spice to Hekate's ancient witches, who used it in special dishes and to spice wine. Cinnamon has a sustained, fiery energy that can be used for a variety of purposes, from improving wellness to kindling passion, and for rebirth work. Because of the high price of cinnamon, the spice has been associated with abundance. Wrap a dollar bill around a stick and tie with green string for a quick money spell.

Fiery mythical creatures, including the serpent, dragon, and phoenix, are all strongly associated with this botanical. The phoenix nested on a bed of cinnamon, which became its fire of rebirth. Known as the dragon spice, cinnamon can be used to summon their spirits and for your own renewal. Dragons protected the ancient fields where cinnamon grew, so make an offering to these guardians and ask them to watch over you. If dragon or phoenix are your allies, cinnamon is an excellent way to connect with them and to appease them.

Although the associations with such fierce creatures might make you think that this pharmakoi is imposing, cinnamon is a nourishing fire that burns away what blocks, opening the path to abundance, healing, and success. Cinnamon motivates you to bring about the change after rebirth work, just as it fueled the phoenix to rise up from the ashes.

Properties and Correspondences

- ⚜ *Latin name*: Cinnamomum verum (true cinnamon)
- ⚜ *Genus*: Cinnamomum
- ⚜ *Classification*: Tree
- ⚜ *Spiritual properties*: Cinnamon is especially useful for adding sustained passionate energy to all spiritual undertakings, from psychic skills to rebirth. It is also excellent for entering into a state of grace within while connecting to the eternal torch of Hekate. It is excellent for rites evoking Hekate Enodia, she who lights our way, as well as in her role as dragon tamer.
- ⚜ *Physiological properties*: Digestive aid, astringent, antiseptic, improves cognitive functioning, warming.
- ⚜ *Magickal properties*: Removing barriers, sustained attraction spells, rebirth, motivation, sacred rites involving fire and the sun.
- ⚜ *Part used*: Bark
- ⚜ *Planetary correspondences*: Sun
- ⚜ *Elemental correspondences*: Fire
- ⚜ *Archetype*: Pyriboulos (Fiery Counselor)
- ⚜ *World*: Middle

- ♀ *Zodiac*: Aries
- ♀ *Color*: Red
- ♀ *Stone*: Tourmaline
- ♀ *Animal*: Phoenix

Indications

Generally safe for children and adults. Excessive amounts can cause digestive trouble and dizziness.

Formulations

- ♀ Cinnamon sticks are an essential of the apothecary. Keep them on hand for use in spells of abundance, for invigoration, and for simmering on the stove to create a warm atmosphere.

- ♀ Cinnamon oil can be purchased for easy use. Make your own with jojoba as the fixative for a heavy-duty skin treatment for tired hands.

- ♀ Use cinnamon in your daily tonic to bring back your inner fire, add to heated almond milk with a bit of honey, or make yourself a chai. Adding cinnamon to your daily diet benefits mind, body, and soul.

- ♀ Add a pinch to wine to serve as an offering to the Triple Goddesses, especially to evoke their passionate energies, and to unleash your own erotic divinity. Don't be surprised if the horned god himself shows up.

Pharmakeia

To sweeten the deal, mix 1 tsp of cinnamon in ¼ cup sugar. Mix into ½ cup coconut oil for a scrub to warm you up on chilly winter nights. Place in a bowl with juniper berries to banish and bless your home.

Cinnamon is excellent for bringing back the light and for anytime you need to rekindle your zest for life. As an ally for rebirth work, it represents the fire of Hekate's torch, shining our way out through the womb.

Hekate's Cauldron Incense

The witch's cauldron symbolizes the womb, and Hekate's resides in the heart of her Cave, full of the spirits from her Garden. It is the source of all her power, the font of her Anima Mundi. Return to the cauldron using this blend.

This incense is wonderful, especially to celebrate the rebirth of the sun at the Winter Solstice, while honoring the Darkest Night as the most sacred of all times for Hekatean witchcraft.

SUPPLIES

- ⚜ Small cauldron
- ⚜ Charcoal disk
- ⚜ Mortar and pestle
- ⚜ Glass jar for storage

INGREDIENTS

½ tsp cinnamon

1 tsp mugwort

½ tsp rosemary

½ tsp crushed pine cone

DIRECTIONS

- ⚜ Crush the pine cone in the mortar and pestle, then add the rest of the ingredients, blending in a clockwise direction and concentrating on your own journey and desire for rebirth.

- ⚜ Store in the glass jar until you are ready to journey into Hekate's cauldron.

- ⚜ When you're ready, place the charcoal disk in the bottom of the cauldron, then light it. Add the incense. Then recite the following petition:

Hail, Hekate, Witch Mother, Dark Queen,
She who spins the Wheel of the Year!
Anima Mundi, World Soul!
Keeper of time,
Mistress of the Moon,
That rises and sets in her Cave.
Dark Mother, grant me entrance
Into your secret lair,

Shine your torchlight
To the inner chamber
Where your eternal cauldron
Of rebirth resides.
I come, as your witches have since before time,
To be undone
Reduced to my soul fire,
To be rebuilt in truth.

Corn and Grain

Corn has an interesting history as a symbol of the fall harvest. Corn symbolizes Hekate as the Mother of All. Make corn dolls in her honor during the harvest season, celebrating her most ancient role as a goddess of the harvest. Hail to the pharmakoi maize.

Corn Mother

Prior to it becoming associated with North American maize, the word "corn" was used, and is still, to describe any grain. This makes it confusing when reading ancient texts—for instance, when Demeter is referred to as the "Corn Mother." Obviously, the ancient Greeks didn't have what we now call corn, since it's indigenous to North America. However, Demeter, Persephone, and their close companion, Hekate, are well-honored with offerings of corn.

Corn has become such a widespread crop that most of us can claim it to be local. While the politics of corn are worthy of thoughtful consideration, the importance of the grain is not to be dismissed. Rather, honoring corn as a symbol of plenty reminds us that agriculture is both necessary and problematic. Mindful use of it, as with everything, is part of a witch's prerogative. Corn is humble and noble, a symbol of the bounty of the land, and is sacred to Hekate as Pammetor.

THE
KNOWLEDGE

Properties and Correspondences

- ⚘ *Latin name:* Maize

- ⚘ *Genus:* Zea

- ⚘ *Classification:* Grain

- ⚘ *Spiritual properties:* Corn symbolizes a bountiful harvest, nourishing body and spirit. Useful for connecting with maize as you prepare for rebirth.

- ⚘ *Physiological properties:* Nourishing grain, especially for energizing B vitamins and other nutrients.

- ⚘ *Magickal properties:* Abundance, blessings, harvests, autumn, government issues.

- ⚘ *Part used:* All

- ⚘ *Planetary correspondences:* Sun

- ⚘ *Elemental correspondences:* Fire

- ⚘ *Archetype:* Pammetor (Mother of All)

- ⚘ *World:* Middle

- ⚘ *Zodiac:* Leo

- ⚘ *Color:* Yellow

- ⚘ *Stone:* Citrine

- ⚘ *Animal:* Hen

Indications

Safe.

Formulations

- ⚘ Keep cornmeal on hand for offerings when petitioning for abundance; use to attune your tools to the power of abundance.

- ⚘ Fill a green bag with cornmeal, add your specific intention for abundance, and hang over the kitchen table to bring bounty to your cupboards.

- ⚘ Fully grown corn is both food and seed, simultaneously representing completion and beginning.

- Corn cobs represent all parts of the life cycle and the power of creation.
- Corn is used to make several types of alcohol, including bourbon, which is one of my favorite bases for making abundance tinctures.

Pharmakeia

Wrap a spell in a cornstalk to bind it. Write sigils and incantations on corn-stalks and burn to activate. Ears of corn represent the reproductive cycle. Use dried seed corn to support your spells of beginnings.

Corn attracts some animal spirits, like certain birds (especially jays) and deer. To use it in this way, place an offering for the animal on an energy grid containing their symbols. Then meditate on the symbols, envisioning offering them the corn and opening to the animal spirit.

Use an ear as a coffin to bury that which needs to die. Carefully open the cob, then write your intention directly on it. Close the ear back around it, securing it with black string. Then bury it away from your home.

Use a corn husk as a conduit to speak with the departed. Remove the cob and replace with an image, the name, and some personal belonging. Write your message/question and put that in as well. Wrap the husk around your spell, then seal with a white cord. Perform a ritual honoring this ancestor to attract his or her attention. When the ritual is complete, open the ear and you will receive your reply.

Charge cornmeal with botanicals to enhance them both.

Bread of the Goddess

This is a super-easy recipe that requires no fancy tools.

Supplies
- Large bowl
- 2 smaller bowls
- Measuring cup
- Spoon
- Greased pan

I usually use an 8 x 8 square pan, but this also makes six to eight good-sized muffins or those little corn-shaped molds. I've doubled and tripled the recipe many times.

INGREDIENTS

2 tsp white vinegar

1 cup full-fat milk

½ cup butter

1 egg

1 cup all-purpose flour

1 cup cornmeal

¼ cup white sugar

1 tsp baking powder

½ tsp baking soda

1 tsp salt

DIRECTIONS

☥ Heat the oven to 350 degrees and grease the pan well.

☥ Mix the white vinegar into the milk.

☥ Let rest at least ten minutes on the counter. This will curdle the milk, making it much better for helping the bread to be fluffy.

☥ Melt the butter and let cool a bit.

☥ Beat the egg lightly.

☥ Mix the flour with the cornmeal.

☥ Add the white sugar, baking powder, baking soda, and salt and mix well.

☥ Pour the butter into the milk mixture, combine, then add the egg.

☥ Now pour this wet mixture into the dry mixture, mixing just until everything is blended. Don't over-mix.

☥ Pour into the prepared pan and bake for about twenty to twenty-five minutes.

☥ Once you take it out of the oven, butter the entire top of the bread.

Damiana

A native of the American southwest, damiana has a long history of association with fertility and sexuality, and as healer for myriad health problems. It is perhaps due to the hypersexual Victorian herbalists who highly extolled damiana as an aphrodisiac that the herb has become narrowly viewed as useful only in this manner. However, traditional uses and modern scientific investigations both reveal that this botanical has a broad range of abilities.

My experience with damiana is deeply personal. At a time when I was immersed in my own healing from trauma and doing soul-retrieval work, damiana appeared to me. Since then, it has been a stalwart companion, reminding me of my own sexual nature while helping me to heal from the past.

Damiana is evocative of Hekate Erototokos, the Bringer of Love. As damiana's healing properties were restricted to sexual abilities, so was our Mother's sexuality removed from her general knowledge. However, to the ancients, she was a great Mother Goddess, associated with fertility. At times, she was the maiden; at others, the crone. She was all phases of life at once. She is *Triformis*. Turn to damiana to understand your multifaceted nature, for sexuality, and for healing through regression.

Properties and Correspondences

- ⚥ *Latin name*: *Turnera diffusa*

- ⚥ *Genus*: *Turnera*

- ⚥ *Classification*: Shrub

- ⚥ *Spiritual properties*: Mild euphoric and trance inducer, soul retrieval, mending broken relationships, sexual healing.

- ⚥ *Physiological properties*: Damiana has many healing properties for the body and mind, especially in reducing anxiety, depression, inflammation, and pain. It is also an antitussive, antibacterial, analgesic, and antifungal.

- ⚥ *Magickal properties*: Attraction spells of all kinds, anxiety relief, happiness, healing through past-life and younger-self regression, igniting sexual passion.

- ⚥ *Part used*: Leaves

- ⚥ *Planetary correspondences*: Venus

- ♀ *Elemental correspondences*: Fire
- ♀ *Archetype*: Erototokos (Bringer of Love)
- ♀ *World*: Middle
- ♀ *Zodiac*: Scorpio, Aries
- ♀ *Color*: Yellow, dark gray
- ♀ *Stone*: Smoky quartz
- ♀ *Animal*: Coyote

Indications

Not for children, pets, or those who are pregnant or breastfeeding. It is safe to consume in small amounts for up to three months. Damiana can stimulate libido, so test out a small amount to gauge your reaction.

Formulations

- ♀ Damiana can be used in tinctures, infusions, oils, and as a poultice.
- ♀ Slightly bitter, the taste can be sweetened with honey.
- ♀ A liqueur is available for purchase.
- ♀ A bowl of damiana in the bedroom will kindle sexual energy, whether for solitary adventures or liaisons with other partners. To use it in this way, bless a bowl of damiana with a bit of your own magical sex fluids.
- ♀ Attune to damiana as a guide for healing sexual trauma.

Pharmakeia

Damiana heats up any formulation, although her natural inclinations tend to soul restoration, time travel, and erotic adventures. Her reputation as an aphrodisiac may be based in her core characteristic of recollection; if the good old days were sexy, then she'll kindle your fire anew. However, if there is trauma in your past, she'll want you to heal that. This is a complex herb that rewards pharmakas who are willing to see how damiana mirrors themselves.

To use as a sexual stimulator, keep a paquet of damiana with any erotic clothing or gear. Also serve an infusion mixed into a cocktail with Triple Sec, gin, and fizzy water over ice to really get the mood going.

For soul-retrieval healing work, damiana has a key role to play in supporting our kairos magick, going back through the years to heal our wounded earlier selves or to extend healing to the younger versions of people we have wounded.

Time-Travel Tincture

This tincture is excellent for traveling back into the past to retrieve missing pieces of yourself, to find resolution, and to connect with younger versions of you. It is a very healing tincture.

INGREDIENTS

  1 tbsp damiana

  1 tbsp mugwort

  1 tbsp yarrow

  ¾ cup alcohol, glycerin, or apple-cider vinegar

DIRECTIONS

- ⚜ Place the botanicals in a clean jar, then add the liquid. I generally pour just enough boiled water over the botanicals to loosen them up, speeding up the distillation process.

- ⚜ Cover the jar.

- ⚜ Shake gently daily. The tincture will be ready for use after about four to six weeks for alcohol-based mixtures—shorter times for glycerites and vinegars.

- ⚜ Test by dropping a small amount under the tongue.

Kairos Incense

This incense is another time-travel companion. It combines the power of damiana with the zeal of foxglove, aided by mugwort's ease of opening the way to the past.

INGREDIENTS

  About 1 tsp dried foxglove flowers or leaves

  1 tbsp mugwort

  2 tsp damiana

- ⚷ Blend in a black bowl, preferably of obsidian or dark granite, stirring in a counter-clockwise direction, drawing Under World energy into it as you blend.

- ⚷ Burn a small amount of this on a ¼ charcoal disk for about five minutes to evaluate your response to it.

- ⚷ Proceed with caution from there.

- ⚷ Don't breathe in excessive amounts of the smoke.

You can make an oil to heat in a diffuser as well, but do not consume any or anoint yourself with it.

Dandelion

This humble plant offers us a great deal of symbolic energy. Like Hekate, the dandelion represents the Three Worlds and our Three Selves. The pervasive roots remind us of the importance of Under World energy—that all that exists is borne from the dark depths of the Earth. The emotions, the dominant force of the Lower Self, are deep and vast. They nourish our minds and inform our actions. The golden flower reaches toward the Upper World, showing us that the abilities of the Higher Self stretch up to the mysteries of intellect and mysticism. At the Middle World, the stalk and leaves are the active part of the plant, growing and spreading, like our actions.

The persistence of dandelion to grow anywhere and its refusal to yield to attempts to destroy it are a mighty lesson in living our truth. There was a time, when I lived in suburbia, that I conformed to the neighborhood practice of destroying dandelions to have a weed-free lawn. The dandelions persisted and, eventually, I did as well. Dandelion reminds us that conformity is quite boring and requires way too much effort.

Thus, the message of dandelion is just to be you—from your emotional roots to your intellectual curiosities. Hekate comes to her devotees in many different forms as well. Let you be you and let your Hekate be yours.

Properties and Correspondences

- ⚷ *Latin name: Taraxacum officinale*

- ⚷ *Genus: Taraxacum*

- ⚕ *Classification*: Plant
- ⚕ *Spiritual properties*: Cleansing; all healing, especially emotional; protection; psychic abilities.
- ⚕ *Physiological properties*: Promotes digestion, stimulates the kidneys, cleanses the liver, boosts immune functioning, and reduces stress.
- ⚕ *Magickal properties*: Clarity, communication, freedom, messages, money, power, prophecy, summoning spirits.
- ⚕ *Part used*: Roots, young tops, leaves
- ⚕ *Planetary correspondences*: Jupiter, Mercury
- ⚕ *Elemental correspondences*: Air
- ⚕ *Archetype*: Nyssa (Initiator)
- ⚕ *World*: Upper
- ⚕ *Zodiac*: Aquarius
- ⚕ *Color*: Yellow
- ⚕ *Stone*: Lepidolite
- ⚕ *Metal*: Brass
- ⚕ *Animal*: Lion

Indications

Very safe.

Formulations

- ⚕ Dandelion can be formulated as an infusion, decoction, or tincture. The root is typically used for these formularies, although the entire plant can be used when fresh.
- ⚕ Craft an entire root as a healing poppet.
- ⚕ The leaves are excellent cooked or served in a salad.

Pharmakeia

Dandelion is a powerful all-purpose healer. Dandelion is most useful in cleansing and purification. You can add dried dandelion root, leaves, or flowers to an incense. Drinking a daily tonic of dandelion root is beneficial for mind, body,

and soul. Add the greens to salads and smoothies for a similar benefit. A dandelion potion consisting of a concentrate of the root tea can be used as a base for other potions and makes a great ritual-bath ingredient.

Carrying dandelion with you as part of a charm can also be very beneficial. Of course, you can use the waning dandelion flower as a conduit to activate a spell by blowing the fragile petals onto the wind. Not surprisingly, dandelion is associated with the element of Air. You can adapt dandelion energy to your specific focus, add appropriate correspondences, and cast a spell into it with a great incantation.

Offering to Hekate

A wreath made of dandelion would be an excellent offering to Hekate on the Dark Moon or at anytime. You can wear it during your ritual and then offer it to her by placing it around a statue or leaving it at the crossroads.

Spiritual Upgrade Soother

Drinking dandelion-root tea after deep work helps us manage the post-ritual mess. Dandelion brings the body, spirit, and mind into synchrony, while synthesizing our experiences and guiding us through the muck of transformation.

As a root, dandelion releases its properties much more easily through the decocting process. To make a decoction, simply add a spoonful of plant material for every two cups of water. Bring the mixture to a gentle boil for about five minutes, then cover and let steep for five more. If you're feeling too fiery from your ritual, chill the decoction and drink it cold. Too cold? Drink it warm. Add honey and lemon to taste for enhanced support. You can also make this ahead and freeze it into ice cubes to have ready for after your ritual. Defrost it in boiled water and mix with honey and lemon.

Reality Check Spell

Unrealistic expectations can be very damaging. Whether we think that our homes must be always be tidy or our lovers must be free of faults, there's no benefit to be found in hoping for perfection. A better approach is to expect things to be whole—flaws and all. Dirty dishes are a sign of a busy life. Does your potential partner really need to satisfy every item on your checklist?

Transmutation is a type of spellwork that has us changing the energetic properties of an object to achieve our desired outcome. In this case, the intention is to change unrealistic expectations into realistic ones. That's a lofty goal, but using the energy of the dandelion can be quite helpful in this situation.

SUPPLIES

- ⚜ A fresh dandelion or dried plant material—it's widely available as an herbal tea.
- ⚜ Paper
- ⚜ Pen
- ⚜ Candle (if possible, yellow)
- ⚜ Small bag (yellow is best)

DIRECTIONS

- ⚜ Create your protective circle as you usually do. A simple technique is to sweep your space clean with three rounds in a clockwise direction before beginning the spell with a fresh broom or your clean right hand.
- ⚜ Sit inside your circle and make a list of your unrealistic expectations.
- ⚜ Place the dandelion and the list in the bag.
- ⚜ Light the candle and place your talisman in front of it.
- ⚜ Envision all those expectations being transformed into more realistic ones by the energy of the candle.
- ⚜ Open the circle by sweeping three times counter-clockwise with the broom or your clean left hand.
- ⚜ Carry your talisman with you. Light the candle daily to help the transmutation process.

Dittany of Crete

Dittany can be added to any magickal working and used as an all-heal for corporeal complaints. It is a true panacea. There are two common types of dittany that are closely related—American and Cretan. Both are similar to oregano and marjoram, although there are important distinctions. They share the same properties and characteristics. If you can access the American

version through foraging, I recommend doing so. Otherwise, ordering live dittany of Crete plants and growing them yourself is the best option.

Dittany of Crete (*Origanum dictamnus*) is also referred to as eronda, diktamo, Cretan dittany, hop marjoram, wintersweet, and wild marjoram. The Cretan word for the plant is *erontas*, meaning "love herb." American dittany (*Cunila origanoides*) is also known as wild dittany, wild oregano, frost flower, feverwort, mountain dittany, gas plant, and stone mint. Both belong to the *Lamiaceae* (mint) family.

Lepidium latifolium, sometimes called dittany, but more commonly known as pepperweed or pepperwort, belongs to the mustard family and, as such, has properties reflective of this classification rather than the true forms of dittany. And there is yet another dittany imposter (*dictamnus alba*) known as dittany or burning bush. My advice is to stick to *Origanum dictamnus* or *cunila origanoides*. Finally, there are some retailers who falsely label oregano or marjoram as "dittany."

The Real Thing

True dittany from Crete is a rare commodity, given that it grows naturally only in dangerous places, like cliff tops, on the island for which it is named. Cultivated dittany of Crete is available from reputable retailers. If purchasing the dried plant online, ensure that you are getting true dittany. Look for the fuzzy leaves and purple flowers.

Dittany of Crete is sacred to several goddesses of the ancient Mediterranean cultures, dating back to the Minoans. Aphrodite/Venus, Artemis, Circe, Diana, Hekate, Hera, and Persephone can be evoked using either the European or North American variety. Jupiter/Zeus is associated with it as well. According to mythology, Zeus gave the plant to Crete in gratitude for being raised there.

There is a great deal of lore surrounding this botanical, especially regarding its use in all matters to do with love—from finding it, to its ultimate result of pregnancy and childbirth. Venus is said to have healed Aeneas with it. Artemis and others were depicted wearing crowns of dittany. It is a most royal plant for connecting with the divine feminine. Dittany is excellent for repelling poisons from the body, mind, and spirit. It is particularly useful for soothing digestion. Dittany brings loving connection to the dead and is excellent for deathwalking.

The amazing and diverse healing powers of dittany are legendary, ranging from healing knife wounds to facilitating birth. Colonizers recognized comparable properties in the North American species and named it accordingly.

Dittany of Crete is not widely available, although there is increasing interest in it for pharmakeia, culinary uses, and in liqueurs (Diktamo Amaro). Extract from dittany of Crete is used to flavor Italian dry vermouth, which can be used as a base for potions and more.

Properties and Correspondences

- ⚜ *Latin name*: Origanum dictamnus
- ⚜ *Genus*: Origanum
- ⚜ *Classification*: Herb
- ⚜ *Spiritual properties*: Soothes mind, body, and spirit. Excellent for healing and for connecting with the Other Worlds. Evoking, merging, and invoking the divine feminine. Sovereignty, agency, and personal power. Brings comfort to the lonely and symbolizes true love.
- ⚜ *Physiological properties*: Digestion, reproduction, anti-inflammatory, wound healing, rejecting poisons, drawing out splinters.
- ⚜ *Magickal properties*: Abundance, astral travel, beauty, deathwalking, divination, drawing out toxins (harmful people and spirits), healing, journeying, mysticism, passion, protection, spirits, and visions.
- ⚜ *Part used*: Leaves, flowers
- ⚜ *Planetary correspondences*: Venus, Jupiter
- ⚜ *Elemental correspondences*: Water, Air
- ⚜ *Archetype*: Pandoteira (Giver of All)
- ⚜ *World*: Middle
- ⚜ *Zodiac*: Virgo, Taurus, Libra
- ⚜ *Color*: Gray, purple
- ⚜ *Stone*: Selenite
- ⚜ *Animal*: Bee

Indications

Whether this botanical is safe for use during pregnancy or by children has not been established through clinical trials. Caution is advised for those with mint, oregano, or marjoram sensitivities.

American dittany can be used as a substitute for many magical purposes, but is not as skilled for deathwalking. You can substitute oregano, marjoram, or mint, as long as you do so in accordance with the specific focus of your working, since none can be considered a general substitution. Marjoram and mugwort together may yield similar results for spirit work.

Formulations

- ❧ Dittany can be used in all manner of formulations. In Crete, it is popularly consumed as a daily tea for its prophylactic and remedial healing properties. An infusion of ½ tsp botanical to 2 cups of boiled water is recommended. It is also excellent in tinctures, which can be made by adding about 1 tsp plant material to ½ cup 80-proof or above alcohol. It is amenable to being added to oils as well.

- ❧ Dittany is excellent in a healing poultice, for physical wounds, and to heal or open the Middle Self and the heart center.

- ❧ Plant dittany by your home's threshold to ensure abundance and health, and to attract good spirits and protect against harm. A dish of dried dittany can be substituted.

- ❧ This beloved botanical has an amazing scent, both in its natural form and burned as an incense.

Pharmakeia

Dittany of Crete is an amazing super-botanical that can be used in many ways. It is superior for connecting with departed loved ones. To use it in this manner, instruct the plant that it is to facilitate your connection with your beloved. Set up an altar including photos and *memento mori*. Burn a sprig of dittany while you call to mind your memories of the person. Your loved one's image will appear in the smoke. To enhance the experience, drink an infusion.

Diktamo

Make a tincture of dittany using about 2 tbsp of the fresh leaves per ½ cup of alcohol. Allow to settle for six weeks, shaking daily. Mix several drops of the tincture in a few ounces of orange juice about thirty minutes before beginning any ritual to deepen your ability to journey in the spirit world. This tincture is especially useful for invoking Hekate and Circe.

Fennel

An ancient member of Hekate's Garden, this licorice-flavored plant was consumed for courage, protection, and strength, and for victory in competitions by the ancients. Fennel is a breaker of chains, meaning that it has the power to remove blockages, especially for all forms of communication.

Fennel is sometimes used in love philters, to encourage sending off the right signals regarding romance and sex, giving it a reputation as a sexual stimulant. Its applications extend to all manner of communication problems, from breaking curses to removing barriers for successful engagement with authority figures and government, rendering it an apothecary necessity.

Properties and Correspondences

- ⚶ *Latin name*: Foeniculum vulgare
- ⚶ *Genus*: Foeniculum
- ⚶ *Classification*: Vegetable
- ⚶ *Spiritual properties*: Communication, courage, healing of the mind, sexuality.
- ⚶ *Physiological properties*: Aromative, digestive, pesticide.
- ⚶ *Magickal properties*: Breaking curses and bad luck, clarity, communication, courage, dealing with authority and government, prevention, protection, psychic witchcraft, visions.
- ⚶ *Part used*: Seeds, bulb, stems
- ⚶ *Planetary correspondences*: Mercury
- ⚶ *Elemental correspondences*: Air
- ⚶ *Archetype*: Rixipyle (Breaker of Chains)
- ⚶ *World*: Upper

- ⚜ *Zodiac*: Aquarius, Gemini
- ⚜ *Color*: Blue
- ⚜ *Stone*: Blue agate
- ⚜ *Animal*: Magpie

Indications

Generally safe in small doses, but not for use during pregnancy. Take caution with children and pets.

Formulations

- ⚜ Given that all parts of this vegetable are suitable for consumption, fennel is an excellent addition to the menu when the goal is improved communication. It is great for romantic dinners, as well as those times when the subject matter is difficult. Make fennel for yourself when you need to get clarity.

- ⚜ The seeds are very easy to work with. Release their properties by lightly grinding them in a mortar with a pestle. To enhance communication, grind clockwise; to remove barriers, reverse the direction.

- ⚜ Five is the number most associated with fennel. Release its properties using multiples of five when grinding and use seeds in multiples of the same number.

- ⚜ Fennel is excellent as part of a tonic, although continued daily use beyond six weeks is not recommended. To make a tonic, add ½ tsp seeds to a cup boiled water. Let the mixture steep for fifteen minutes, as fennel is a bit slow to release. Use on its own or mixed into your daily tonic.

- ⚜ Drink a fennel infusion before doing any sort of communicative witchery, like sigilcraft or *voces magicae*.

- ⚜ Keep an open dish of gently ground seeds for ensuring smooth communication.

- ⚜ Carry fennel seeds in a glass vial. They are excellent for digestion and for on-the-go witchery. Slip a few seeds in where needed. Chew the seeds to ease digestion and to speak the truth. Five will do the trick.

- Fennel is strongly associated with Mercury. Adding this planetary symbol to any working will increase its potency.

Pharmakeia

Fennel is a very specific botanical that is eager to help with a variety of situations involving breaking barriers to communication. It is excellent for breaking down resistance. Drink a tonic and watch your procrastination dissolve.

Fennel at the threshold ensures that only the truth is spoken within. Add it to your home wards—those protective barriers placed at the entrances or around the perimeter.

If you have a familiar spirit, as I do, fennel seeds can be an excellent snack. I leave a dish by LeRoy's spot, activated with the intention that they nourish his ability to communicate with me. By giving them to him, I strengthen my connection to him.

Rixipyle Uncrossing Tincture

This tincture can be made in advance so that it is ready to use whenever communication goes awry—or for when you need to make sure it doesn't. Rixipyle means "breaker of chains," so it is an excellent archetype to evoke for this tincture. Consider it a sort of Mercury-retrograde antidote.

This tincture is excellent when applied to any written documents, especially those involving legal situations and the government. It's a red-tape uncrosser. Make a copy of the document if using the original is not advisable, then apply a few drops while envisioning a successful resolution. Rub it on your Third Eye when messages from the Other Side are murky.

This tincture is safe to consume when you want to ramp up your communication skills or remove curses quickly. Speak unto fennel your directions and he will gladly comply, as long as it's in his skill set.

SUPPLIES

- Glass vial with stopper
- Mortar and pestle
- Funnel
- 5 grams (roughly 1 tsp) fennel seeds

- ⚜ 25 milliliters (roughly ¼ cup) high-proof alcohol like vodka
- ⚜ Blue cord

DIRECTIONS

- ⚜ Gently grind the seeds in a counter-clockwise direction, then add to the vial, speaking this incantation:
  Fennel, your spirit I now release. All barriers shall cease.

- ⚜ If the tincture is being made for a specific purpose, adjust the incantation appropriately—for instance:
  All barriers between me and (the goal or person) now cease.

- ⚜ Sing the spell as you grind the seeds, then combine them with the alcohol.

- ⚜ If you aren't using the tincture right away, seal it with wax to keep it ready for use.

MAKING A WAX SEAL

- ⚜ In a small stainless-steel pot, place about 1 tbsp of beeswax pellets.

- ⚜ Stirring constantly with a skewer, melt the wax over a low heat.

- ⚜ Let cool for a couple of minutes, then dunk the top of the bottle (with the topper in) into the wax, swirling it around until a good seal forms.

- ⚜ You can add a few drops of blue food coloring or acrylic paint to make the wax blue, then tie it with a blue cord.

Foxglove

Foxglove is an amazing plant to incorporate into Under World witchery, but it is for skilled practitioners only. It is a temperamental plant, given to doing as it pleases. If you're up for the challenge, proceed with a steely mindset. You'll need that to control the incredibly poisonous and willful foxglove. You can add it to a mugwort-and-mint base to form an Under World journeying incense.

Standing at the entrance to Hekate's Garden, foxglove, also known as digitalis, banishes the profane while keeping in the secrets of those of us who enter. As with many of the master teachers, foxglove prefers their own company. I wrote "their" because foxglove is a hermaphroditic botanical, containing both male and female organs. As such, it is an excellent healer for those who also resist traditional gender norms and sex roles.

Foxglove is often associated with the fair folk and other types of small land spirits. The beautiful glove-like blossoms have traditionally been attracted to these spirits, and lore has them gathering round the plants, wearing the blossoms themselves and sharing them with foxes. Leave offerings to these spirits under the leaves of foxglove and you'll be rewarded. Possibly. Like foxglove, the fair folk are willful, lending their favor on their own terms. Both are best left in the natural state except by the most confident witches. Dancing with digitalis or the wee ones can be a wild ride, and not without risk.

In my personal practice, foxglove is one of my master teachers. It grows on the left side of my front door, representing the left-hand Poison Path.

Because of foxglove's centuries of popularity and the extensive folk tales that surround it, the plant is known by many names, including bloody fingers, dead man's bells, fairy finger, fairy bells, fairy thimbles, fairy cap, goblin gloves, gloves of our lady, ladies' thimble, lady-finger, lion's mouth, rabbit's flower, throatwort, Scotch mercury, virgin's gloves, and witch's gloves.

Foxglove offers a boost to those feeling low, but amplifies those effects greatly when the practitioner is already in an excited state. Thus it is not a suitable companion for anxious witches, although it can be healing when we are depressed.

Foxglove is ruled by Venus and strongly linked to the emotional depths. Its resistance to being told what to do can be overcome through sincerity and persistence by an even stronger mind. It can make for an excellent study for those willing to explore their own shadow sides, but be well-advised of its capricious nature. Venus has a talent for keeping secrets, so add foxglove to anything that you wish to keep hidden.

Time-travel witchcraft, like journeying into the past to recover missing pieces of ourselves or healing the ancestral line, benefits from the addition of foxglove, as it is a portal to kairos, the nonlinear time of the etheric world.

All parts of foxglove are poisonous, so it is best handled wearing gloves in well-ventilated areas, although it is not overly toxic to the touch.

Properties and Correspondences

- *Latin name*: *Digitalis purpurea*
- *Genus*: *Digitalis*
- *Classification*: Plant

- *Spiritual properties*: Healing the past, lifting spirits, Under World work including soul retrieval and rebirth (for the strong-willed practitioner).

- *Physiological properties*: Digitalis, a compound of foxglove, was long used as a treatment for cardiac problems, although it has been replaced with a synthetic version in allopathic medical practice. Foxglove rapidly increases blood pressure, so spending time with a beautiful specimen can be helpful for those with chronic hypotension.

- *Magickal properties*: Banishing, cunning, keeping secrets, protection.

- *Part used*: All

- *Planetary correspondences*: Venus

- *Elemental correspondences*: Water

- *Archetype*: Daidalos (Cunning One)

- *World*: Under

- *Zodiac*: Taurus

- *Color*: Purple or white

- *Stone*: Opal

- *Animal*: Fox

Indications

All parts of the plant are poisonous. Do not ingest or rub directly on the skin. This plant is not to be used in conjunction with aconite, as they cancel out each other's medicine.

Formulations

- Foxglove is a popular garden plant because it grows so easily. All parts of the plant can be harvested for use in pharmakeia. The seeds can be purchased online.

- Use all parts of the plant in infusions, tinctures, oils, etc.

- When blending with other botanicals, be very directive as to how you wish digitalis to perform. They may or may not comply if you haven't taken the time to build a strong relationship with them.

- Foxglove demands respect and will come to trust only you over time.

Pharmakeia

Grow foxglove in your garden as energetic sentinels who will keep all intruders at bay. Foxglove is an excellent self-propagator that will spread happily, even when neglected. For novice practitioners, I recommend leaving foxglove to do as they wish and allowing the plants to grow as they wish.

For those confident in their ability to work with foxglove, all parts of the plant can be utilized in banishings, keeping secrets, and emotional healing. Note that foxglove is hot in temperature and quite moist, like the air in a sauna, so if this climate doesn't appeal to you, best avoid this botanical. If you wish to work with foxglove in a less intense manner, a plant oracle card is suitable.

Banishing Besom

I keep a besom of foxglove hanging in the kitchen that continually banishes the unwanted. I use it for quick sweepings when the harmful enters. I also use it to connect with the spirit of digitalis when I need to make tough decisions and for my own emotional healing.

To make a besom, collect thirteen large leaves and bind them with a black cord. Add charms to please foxglove, like symbols of witchcraft. The leaves will perform for a year, while the blossoms tend to wear out much faster in my experience.

Witch's Glove of Secrets

Use this spell to ensure that your secrets aren't revealed. You can continue to add your secrets after the spell is cast.

Supplies

- ✣ One black glove
- ✣ Black cord
- ✣ Paper
- ✣ Black pen
- ✣ Foxglove seeds
- ✣ Glass jar with lid

- Stuff a bit of foxglove into each finger of the glove or drop in the seeds, while reciting:

  Fairest foxglove, heed my request, keep my secrets in your grasp. With your powers contained inside, my secrets within this glove abide.

- Write your secrets on the paper with the black pen and stuff it inside the glove while reciting the incantation.

- Tie up the glove and keep it in a cool, dark place.

- Add secrets as you wish, always reciting the incantation.

Frankincense

Frankincense is essential for ritual witchery. It is a more formal sort of spirit than many of the other members of Hekate's Garden. The medicinal and magickal uses of frankincense are diverse, from its remarkable properties as a healer of wounds to its power of initiation.

Frankincense is the resin of five different species of Boswellia trees, obtained by cutting the bark and letting the sap form nuggets. The resin can be burned in small chunks as incense, following the ancient practices. Frankincense was a very common incense in rituals in ancient Mediterranean cultures. In *The Greek Magical Papyri*, it is the second most common incense after myrrh. It was used to anoint everything from infants to the dead, bringing the energy of purification while summoning the spirits to the person or object being anointed.

Properties and Correspondences

- *Latin name*: Boswellia caterii, sacra, frereana, serrate, and papyritera

- *Genus*: Boswellia

- *Classification*: Tree

- *Spiritual properties*: Anointing, cleansing, focus, opening, self-discipline, expanding consciousness.

- *Physiological properties*: Astringent, improving circulation, diuretic, skin-healing, relieving stress, breathing aid.

- *Magickal properties*: Anointing, initiation, clarity, connecting to the spirit world, devotional work, deathwalking.

- ✢ *Part used*: Resin
- ✢ *Planetary correspondences*: Sun
- ✢ *Elemental correspondences*: Air, Fire
- ✢ *Archetype*: Amphiphaes (Illuminator)
- ✢ *World*: Upper
- ✢ *Zodiac*: Aquarius, Aries, Leo
- ✢ *Color*: Deep golden
- ✢ *Stone*: Yellow calcite
- ✢ *Animal*: Lion

Indications

Not for use while pregnant or breastfeeding. Not to be used on children. It is safe to consume in very small amounts (i.e., 1 to 2 drops of the essential oil blended into a carrier).

Formulations

- ✢ Frankincense is used as a raw resin or as an essential oil. Make an infused oil using a few chunks in about a cup of carrier oil, especially olive or almond. Let blend for a few weeks, starting when the moon is full. Tinctures can also be made.
- ✢ Burn chunks as an incense or add drops of the oil to botanical blends. The essential oil is excellent in a diffuser.
- ✢ Experiment with the different types and grades of frankincense. In general, silver and hojari are considered the highest grades, although they are not widely available.

Pharmakeia

Frankincense is a mighty master for almost any ritual. It is especially useful for preparing the body for trance. Taking a ritual bath infused with frankincense, either with a few chunks or several drops of the essential oil, relieves distress, soothes the mind, and prepares the soul for ritual and trance.

Anoint the seven power centers of the body at the beginning of ritual, for initiation, and for rebirth workings. Dilute 7 drops of essential oil in ¼ cup

THE
KNOWLEDGE

135

olive oil for a week, shaking daily, to make a frankincense-infused oil that can be used for anointing the body and sacred objects. Dress candles with frankincense-infused oil to prepare them for ritual work. As previously mentioned, frankincense is very appropriate for anointing/activating all Hekatean icons and objects.

Oleum Spiritus

Frankincense is a spirit that brings magick, medicine, and mystery and makes all three readily available for the pharmaka, rendering us truly unbeatable. Make a mugwort base oil by blending ¼ cup dried mugwort with ½ cup olive oil. Let this rest for six weeks, shaking daily. On a Full Moon, drain the mugwort from the oil, then add several drops of frankincense. This oil should be applied to the energetic centers of the Septem Novum about thirty minutes before journeying to the spirit world. Anointing the Third Eye is also recommended.

Garlic

Garlic was sacred to the ancient Hekateans. It was revered for its diverse healing powers and for its ability to banish just about anything. Garlic purifies, protects, and activates, making it an excellent herb for Hekate Enodia, the guide of our Middle World journey. It is indispensable for modern witches; always keep several cloves on hand.

One of the most sacred pharmakoi, garlic should always be included in the evening meal, whether as simple cloves or in more elaborate creations like garlic jam. Ancient Hekate's suppers always included garlic, eggs, fish, bread, and cheese. The ancient use of garlic to ward against evil was undoubtedly why it was included in the meal, since Hekate was seen as both household protector and imminent threat if she wasn't honored each month on the Dark Moon.

Garlic is one of the most healing botanicals, applicable to many health complaints from the common cold to stiff joints. Spiritually, it is a very strong ally when venturing into the Other World and will greatly enhance any encounters with Hekate. Garlic will always pull you back to the Middle World wherever you wander in the astral realms. Wise, undemanding, and energetic, this botanical stands on guard for witches always.

Garlic has a fiery, passionate side that can be coaxed out for sex magic, but watch out—this plant of Mars means business.

Properties and Correspondences

- ✠ *Latin name*: Allium sativum
- ✠ *Genus*: Allium
- ✠ *Classification*: Plant, bulb
- ✠ *General properties*: Cleansing, emotions, shadow healing, invoking, offerings, protection, sacred rituals.
- ✠ *Spiritual properties*: Cleansing, healing, purification, sacred rites.
- ✠ *Physiological properties*: Revered for myriad healing properties, garlic should be part of a witch's daily diet. It is antiseptic, anti-inflammatory, diuretic, expectorant, and stimulant.
- ✠ *Magickal properties*: Banishings, courage, envy, healing, hex-breaking, home protection, prevention of psychic attacks, purification, sex magic, and sacred Hekatean rites.
- ✠ *Part used*: Generally the bulb (clove), although the greens and even the blossom can be used
- ✠ *Planetary correspondences*: Mars
- ✠ *Elemental correspondences*: Fire
- ✠ *Archetype*: Propolos (Guide)
- ✠ *World*: Middle
- ✠ *Zodiac*: Aries
- ✠ *Color*: Red
- ✠ *Stone*: Red jasper
- ✠ *Animal*: Horse

Indications

Very safe for all.

Formulations

- ✠ Generally, the strong taste of garlic renders it difficult to consume on its own. Add small amounts to infusions for banishing colds, stress, and stiffness, as well as to degunk any miasma you've accumulated.

- One of our enduring family jokes is that, no matter what the situation, sleeping with a clove of garlic in your sock is the cure. There is quite a bit of truth in this, because garlic, as it is absorbed through the foot, releases calming energies as well as antiseptic properties. It cures nightmares, draws impurities to the surface, and banishes colds and viruses. A general remedy of an entire freshly chopped clove of garlic mixed with a bit of olive oil is a common sight whenever one of us is feeling a bit off.

- Growing garlic is simple and rewarding. Cut off the top of a clove, then turn it upside down in a tall glass so that the top (now the bottom) is immersed in water. Place this in a warm, sunny spot. Edible garlic shoots (known as "scapes") will soon grow out of the bulb.

- Add bits of the skin to incense.

Pharmakeia

Hekate, as the protector of the household, is evoked using garlic. Make an offering to Hekate of three garlic bulbs, placing them on your altar. This is especially suited for the dinner ritual.

To make a garlic banishing spell, write the name or intention of that which you seek to banish on a piece of paper with black ink and wrap it around a clove of garlic. Place the talisman in a piece of black fabric and tie tightly. Bury it or place it in the compost bin.

To create a shut-the-fuck-up spell, make a poppet with a slit for the mouth and then insert a clove of garlic. For a leave-me-alone spell, take a picture or write the name of the target on paper and pin on a bulb of garlic with two crossed pins.

Cooking with garlic purifies mind, body, and spirit. It connects us to sustained energy for getting the job done, while maintaining health. Place bulbs around your property to banish all evils.

Garlic Jam

This garlic jam is excellent as part of Hekate's Feast. It can be made up to three days in advance. It can also be used for its antiseptic qualities to cleanse germs from the body, especially when cold symptoms are first starting. Smear it on the photos of your enemies to banish them. In fact, it is an all-around super-useful witchy recipe.

SUPPLIES

- ⚜ Foil
- ⚜ Baking sheet
- ⚜ Bowl
- ⚜ Sharp knife
- ⚜ Fork
- ⚜ Pepper and salt

INGREDIENTS

6 bulbs garlic

1 to 1½ cup olive oil

DIRECTIONS

- ⚜ Preheat the oven to 350 degrees.
- ⚜ Cut the tops off the garlic bulbs, just enough to expose the individual cloves. Place each one on a separate sheet of foil. Pour olive oil directly into the bulb until it flows over the top. Wrap each bulb tightly in the foil.
- ⚜ Place the completed bulbs on the baking sheet.
- ⚜ Bake for thirty-five minutes, until the packets feel soft.
- ⚜ Allow to cool completely while wrapped in the foil.
- ⚜ Once cooled, remove the bulbs and squish the garlic out of them into the bowl. This is easier than it sounds.
- ⚜ Mash the garlic well, adding olive oil if the jam is too thick. I always add hot chili oil as well.
- ⚜ Season with pepper and salt.

This jam makes an excellent offering and can be used to banish unwanted spirits without and within. Serve with the Goddess Cornbread as part of Hekate's Feast.

Juniper

Sacred to Hekate, Medea, and Circe, as well as to many other deities and spirits, juniper is a most useful botanical. The seed cones, known as berries, are

potent for cleansing the body of toxins. Grind the berries or soak them well to use in tonics. The wood of the juniper is excellent for wands used to conjure fire energy, its ruling element. Juniper is ruled by Mars and is thus excellent for promoting courage and going into battle.

Juniper is a phenomenal bodyguard, protecting against all evil. Traditionally, it was used to protect against witches and all manner of malevolent spirits. It was often planted near the threshold, and boughs were placed over the door to ward off evil.

I collect wild coastal juniper along the seaside cliffs surrounding my home. This is *Juniperus horizontalis*, which varies from common juniper in appearance and growth pattern, although they share similar attributes and applications. Juniper is one of my personal pharmakoi. I use it to treat toxins of body, mind, spirit, and space. Juniper has two broad growing styles: some, like my coastal juniper, clings to granite outcroppings and spreads along the ground; other varieties twist their way upward.

The Power of Place

The influence of the local environment on botanicals is powerful. Soil, weather, other botanicals, wildlife, the landscape, and human factors can all influence plants, in both their physical form and their energetic signature. My coastal juniper is raised on sea spray and soil dense with mica, a very different diet from that of its desert companion. The influence of place on botanicals is a factor to consider when growing, wildharvesting, and purchasing them. More important, these possible influences should be explored when using them.

Juniper is commonly found across North America and Europe. It's used in landscaping extensively here, making it easy to acquire for our witchery. Juniper wood is highly purifying and makes a most excellent smoke. Boughs of juniper can be used for the energetic cleansing of your home and your magickal workspace. This is one of my favorite techniques. I usually have a juniper "broom" on the front doorstep that I change up when it gets too dried out (then it's time to burn it). Boughs and wreaths are traditional decorations for holy days and celebrations like Samhain and Yule. Juniper berries are excellent for purging toxins from the body. And then there's gin (made from the berries). How useful the ubiquitous juniper is for mind, body, and soul.

Medea used juniper in her spells—for instance, when she tamed a fierce snake with sprigs placed over its eyes while dousing it with other herbs and singing her incantation. Ancient statues of Hekate sculpted from juniper have been found. It was also special to Circe, who burned it as an incense. Heed her practice: snip a sprig and burn it—fresh or dried. The smoke is a lovely white and the smell speaks of comfort, clarity, and clairvoyance.

Other names for juniper include aiten, aiteal, aittin, bastard killer, enebro, fairy circle, hackmatack, gin berry, gorst, genevier, genévrier, ginepro, gemeiner, mother's ruin, mountain yew, reckholder, saffron (just to confuse things), samh, savin, and wachholde. The names dwarf juniper, fairy circle, mountain common juniper, old field common juniper, and prostrate juniper are usually applied to low-growing varieties.

Properties and Correspondences

Note that most junipers share very similar properties, but the junipers of the ancient practitioners of Hekatean witchcraft were of a different species than the most common ones we know today.

- ⚘ *Latin name*: *Juniperus communis* and others

- ⚘ *Genus*: *Juniperus*

- ⚘ *Classification*: Shrub

- ⚘ *Spiritual properties*: Juniper calms through instilling courage and banishing toxins. It activates assertiveness and stimulates the soul. It gives a very different calming experience from lavender, for example. Protects the home and self during spiritual workings, encourages visions.

- ⚘ *Physiological properties*: Folk names for juniper including "bastard killer" and "mother's ruin" refer to juniper's ability to induce miscarriage. As with spiritual uses, juniper banishes that which doesn't serve the individual's truth. It makes an excellent tonic and stimulates appetite and digestion. It is a diuretic and treatment for urinary-tract infections.

- ⚘ *Magickal properties*: Banishing evil, clarity, courage, defensive magic, protection, purification, release, strength, truth, willpower.

- ✤ *Part used*: Cones (known as berries), resin, needles, and wood
- ✤ *Planetary correspondences*: Mars, Sun
- ✤ *Elemental correspondences*: Fire, Earth
- ✤ *Archetype*: Triformis (Shapeshifter)
- ✤ *World*: Middle
- ✤ *Zodiac*: Aries, Leo, Sagittarius
- ✤ *Color*: Dark blue, creamy white, sage green
- ✤ *Stone*: Beryl
- ✤ *Animal*: Hawk

Indications

Generally, juniper berries are what is consumed, although the leaves (needles) are also safe. The berries may contain a hard seed that can stick in the teeth. It is not safe for those with kidney disorders and those who are pregnant or breastfeeding. No research has been done on its use in children. My experience with juniper is that it is best used for periods no longer than four to six weeks.

Formulations

Since juniper is a tripartite botanical with the leaves, berries (seeds), sap, and wood being amenable to our witchery, the ways of using this beautiful tree are innumerable.

- ✤ Generally speaking, berries are used for brewing and needles are used for burning.
- ✤ Branches are excellent conductors of the plant's properties, rendering them most useful as wands for summoning powers and connecting to corresponding forces and spirits.
- ✤ The berries can be purchased in most grocery stores if you can't find them to harvest. Sprigs of juniper can be snipped from shrubs used in landscaping. Longer branches can be used as besoms (sacred brooms), boughs can be hung, etc. Juniper essential oil can be added to a spell candle for all matters requiring courage, clarity, and banishing.

- ⚜ Infusions of the berries are useful for mind and magic. Use about 10 per cup of boiled water.
- ⚜ Tinctures using ¼ cup of berries per cup of gin are excellent.
- ⚜ Shave the needles off the branches to use in infusions, decoctions, and tinctures.
- ⚜ Collect resin for use as seals and in poultices.

Pharmakeia

Perhaps my favorite use of a juniper sprig is as an easy incense to cleanse my workspace and clear my mind, helping me settle down to work when I am having difficulty getting grounded.

The distinctive flavor in gin comes primarily from juniper berries, so a true gin can be made using them. Use gin as the basis for spells and tinctures. Blend juniper, mugwort, and oak for an excellent visionary incense. One of my personal favorites for stable journeying in the spirit world.

I keep a juniper broom on my doorstep for sweeping away all unwanted energies, from the human kind to curious spirits. Collect branches and bind them with black cord, adding appropriate charms—especially symbols of Mars, Hekate's Wheel, and a charm representing a hawk.

Juniper is excellent for use in the khernips ritual for workings that require cleansing, clarity, clairvoyance, and courage. Juniper tincture is wonderful as a cleaning product. Just add to a vinegar dilution.

Juniper Nightmare Banishing Paquet

Ward off nightmares with a juniper paquet under your pillow. Make one of juniper and mugwort to inspire dream visions while maintaining protection from troublesome dream spirits.

Lavender

Mighty lavender is an essential herb in the witch's apothecary. It has been used in magick and medicine for thousands of years. To the ancient Greeks, lavender was used as a heal-all, for sleeping, and for purification. It may have sometimes been called nard in ancient texts like *The Greek Magical Papyri*. Canidia, one of Hekate's ancient witches, laments that "he is soaked in nard better than any made by my hands" (Horace, *Epodes* 5), perhaps referring

to the power of lavender to induce deep sleep. It was known to the ancient Romans, who used it in their spiritual and practical purification. Indeed "lavender" comes from the Latin word *lavare*, which means "to wash." Hekate's ancient priestesses, including the Sibylla, most likely used it in their rites, including their oracles. Lavender is associated with serpent energy, specifically the asp viper from Roman lore.

Lavender is used in spiritual, magickal, physiological, and psychological ways. It is a wonderful culinary herb. There are over 115 cultivated varieties of the herb, the most common being the English variety.

Lavender is stalwart, steady, and calm. It is excellent for calming the body, the mind, and the spirit and for allowing truth to surface. It is perfect for prophetic work of all forms and provides wonderful support for sovereignty endeavors.

Properties and Correspondences

- ⚜ *Latin name*: English lavender is *Lavandula Angustifolia*
- ⚜ *Genus*: *Lamiaceae*
- ⚜ *Classification*: Herb
- ⚜ *Spiritual properties*: Calm, clarity, love, protection, purification.
- ⚜ *Physiological properties*: Nervine, deodorant, diuretic, emmenagogue, headache treatment, parasiticide, insecticide, sedative, stimulant.
- ⚜ *Magickal properties*: Banishing, calming, clarity, deathwalking, divination, dreams, prophecy, protection from evil, rebirth, renewal.
- ⚜ *Part used*: Flowers, leaves
- ⚜ *Planetary correspondences*: Mercury, Virgo
- ⚜ *Elemental correspondences*: Air
- ⚜ *Archetype*: Aregos (Helper)
- ⚜ *World*: Upper
- ⚜ *Zodiac*: Aquarius, Gemini, Virgo
- ⚜ *Color*: Purple, blue
- ⚜ *Stone*: Fluorite
- ⚜ *Animal*: Wren

Indications

Not to be consumed while pregnant. Juniper or valerian can usually be used as substitutions.

Formulations

- ⚜ Lavender is an endlessly versatile plant that can be consumed, burned, and made into essences, oils, tinctures, and infusions. Fresh or dried, it can be used without formulation with amazing results.

- ⚜ For formulations that will be consumed, keep in mind that a little goes a long way. Lavender can be very overwhelming to the palate, which may be why those ancient witches used it to mask the taste of poisons.

Pharmakeia

Lavender is so useful, from bringing calm clarity to helping us journey in the spirit world. Lavender paquets (sachets/witch bags) have many uses. Attune the lavender being used to the specific purpose, whether it's sleep or protection.

Clarifying Lavender Bath

This bath is detoxifying and restorative, and will bring you deep awareness of what is important when you are faced with a big decision.

Make an infusion by steeping 1 tsp chamomile and ½ tsp lavender in 2 cups boiling water for ten minutes, then add to the bath. Take this deeper by blending dried lavender into a mixture of activated charcoal (about 1 tsp) to $^{1}/_{3}$ cup sea salt with just enough olive oil to blend into a scrub.

Moss

This botanical has often been overlooked by practitioners, but she offers us the opportunity to contemplate how what is spiritually true can diverge from scientific thought because of the difference in common understanding of the many plants known as mosses in comparison with the scientific classifications. The Moss Queen is the wisdom of the ages. Moss offers us entrance into the deeper world beyond the whims of the structures man imposes on nature. Spend time connecting with your local mosses to experience the timelessness

of the Green World. They are connectors to the primal. Moss is a master teacher that nourishes our emotions, connects us to the earth, and reminds us that we are eternal.

The Moss Queen first came to me in a dream as a guide into Hekate's Cave. She has borne witness to all of history. She is one of the oldest members of Hekate's Garden, having been created to be the steady presence of our Mother, the velvet carpet on which Hekate and her witches tread. Moss is revered as the wisest pharmakoi, for she has known it all. Since she knows all, she can easily absorb whatever comes her way, making her an excellent spirit for all releasing work. Turn to moss for deep nourishment of your soul.

Moss keeps her own time. She is a plant that grows slowly, according to the time of the gods. She, thus, is a plant of kairos rather than chronos. Keep this in mind when working with her. Moss is as ancient as our planet. She adapts to the changing environment but remains unique.

In the scientific classification of plants, moss refers to a specific family of plants, but in common practice, the term "moss" refers to plants that may or may not be classified as such by botanists. Generally, in herbalism, mosses can include plants outside of the botanical classification, especially certain lichens, which are related to moss. Liverworts and hornworts are also often considered as mosses, while Spanish moss is an altogether different species. Then there's Irish moss, which is actually a type of seaweed. Club moss is another example of a species that is energetically a moss, while not classified as such. Sphagnum, commonly known as peat moss, is a traditional form of fuel and used to keep wounds from turning septic.

What is it that binds these very different plants together into the practitioner's understanding of them? It is that they are ancient, enduring, and uniquely suited for workings that need sturdy stability. Mosses can be added to just about any spell to perform this role.

In addition to sphagnum, I am also partial to broom moss (*Dicranum scoparium*). This beautiful plant is found all over North America. Look for the broom-like fans of leaves, often mixed in with other types of mosses.

Moss teaches patience and increases perseverance, all leading to sustained sovereignty. It acquires the properties of the plant or rock on which it grows, so keep this in mind. For example, moss found on granite will be especially useful for prolonged emotional healing.

Properties and Correspondences

- ⚜ *Latin name*: Many, including *Sphagnum* and *Dicranum scoparium*
- ⚜ *Genus*: Bryophyta
- ⚜ *Classification*: Plant
- ⚜ *Spiritual properties*: Emotional healing, especially for deep wounds from childhood; entering the Under World; purification; releasing; and wisdom.
- ⚜ *Physiological properties*: Antiseptic (peat), febrifuge, treatment of skin conditions (club).
- ⚜ *Magickal properties*: Absorbs the energy of other botanicals well, so can be adapted to any spell. Specifically, for spells of purification requiring absorption of existing toxicity, and for those designed to endure. Patience and persistence.
- ⚜ *Part used*: All
- ⚜ *Planetary correspondences*: Jupiter
- ⚜ *Elemental correspondences*: Earth
- ⚜ *Archetype*: Presbeia (Ancient One)
- ⚜ *World*: Under
- ⚜ *Zodiac*: Pisces
- ⚜ *Color*: Brown
- ⚜ *Stone*: Moss agate
- ⚜ *Animal*: Turtle

Indications

Most mosses are considered nontoxic, although consuming them should be done with caution, except in the case of Icelandic moss, which is very healing.

Although mosses (*bryophytes*) constitute the second largest plant group on the planet, they remain quite a mystery in terms of their uses in witchcraft medicine. This is one pharmakoi where our intuition is our best guide.

Formulations

- ⚜ Moss keeps her own counsel, so she typically needs a bit of prompting for use in pharmakeia. Not that she is stubborn, like

mandragora, or willful, like foxglove, but she is very self-contained. In all my experimentations and communications with various mosses and lichens, I've found that she responds best to flame. As such, using moss with candle magick is recommended.

- ⚜ Moss can be added to tinctures and infusions as a stabilizer. Icelandic moss tea can be purchased and is quite safe for all uses.

- ⚜ Commercial peat moss is generally treated with chemicals, so avoid it.

- ⚜ Wildharvesting moss is the best approach. Only take what you need.

- ⚜ Allow moss to air dry if you are going to be burning it as part of an incense. Be mindful that it is quite flammable. A small pinch will add longevity to the other botanicals in your blend.

- ⚜ Moss is often home to land spirits who are somber and given to shyness. They can become wonderful allies for those patient enough to establish a relationship with them, however. Offerings of water are often well-accepted.

Pharmakeia

I've used moss in many spells to give them persistence and endurance. Keep in mind that moss is slow-acting, so it is best suited to those workings that you want to play out over months and years. Use moss on your altar to connect with Hekate's primal force.

Magickal Moss Balls

This is one of my favorite techniques for long-term spells. Use the moss as a stabilizer and binder, in addition to giving the spell endurance. Add botanicals, stones, animal-spirit medicine, and other correspondences, as suited to your goal.

This is a great spell to create using your intuition. Find your moss and then allow the rest of the spell to come to you while meditating on your intention. The more natural, the better. Moss is primal wisdom; let her connect you to yours as you develop this spell. Once you've collected the spirits who've answered the call of your intention, write an incantation.

- ☘ Rose bowl or other wide-mouth glass jar
- ☘ Candle in a color corresponding to your purpose, either in glass or in a heavy drinking glass or jar to keep the moss from catching fire
- ☘ Moss—broom, Icelandic, or whatever one presents herself to you

Directions

- ☘ Make a nest in the bottom of the bowl using the moss, while reciting:
  Lady Moss, she who endures, make this spell true and pure. Ask I of you, and you so do.
- ☘ Add your chosen spirits while singing your incantation. Moss is of very low vibration and appreciates a deeper voice than most botanicals.
- ☘ Place the candle in the nest and light it, reciting your incantation.
- ☘ Relight the candle at least once a week to boost the spell.

I've found that moss never fails in her assignment and requires little attention, but occasionally lighting the candle will reawaken the spell.

Mugwort

The witches' best friend. Excellent for opening psychic abilities because it has the dualistic actions of enhancing connection while offering protection. Mugwort is often thought to be named after the goddess Artemis, but it is actually named for a benevolent healing queen in ancient Greece. The association of mugwort with witches predates even this story, however. It is a core herb of witchcraft. Easy to get to know, strong, steady, and sure, mugwort is a most helpful spirit for medicine and magick.

Mugwort grows almost anywhere, making it an excellent choice for your witch's garden. Choose a variety that grows well in your climate and geography.

Properties and Correspondences

- ☘ *Latin name: Artemisia Vulgaris*
- ☘ *Genus: Artemisia*

- ✤ *Classification*: Herb
- ✤ *Spiritual properties*: Integrity, healing, purification, protection, psychic development, soothing the worried mind, astral travel, dream work.
- ✤ *Physiological properties*: Emmenagogue, eases the symptoms of uterine distress, calms, relaxes female reproductive system, calms overactive nervous systems.
- ✤ *Magickal properties*: All spells, activating altars and energy grids, astral travel, Third Eye work, mild trance inducer, meditation helper, revelations.
- ✤ *Part used*: Leaves, stems
- ✤ *Planetary correspondences*: Venus, Moon
- ✤ *Elemental correspondences*: Air, Earth
- ✤ *Archetype*: Kleidoukhos (Keeper of the Keys)
- ✤ *World*: Upper
- ✤ *Zodiac*: Gemini, Cancer, Libra
- ✤ *Color*: Purple, white, green
- ✤ *Stone*: Clear quartz
- ✤ *Animal*: Raven

Indications

Not for use while pregnant or trying to conceive. If you have a ragweed allergy, you may also react to mugwort.

Formulations

Mugwort can be used fresh or dried. There are many varieties available. It is applicable in any type of formulation.

Pharmakeia

A basic infusion (known as a "simple") of 1 tsp mugwort steeped in a cup of boiled water has endless uses in medicine and magick. Mugwort also burns exceptionally well as an incense. Burn a small amount on ½ charcoal disk before any ritual to cleanse, protect, and activate the space. Use as a base for just about any incense.

As part of your daily tonic, mugwort boosts magickal abilities and eases inflammation of the body, mind, and spirit. An equal mixture of mugwort and pennyroyal in an infusion can be taken to soothe menstrual distress, for example. A mugwort paquet made by stuffing purple fabric full of mugwort and keeping it under your pillow will empower your dreams. Keep it in your pocket for calm awareness.

Mugwort Medicine Patch

One of my favorite ways to use mugwort is in a psychic patch, a Third Eye-opening poultice. Wrap about 1 tbsp mugwort in white gauze, then cover it with boiling water (just enough to get it wet). Cover the mixture until completely cool. Place on your Third Eye to cleanse and open it. This is an excellent way to augment trance in any journey. Use it for several days to detoxify your Third Eye and strengthen your psychic vision.

Myrrh

Myrrh is the pharmakoi of initiation. This resin has the power to raise our vibrations right up to the heights of possibility. It is a gate-opener to the unborn soul and mysticism.

Myrrh is the incense most used by the ancient creators of *The Greek Magical Papyri*, those Hekatean sorcerers who stretch across time to share their wisdom. In spells and offerings, myrrh represents the mystery of Hekatean witchcraft. Complex and challenging, myrrh is not for the weak. It is ancient, wise, and intimidating. Very much like our Mother, it opens the way to the mysteries within and without, but we must initiate ourselves.

The *Ophies Pteretoi* were feathery winged serpents who guarded the myrrh fields in ancient Arabia, revealing that only the bravest could access their bounty. Thus, myrrh is strongly associated with dragon energy. The phoenix, as a harbinger of the rebirth process, often comes forward when we are connected to this botanical.

The resin is said to be the tears of the mother of Adonis, the original Myrrha, who was accused of tricking her father into sexual relations—a sin for which she was transformed into a tree, whose resin is her tears. Were they tears of regret or of the wrongly imprisoned? One retelling of this myth paints Myrrha as the innocent victim whose power threatened her father, rather than as an evil woman. As a woman defiled and denied proper burial, she is a member of Hekate's Horde. She is a sad spirit, who wishes only to have her honor restored. She may also come forward when myrrh is utilized.

Myrrh's properties are an excellent addition to all sorts of psychic workings, especially for death-rebirth magick. It is also a potent psychic-ability activator. A quirky side of myrrh is that it is a powerful addition to abundance spells.

Properties and Correspondences

- ♀ *Latin name*: *Commiphora myrrha*
- ♀ *Genus*: *Commiphora*
- ♀ *Classification*: Tree resin
- ♀ *Spiritual properties*: Myrrh brings lightness of being and connection to the unborn soul, the higher mysteries, ascended masters, angels, and the Starry Road.
- ♀ *Physiological properties*: Antiseptic, used in mouthwash and toothpaste; can also be applied to the skin to treat wounds and to ease toothache.
- ♀ *Magickal properties*: Abundance, afterlife, blessings, death, hex-breaking, initiation, purification (ritual), rebirth, sacred rites.
- ♀ *Part used*: Resin
- ♀ *Planetary correspondences*: Jupiter, moon
- ♀ *Elemental correspondences*: Air
- ♀ *Archetype*: Daeira (Knowing One)
- ♀ *World*: Upper
- ♀ *Zodiac*: Scorpio
- ♀ *Color*: Amber
- ♀ *Stone*: Moonstone
- ♀ *Animal*: Dragonfly

Indications

Not for animals, children, or pregnant women. This resin should only be consumed occasionally, at a dose of less than 2 grams.

Formulations

⚜ Myrrh can be purchased as an essential oil, already ground, or in chunks that you grind yourself in a mortar and pestle.

⚜ Make a tincture using gin for a potent spiritual voyager that opens the way while banishing the unwelcome.

Pharmakeia

Burning myrrh as an incense or vaporized in a diffuser creates lightness of being by encouraging separation from the physical self. Place a small amount (pinky-fingernail size) on a slightly larger piece of charcoal. It can also be placed in a warming pot that's heated by a candle. In a pinch, myrrh can be heated in a 350-degree oven for thirty-five minutes to release its powers.

Wear a chunk of the resin around your neck to invoke the power of myrrh without sacred smoke. To inhale the sacred smoke of myrrh, use a series of short, quick, shallow breaths, like you would use in holotropic breathing or kundalini activation. This will greatly enhance its effects.

Myrrh Ink

Ancient Hekateans reserved myrrh for their most sacred rites, including writing spells using it as an ink. Create myrrh ink to use for spells and rituals that summon the heights of the Starry Road and for connecting to your unborn soul. It is especially useful for writing proclamations of initiation.

Black or gold ink works best. Purchase a small pot of ink with an opening wide enough to drop in the small pieces. Use a glass fountain pen that can be dipped into the inkwell for best results, or a suitable feather. Grind the myrrh into pieces about the size of your pinky fingernail, then place several in the bottle of ink. Let it rest for seven days and use when the moon is full or new to write your spell or ritual.

Oak

In the center of the Garden, the mightiest tree of all holds court—the King of the Wood, blessed oak. This botanical brings the masculine energy of virility, knowledge, and strength. Oak is ancient, primal, and omnipotent, standing as Zeus did before Hekate, bowing to her power while maintaining his own.

Oak represents the sometimes-complicated relationship we have with powerful men. This master also knows all the secrets of Hekate's witches, but loves us anyway.

The feeling is mutual. Even Medea, who harbored some resentment for this spirit after he yielded that sheepskin to Jason, realizes that this tree is a powerful ally. After all, it was her spell that released the sacred fleece from the grip of the oak when she put the guardian dragon to sleep. Herein we find the symbolic cautionary tale of giving up our own power. Hold on to the sacred serpent within who guards your soul and honors the source from which it came.

Sacred objects have been carved from oak since antiquity and, as the royal wood of kings and queens, it is most suitable for statuary and other icons. My two beloved statues of Hekate are both handcrafted in oak. While oak is highly masculine in personality, the oversoul of this pharmakoi is one of sacred sovereign power, making it an excellent offering to our Mother and for helping us to claim our own crown.

Wands made of oak are excellent for connecting to the Starry Road, dragon energy, and Hekate as the Star Walker. It is also excellent for summoning masculine energies and useful for instilling persistence when we are drained. It can lend power to all spells. Although ancient and wise, oak is also virile, lending his spirit to our rites of fertility and sex magick. Oak is the experienced teacher who's seen and done it all.

Properties and Correspondences

- *Latin name*: There are over 200 varieties of oak. The most common include *Quercus robur* (English oak), *Quercus alba* (white oak), and *Quercus Velutina* (black oak).
- *Genus: Quercus*
- *Classification*: Tree
- *Spiritual properties*: Loyalty, personal power, sovereignty, freedom, strength, divine masculine, offerings, rebirth, wisdom.
- *Physiological properties*: Different species can have specific health benefits. White-oak bark is good for inflammation, for treating minor skin problems, and as an antidiarrheal. Acorns also have many nutrients and are high in fiber.
- *Magickal properties*: Abundance, ancestors, blessings, courage, justice, power, sex, wisdom.

- ✤ *Part used*: Leaves, bark, wood, and seeds (acorns)
- ✤ *Planetary correspondences*: Jupiter
- ✤ *Elemental correspondences*: Air, Fire
- ✤ *Archetype*: Kyria (Supreme)
- ✤ *World*: Upper
- ✤ *Zodiac*: Taurus, Gemini, Cancer, Leo, Sagittarius
- ✤ *Color*: Brown
- ✤ *Stone*: Emerald
- ✤ *Animal*: Dragon

Indications

Generally, wildharvested oak requires careful preparation to remove any toxins. Commercial teas are safe to consume by most.

Formulations

- ✤ White-oak bark is used in teas and tinctures for its health benefits and can be purchased ready to consume.
- ✤ Use the leaves as offerings, for wreaths, and to make crowns celebrating your sovereignty, especially for celebrating the seasonal transitions.
- ✤ Acorns are amazing magickal gifts from the mighty King of the Wood. Besides being used as talismans, they can be consumed after careful preparation. Acorn flour, noodles, and oil can be purchased to make dishes suited for Hekate's Feast.
- ✤ Oak tincture, also known as essence, is a staple of the apothecary. It can be diluted into a wash to activate your own persistence and sovereignty, and for vivifying and cleansing sacred objects.

Pharmakeia

The tannins in oak were used by the ancients for tanning leather. Make a decoction of the bark and acorns for dying papers and fabrics. A concentrated decoction, cooled with added gum arabic for stabilizing, makes an excellent ink for writing initiation pledges. Anoint your sacred objects with oak to honor Hekate.

Acorn Magick

Acorns are great for sympathetic magick, for blessing, and for bestowing wisdom on those taglocked to the seed. Write a sigil for the person on the nut, then keep it in your blessing grid. A basic blessing grid consists of talismans or poppets, or other symbols of the people involved, encircled within a ring of botanicals, stones, and animal spirits that bring abundance and healing.

Medea's Flying Ointment

This ointment is used during sacred rituals for inducing mild trance states. It is specifically designed to open your inner sacred serpent and connect with the serpent that is the guardian of the Tree of Wisdom. Medea's serpents flew, so expect this ointment to connect you not only to our Regina Venificarum, but also to the heights of the Starry Road. You may find yourself riding alongside her, playing charioteer to her team of winged serpents—aka dragons.

This ointment consists of five of her sacred botanicals: frankincense, lavender, juniper, mugwort, and oak. I'm sharing this formula as a large batch so you can give the ointments as gifts or keep them all for yourself. The ointment will last in the refrigerator for about a year, or for six months at room temperature.

Supplies

- ☥ Tins with lids (about 6 medium or 12 small ones)
- ☥ Stainless-steel pot
- ☥ Wooden spoon
- ☥ 4-cup heat-proof glass measuring cup

Ingredients

7 drops each frankincense, lavender, and juniper essential oils

2 tbsp dried mugwort infused in ¼ cup olive oil for seven days. Strain off the mugwort if you don't want the botanical matter in the ointment.

7 drops oak tincture. Make your own by steeping several oak leaves in ½ cup alcohol, or purchase the essence. Bach's Flower Essences are excellent.

2 cups shea butter

¼ cup beeswax pellets

- ⚜ Place the shea butter and the beeswax in the measuring cup.
- ⚜ Immerse the cup in a pot filled halfway with water.
- ⚜ Bring the pot to a boil, stirring frequently to encourage swift melting.
- ⚜ Once the mixture is melted, add the mugwort oil and the essential oils.
- ⚜ Stir well and pour into the tins.

ALTERNATIVE EASY-BAKE METHOD

- ⚜ Fill all the metal tins with ¾ shea butter and ¼ beeswax and place on a cookie sheet.
- ⚜ Bake at 300 degrees until melted—about ten minutes depending on the size of the tin. Stir in the oils and the oak tincture.
- ⚜ Let the ointment cool to room temperature.
- ⚜ Test your sensitivity to the ointment on the inside of your right elbow. Wait about an hour to gauge how sensitive you are to it.
- ⚜ Apply to the crown, heart center, root, top of feet, and inside of wrists for complete activation.

Olive

The olive was well-favored by Hekate's ancient witches. We have learned from Medea that she used a wand made of olive to stir her rebirth potion in her cauldron. As she cast the spell and spiraled the dead branch in her potion, it was reborn. Then she used the branch to return the Earth to splendor and, finally, to rejuvenate her father-in-law. She's here now as our guardian, after all. Instead of letting him die, she poured her tonic into the wound and his youthful self was restored.

Olive oil was the most sacred in ancient Hekatean temples, used for fuel in lamps, for anointing, and as offerings. It was also used in potions and as the wood for wands.

Today, olive oil has become so much a part of our diet that we may lose sight of its sacredness. Each time you pour a bit, give silent gratitude to Hekate for blessing the world with such an amazing gift.

Properties and Correspondences

- ⚜ *Latin name:* Olea europaea
- ⚜ *Genus:* Oleaceae
- ⚜ *Classification:* Tree
- ⚜ *Spiritual properties:* Creation, protection, purification, sacredness, wellness.
- ⚜ *Physiological properties:* Olive oil may reduce the risk of certain health conditions, including heart disease. In addition, it is excellent as a lubricant and moisturizer, and great for relieving constipation and generally soothing internal upset.
- ⚜ *Magickal properties:* Abundance, balance, consecration, healing, honor, prosperity, protection, purification, rebirth, success, wealth, well-being.
- ⚜ *Part used:* All parts of the olive tree can be used in witchcraft. The oil is made from the fruit.
- ⚜ *Planetary correspondences:* Sun
- ⚜ *Elemental correspondences:* All
- ⚜ *Archetype:* Pasikratea (Universal Queen)
- ⚜ *World:* All
- ⚜ *Zodiac:* Leo
- ⚜ *Color:* Gold
- ⚜ *Stone:* Labradorite, diamond
- ⚜ *Animal:* Dove

Indications

Safe.

Formulations

- ⚜ Olive oil is used as a fixative, a base, and for pharmakeia formulary. We evoke olive's properties when we use it in this way. The protection offered by the olive will ensure that the other botanicals are secure in their ability to get the job done.

- Olive oil can be consumed and used directly on the skin.
- Note that olive oil has a relatively low burning temperature.

Pharmakeia

Olive oil is excellent for the vivification and consecration of sacred icons, objects, and tools without additional botanicals. To attune your sacred objects to your own energy, charge the oil with a few drops of your blood or locks of your hair. Olive oil is a fantastic sacred moisturizer and lubricant without any additions.

Brimo Oil and Talisman

Brimo is the name given to Hekate at her most terrifying. Uninhibited but wise; angry, yet fair. Evoke the power of Brimo when your righteous anger is in order. This oil works when you must be courageous, do battle, and get justice. Pour it into a small glass vial and wear on a red cord to amplify your inner fierce Goddess. Anoint the seven sacred energy centers to activate your own ferocity.

The mixture contains black pepper for justice, fennel for courage and communication, and oak for success in battle. The olive-oil base provides protection. This spell also uses the power of the number 5, which is associated with conflict and the peace that comes after winning the war.

INGREDIENTS

5 tsp high-quality olive oil (preferably organic and Greek)

5 black peppercorns

5 fennel seeds

5 drops of oak essence (like Bach's)

1 acorn or 1 oak leaf torn into 5 pieces

DIRECTIONS

Supercharge this oil by creating it on the day of the Full Moon and letting it coagulate under its light.

- Combine the ingredients in the order listed. As you add each ingredient, stir clockwise five times, while reciting:

Five times I stir this cauldron round,
To cast this spell true and sound.
Olive's protection a spiral now released,
I summon my Brimo to ultimately bring peace.
Pepper brings justice fast,
Fennel makes my courage last,
And the King of the Wood
Renders my anger strong and good.
As I spin you round and round,
Brimo does pour down,
Her power fierce and true,
This spells now cast,
And the work is through.

If you're not using the oil immediately, it's best to keep it in a brown or black bottle to avoid triggering anger in highly sensitive people (including yourself, possibly). Store it by itself in a dark, cool place.

Peppermint

Mint is one of the most common, but most powerful, Pharmakoi Kyrios. Mint is amenable to the beginning pharmaka, but should not be dismissed by experienced practitioners. It brings calm, content, and connection to the spirits, especially the beloved departed.

Persephone, enraged at Hades' romantic liaison with a nymph called Mentha, turned her into the eponymous plant. Mint refers to a variety of over two dozen botanical species, including the popular peppermint and spearmint. Pennyroyal is a type of mint that is specifically useful for banishing and can be considered an amplified form of mint. Whereas pennyroyal and spearmint are more aggressive, peppermint is soothing.

Peppermint has strong properties as a visionary herb and is excellent consumed as a tonic. In ancient times, mint was used to scent the body after death, leading to its association with the dead and the spirit world. Mint is also traditionally used as an herb of welcome, bringing friendly visitors and goodwill.

The Romans held mint in such high esteem that they wore crowns of it. It makes an excellent offering to Hekate and her companions when welcoming them into your space.

Mint has countless uses in pharmakeia and is as easy to work with as it is to grow. Keep a pot of mint growing by the entrance to your home to ensure good vibes, and to clip for your witchery as needed. It is a staple of the witch's apothecary.

Properties and Correspondences

- ⚥ *Latin name*: Mentha piperita
- ⚥ *Genus*: Mentha
- ⚥ *Classification*: Herb
- ⚥ *Spiritual properties*: Calms the mind, body, and spirit. Excellent to increase awareness of your inner life and of spirits. Facilitates feelings of trust.
- ⚥ *Physiological properties*: Soothes the digestive system, overall tonic.
- ⚥ *Magickal properties*: Can be used for purification if more appropriate plants are unavailable. Used on its own, be sure to direct the cleansing properties through your intentions to ensure the toxic is banished, lest the mint create a contented sort of chaos, in both the physical and etheric worlds (unless that is your goal). Mint is fantastic for quick-acting spells, and for those short in duration. It can be used as a substitute for communication spells when other botanicals, like fennel or licorice, aren't available.
- ⚥ *Part used*: Leaves
- ⚥ *Planetary correspondences*: Mercury
- ⚥ *Elemental correspondences*: Air
- ⚥ *Archetype*: Melinoe (Soothing One)
- ⚥ *World*: Upper
- ⚥ *Zodiac*: Aquarius, Gemini
- ⚥ *Color*: Green
- ⚥ *Stone*: Blue topaz
- ⚥ *Animal*: Finch

Indications

Mint is generally safe to consume, but some people are allergic to it.

Formulations

❀ Mint can be used as an oil, dried, or fresh. Generally, the leaves are the only part used, although you can use the stems in crowns or talismans.

❀ Mint is highly aromatic, rendering the olfactory experience as powerful as consuming it. Mint oil in the diffuser during social engagements will ensure a happy time is had by all. Avoid excessive amounts when using to create a positive social climate, since it may shift into its other main use—that of connecting to the spirit world.

❀ Mint tea can be taken as a daily tonic to enhance the Third Eye and maintain balance in the physical and spiritual selves. Use ¼ tsp to a cup of boiled water. For visionary workings, increase the concentration to ½ tsp per cup.

❀ Mint oil can easily be made by adding ½ cup fresh chopped plant (or ¼ cup dried) to a cup of oil. To activate as a bringer of happy social interactions, make during the waxing moon. For use as a visionary herb, make during the Full Moon.

❀ Pets may be fond of mint. If yours are, add a bit to their meals to soothe them.

Pharmakeia

Mint is soothing and evoking. Generally, as noted above, smaller amounts are advised for creating contentment, while larger amounts facilitate visions, summon spirits, and evoke the Goddess.

Triple Goddess Salad

This light salad is excellent as part of any meal you share with Hekate and her Horde to create the energy of gratitude and evoke her presence. Serve with a side of rice and cornbread for a meal fit for dining with the queens. Tasty medicine.

INGREDIENTS

4 cups chopped and seeded cucumbers, coated with ¼ cup vinegar for one hour (use an infused one, like basil, fennel, or thyme)

1 cup crumbled sheep or goat cheese

½ cup pomegranate seeds

DRESSING

- 2 cups thick plain Greek yogurt
- 1 tsp olive oil
- ½ tsp sea salt
- 3 tbsp finely chopped mint
- 1 tsp minced garlic
- ¼ tsp freshly ground pepper

DIRECTIONS

- ⚜ Combine the botanicals, cheese, and seeds in a large bowl.
- ⚜ Mix the dressing ingredients in a separate bowl, then pour over the salad.
- ⚜ Top with fresh rose petals if available.

Crossing the Veil Tea

This infusion is a gentle aid to walking in the spirit world. The mint connects to the spirits, while the mugwort opens the Third Eye. Yarrow brings healing to all involved, and the juniper berries serve to banish the unwelcome.

INGREDIENTS

- 1 tsp mugwort
- 1 tsp yarrow
- ½ tsp mint
- 13 juniper berries
- 2 cups boiled water

DIRECTIONS

- ⚜ In an infuser, like a tea ball or small strainer, combine the mugwort, yarrow, mint, and juniper berries.
- ⚜ Pour 2 cups of boiled water over the mixture and let steep for ten minutes.
- ⚜ Remove the herbs.

Consume a cup and present the rest to the spirits you wish to connect with.

Pine

Mighty pine—the tree we associate with the holidays, when they often reign over our living rooms—is a bringer of blessings. Our modern association of pine with celebrations and the sacred is rooted in the practices of ancient Hekateans who used the cones in rituals and spells. In fact, pine cones are one of the most common ingredients in the workings contained in *The Greek Magical Papyri*. It was my research on the botanicals used in this ancient grimoire that inspired me to create the Ekdotis Talisman described below when we first purchased our home. That talisman has brought us great bounty, but it is starting to feel tired. My plans for this Winter Solstice include crafting a new one.

Include pine cones in your winter rituals to bring bounty in the new year and to attract good cheer. Try using them in your own talisman. They are suitable for offerings to Hekate Enodia and in workings that bring energy, bestow blessings, and help ensure safety for all possessions. Pine is an excellent gift for another witch.

Properties and Correspondences

- *Latin name: Pinus*
- *Genus: Pinus* (sole species in this genus)
- *Classification:* Tree
- *Spiritual properties:* Pine brings abundance, so it is most useful for all personal-growth workings. Excellent when added to healing and rebirth rituals.
- *Physiological properties:* The bark of certain species, like *Pinus pinaster*, can be consumed and is reported to have anti-inflammatory properties and to be a rich source of many nutrients.
- *Magickal properties:* Abundance, beginnings, growth, happy home, energy, freedom, money, truth, wealth, and wisdom.
- *Part used:* All—seed pods (cones), seeds (pine nuts), needles (leaves), bark, resin, and wood
- *Planetary correspondences:* Jupiter, Mars, Saturn
- *Elemental correspondences:* Air, Earth, Fire
- *Archetype:* Ekdotis (Bestower)

- *World*: Middle
- *Zodiac*: Aquarius, Aries, Scorpio
- *Color*: Deep green
- *Stone*: Shungite
- *Animal*: Deer

Indications

Some species are potentially toxic, so watch out for pets consuming all parts of the pine trees found in the wild. Some species have bark that is safe to consume by adults, and others yield those delicious pine nuts used in many recipes like pesto.

Formulations

- Finding your own pine cones for use in witchery is a most enjoyable adventure. Study the impressive pine, learning the different varieties in your area, and then compare them to the different species you encounter on your travels. I am a long-time student of this botanical, who never fails to bless me in whatever form I find it.

- Given that there are well over 100 different species of pine, there are some subtle differences in their pharmakeiac applications. However, they are all blessers.

- Keep a jar of pine cones in the apothecary at all times because they are so useful.

- Pine essential oil can be blended with a carrier like olive to use in a diffuser, or for gently simmering to release the spirit of blessing.

- Make pine oil by filling a jar with cones, needles, and bark, then pouring oil all around. Let steep for about a month, since pine can be slow to combine with oils.

- To make a decoction, fill a stainless-steel pot with pine, cover with water, and bring to a boil. Continue to boil gently for ten minutes, then cover and let cool.

- Pine ink is sure to bring abundance. Add a few drops of the essential oil or bits of pine cone to your inkwell.

- Instead of disposing of the Yule tree, find a place for it in your yard so you can harvest its bounty for your spells in the coming months.

- Typically, the common wild varieties of pine aren't consumed, but you can purchase pine nuts and bark tea for use in infusions, decoctions, and recipes. Pesto is one of the most Hekatean of sauces: basil, garlic, and pine nuts.

- Given the blessings of pine, using the chips for pet bedding is excellent for their well-being.

Pharmakeia

Make a simple blessing bowl and place it in the heart of your home. Fill a green bowl ⅔ with salt, then add three pine cones, three cinnamon sticks, and three bay leaves. You can also add three juniper berries for banishing the baneful.

Rub pine oil on all money spells. It's also great for attracting the attention of the horned gods and masculine energy, so rub that oil on statues and pictures of gods and guys.

Ekdotis Talisman

A talisman is a combination of spirits, crafted into a material object spell. In this spell, you'll summon the spirits of bay laurel, cinnamon, and pine into a knot working to keep by the entrance to your home. Ekdotis means "Bestower" and this talisman will certainly manifest many blessings from the Goddess.

SUPPLIES

- Green, gold, and white cord

- Metal thread (gold)

- Pine branch or other wood, or bone (I have a coyote rib bone in mine)

- Enchanted home object—for instance, an animal spirit symbol like a feather or bone that you have found

- Other charms that represent abundance to you

- Hole punch

Ingredients

3 pine cones

3 bay leaves (Choose bay leaves that are thicker, so you can punch a hole in the top of each one without cracking)

3 cinnamon sticks

Directions

✣ Bind the 3 pine cones together with the metal thread.

✣ Cut the 3 cords to about five times the length of the cinnamon sticks. You may want to use shorter cinnamon sticks.

✣ Bind the 3 cords to your stick, knotting them tightly, while reciting:
By knot of one, this spell's begun.

✣ Braid about ⅕ of the cord, then slide the 3 bay leaves on, reciting:
Bay banishes all bane from this home.

✣ Knot under the bay to seal this part of the spell, saying:
By knot of two, this spell is true.

✣ Braid the next section, then attach the wire thread on the pine cones to the 3 cords, reciting:
Pine brings plenty to this home.

✣ Knot off the pine cone section, saying:
By knot of three, this spell flows freely.

✣ Braid another segment of the cord, sliding a cinnamon stick onto each cord, reciting:
Cinnamon ensures that warmth abounds in this home.

✣ Add any other charms or beads to complete the talisman. When you are finished, tie the final three knots while reciting (in order as you tie them):
By knot of four, this spell is forever more.
By knot of five, this spell shall thrive.
By knot of six, this spell is now fixed.

Hang the talisman by your household threshold. Touch it daily to further activate its powers, and to check for depletion. The harder it has to work, the sooner it will be depleted.

THE
KNOWLEDGE

Pomegranate

Pomegranate is the sacred fruit of temptation and truth. Depending on your perspective, it was either the poison that bound Persephone to the Under World, or the blessing that freed her from her mother's harsh gaze. Hekate and Persephone are incredibly close, so much so that they can be confused one for the other. Persephone, the benevolent Queen of the Under World, keeps counsel with her trusted companion, Hekate. While our Mother freely wanders her universe, Persephone is bound to the cycle of life, forever obliged to keep humanity going.

Plants of Persephone

Persephone has been my longtime confidante. Not given to practicing pharmakeia herself, she nevertheless oversees the pharmakoi who reside in her realm. The poisons, and particularly botanicals associated with death and the afterlife, are hers to command. We can connect to Persephone through these plants.

Pomegranate is the botanical most connected to Persephone and Hekate's torches shining in the darkness. We can follow those lights or resist them, but the journey is mandatory. It's only a matter of when. That is the message of pomegranate.

Turn to the Hieros Pyr, the sacred fire that flows from pomegranate, for deepening your experience of the feminine mysteries, connecting to the departed, and for honoring Hekate and Persephone. The Hieros Pyr brings rebirth to those who are sincere.

Properties and Correspondences

- ⚷ *Latin name: Punica granatum*
- ⚷ *Genus: Punica*
- ⚷ *Classification:* Tree, fruit
- ⚷ *Spiritual properties:* Afterlife, understanding of the life cycle, spiritual death and rebirth, ancestral healing, forgiveness.

- *Physiological properties*: General tonic, anti-inflammatory, builds immunity, and is an antioxidant.

- *Magickal properties*: As the Hieros Pyr, pomegranate both creates and destroys. With pomegranate spells, ensure that you give clear instructions about how she is to behave. Abundance, banishing, clarity, deception, forgiveness, love, rebirth, trust, and the wisdom of Persephone are some of the uses of pomegranate.

- *Part used*: Fruit

- *Planetary correspondences*: Saturn

- *Elemental correspondences*: Earth

- *Archetype*: Persephone (Destroyer)

- *World*: Under

- *Zodiac*: Scorpio

- *Color*: Deep red

- *Stone*: Red jasper

- *Animal*: Swan

Indications

This plant's seeds are generally safe, and the juice is exceptionally so.

Formulations

- This botanical can be used for most workings and in a seemingly endless variety of ways, from putting the seeds on vanilla ice cream to using as offerings to Hekate and Persephone. Such a versatile, yummy, and amenable pharmakoi.

- Frozen pomegranate seeds can be kept for up to a year and are a staple of the pharmaka's apothecary. The juice is available widely. Fresh pomegranates are generally available only in autumn.

- Pomegranate juice is an excellent addition to infusions. Generally, make the infusion more concentrated—about double strength— and then add an equal amount of the juice.

- Grenadine is a concentrated pomegranate syrup that can be used for infusions and in tinctures. Some commercial products are no

longer made with pomegranates, so read the label to make sure you have a true grenadine.

Pharmakeia

Pomegranate juice makes an excellent basis for magickal papers (papyri). Gently heat the juice over low temperature until slightly steaming, then insert undyed parchment paper using tongs. Spread the paper around and let rest for a few minutes. Dry the paper on towels that can be stained. Add bits of the pith (the white membrane) to incenses. Use the dried seeds in poppets, paquets, and more.

Sacred Fire Water

Basil, skullcap, and mugwort are infused with pomegranate seeds to make this sacred water. Basil is traditionally an herb consumed by initiates as they learn the mysteries, so chosen because it calms the mind while releasing our fire. Mugwort is evoked for protection, psychic awareness, and wisdom. Make sure you direct the energies this way while you make the potion. Skullcap is a supreme binder. A skullcap spell is almost impossible to break. Here, call forth the characteristics of learning, clarity, and success in addition to binding the sacred water together. Pomegranate bears the energy of the price of initiation. A plant of Saturn, pomegranate enhances stability and increases focus.

This is a tried-and-true formulary that my students absolutely love for connecting to their inner fire and the mysteries of Persephone and Hekate. Consume it prior to evoking their presence. It is safe to consume for adults, and you can add gin to the cooled water to make a magickal cocktail.

SUPPLIES

⚕ Stainless-steel strainer or teapot

⚕ Mason jar with lid

INGREDIENTS

3 fresh basil leaves

½ tsp skullcap

1 tsp mugwort

1 cup pomegranate juice

- ⚜ Steep the botanicals in a cup of boiled water for ten minutes, covered.
- ⚜ Place pomegranate juice in a mason jar, then pour in the infusion.

Poppy

Poppy is a somber spirit, for she knows the sorrow of death—the sadness of those left behind and the restless souls of the unquiet dead. Poppy also knows the peace of death, which eases suffering and brings completion. Enter into her embrace for deathwalking and for deep slumber.

Poppy is one of the mistresses of Hekate's Garden, entrusted with teaching one of her most important lessons: without death, there is no life. Sacred to Hekate and Persephone, she is revered as an opener to the mysteries of the dead. Opium, which is produced from *Papaver somniferum*, is a powerful narcotic that has claimed many. Heed this message: poppy is powerful. Her beauty intoxicates the mind and body.

Beautiful corn, or red, poppies are a hardy addition to a witch's Garden. They are especially magical under the waning moon. My earliest memories of red poppies are in my grandmother's vegetable garden, where she always had them around the perimeter to keep out animals. I loved those poppies, although I wasn't allowed to touch them. They enchanted me then, perhaps representing my soul connection to Hekate before I could consciously articulate my belonging to Our Lady.

Poppies are flowers of remembrance, worn to honor those lost in battle. They are deeply connected to Samhain and the Holy Darkness of November.

Properties and Correspondences

- ⚜ *Latin name: Papaver somniferum* (opium poppy); *Papaver rhoeas* (red poppy)
- ⚜ *Genus: Papaver*
- ⚜ *Classification:* Plant
- ⚜ *Spiritual properties:* Excellent for opening the path to spiritual dismemberment and rebirth, and for soul retrieval.
- ⚜ *Physiological properties:* Poppy seeds have many health benefits, including easing digestion, strengthening bones, increasing red-blood-cell production, and improving sleep.

- *Magickal properties*: Afterlife, deathwalking, dream work, necromancy, psychopompery, rebirth, sacred rites, visions.
- *Part used*: Seeds for consuming, flowers for decoration
- *Planetary correspondences*: Moon
- *Elemental correspondences*: Water, Fire
- *Archetype*: Aidonaea (Lady of the Under World)
- *World*: Under
- *Zodiac*: Capricorn
- *Color*: Black, red, white
- *Stone*: Hematite
- *Animal*: Owl

Indications

Commercial poppy seeds are generally safe to consume in small amounts. Poppy seeds are mild narcotics. Consuming them can result in a positive drug test.

Formulations

- Poppy seeds are quite amenable to all formulations, from infusions to baked delicacies.
- An infusion of poppy seed should not exceed ½ tsp to a cup of water, as higher doses can be toxic when consumed.
- I use poppy seeds every autumn in my altars, rituals, and spells. My experience has been that it resists the contamination that plagues weaker botanicals. A simple direction to her to awaken to her full power is all that is required. She has never failed me.

Pharmakeia

Poppy stands watch over the entrance to the Under World. Pluck her at your own peril. For Hekate's witches, she opens the way to our Mother's sacred cave deep within. The following ritual has been profoundly transformative for my students. It is used during Hekate's Holy Darkness, from Samhain to the Winter Solstice, specifically for November 16 and 30.

Deathwalking Oil and Ritual

Whether we seek advice from departed loved ones, wish to connect to our witch ancestors, or just want to wander around the Other Side, the thinness of the veil can be pierced easily by botanical specialists. Deathwalking provides us with the opportunity to understand the mysteries of the afterlife better. If you are new to this sort of witchery, proceed with caution. I suggest contacting a beloved departed for your first time walking on the Other Side.

SUPPLIES

- Glass jar with lid
- Mortar and pestle
- Black cloth

INGREDIENTS

1 cup high-quality organic olive oil

¼ cup poppy seeds

1 tsp dried mugwort

1 fingernail-sized knob of benzoin or 4 drops of the essential oil

1 sprig fresh juniper or 13 berries

1 sprig fresh lavender or 4 drops essential oil

3 aster flowers or 1 large floral aster (sage can be used as a substitution)

1 wild rose blossom (red can be substituted)

DIRECTIONS

- In the mortar, first add the poppy seeds.
- Grind in a clockwise direction until the oil begins to be released.
- Add the mugwort and grind clockwise until blended.
- Crush in the benzoin or add the drops of the oil.
- Add the juniper and lavender, gently blending in the same direction.
- Pour the oil into the jar.
- Stir in the botanical mixture, keeping with the clockwise motion.
- Drop in the aster and rose.

🜊 Close the jar and cover with the black cloth.

🜊 Let the oil rest for three nights.

RITUAL

Create a deathwalking altar honoring Hekate Aidonaea. Add the ancestors you wish to communicate with by including belongings, pictures, and their favorite things.

When you are ready, anoint the objects of the ancestors, the imagery of the deities being evoked, and yourself (last) with the oil. This is a triangular grid. Envision the grid being created between the ancestors (or the Other Side), Hekate, and yourself. Anoint three points on each (top, middle, bottom) in a clockwise direction (Hekate, ancestor, you) while concentrating on creating this grid representing the Higher Self/Upper World mystical energy, the Middle Self/Middle World active energy, and the Lower Self/Under World emotional energy.

Once this grid is activated, a portal will be opened in the space between the three. This is a safe and protected space. Release yourself from your physical being and step into the grid. Your physical being sits comfortably waiting your return.

When you return from visiting with your ancestors on the Other Side, release the grid in a counter-clockwise manner. Make sure you express gratitude to Hekate and to your ancestor(s). Record any messages received, and make sure you consume a sweet snack like orange juice to bring you all the way back into the Middle World of everyday life.

Rose

The most sacred of flowers for Hekatean witches, rose is a necessary member of the apothecary. Her beautiful flowers represent the fire of creation and destruction of our Mother. The hips and the fruit (seed pods) of some wild varieties are her beautiful dark womb, and the thorns banish the profane. Keep all three on hand.

When Hekate came to Persephone during her lament over joining Hades in the Under World, she walked through roses who were saddened by the situation. Persephone is thus strongly evoked by roses, and they soothe our troubled souls, especially when heartbroken. A gift of roses today often symbolizes love, which is very different from the ancients' association of them with death and loss. In Hekate's Garden, rose has a special place near the entrance of Hekate's Cave, a quiet grove where we can seek shelter from our sadness.

The Fiery Rose

In some translations of The Chaldean Oracles, Hekate is referred to as the Fiery Rose. The rose, especially the wild roses that were abundant during the time and place where the Oracles and other ancient texts depicting Hekate were written, is a vibrant symbol of Hekate in the material world and her dominion over nature. The common variety during ancient Roman times was also associated with dogs, giving another connection to Hekate. Roman Hekateans used the rose as symbolic of blood, as in the Rosalia festival, and for funerary rites.

Wild roses, those ramblers and climbers, are symbols of the space between worlds and times. Traditionally known as witch's briar, they are places where we can transcend corporeality to communicate with Hekate and her witches, as well as with other spirits. These ancient roses were used in a variety of magickal ways, including rites honoring the dead, as an ingredient in spells, and in temples for rituals and for adorning statues.

Today, there are so many varieties of roses, and their assorted colors have special properties—for example, red for love and commitment, white for purity, yellow for friendship.

The rose is a primary plant teacher whose diversity reflects that of ourselves and our Mother. Rose is both loss and love, blessing and bane—and the space in between.

Properties and Correspondences

- ⚜ *Latin name*: Rosa
- ⚜ *Genus*: Rosa
- ⚜ *Classification*: Flower
- ⚜ *Spiritual properties*: Ancestors, attachments, beginnings, calmness, psychic abilities, rebirth, sacredness within.

- *Physiological properties*: Astringent, soothes a troubled heart, tonic and ointment for inflammation.

- *Magickal properties*: Diverse uses, from using the buds to activate new ventures, to scattering petals to attract a lover. For banishing, use dead flowers and thorns. For manifestation, use fresh or dried petals. Roses are excellent for emotional healing, for protection, and to rebuild trust in ourselves and others. As aids to psychic witchcraft, use rose petals from wild or hedge roses.

- *Part used*: Buds, flowers, petals, hips, thorns

- *Planetary correspondences*: Venus

- *Elemental correspondences*: Water

- *Archetype*: Anima Mundi (Soul of the World)

- *World*: Under

- *Zodiac*: Taurus

- *Color*: Many

- *Stone*: Sugilite

- *Animal*: Butterfly

Indications

Rose petals and weak rose water are safe to consume by adults in small amounts. Rose water is safe for the skin. Rose hips are generally safe to consume.

Formulations

- Brew rose petals into an infusion, oil, tincture, or incense. Lovely when added to blends used for sacred rituals, especially with mugwort and thyme.

- Rose petals are widely available for purchase, as is rose hip tea. Rose essential oil can also be used.

- Roses are amenable to most types of spiritual witchcraft. Add the energy of the moon phase to attune this botanical.

- Rosebuds are symbolic of beginnings and new life. Excellent for including in spells for new projects.

Pharmakeia

Use rose petals, hips, and thorns for different forms of witchery. The petals are most associated with heart-warming properties like kindness and passion. The hips are evocative of the emotional depths and are thus well suited to emotional healing. Thorns are excellent for banishing. The flowers on their stems are symbolic of Hekate as Anima Mundi, Soul of the World. Roses make a most excellent offering and are useful for attuning to the primal force.

To keep a secret, write it on a piece of paper using black ink and then place it in a black bag. Add rose petals. Knot the bag and then bury it or hide it well.

Rose Water

Rose water is a basic ingredient of the apothecary. While you can purchase prepared versions, making your own is highly rewarding. Wild roses are especially Hekatean, so use those if you can. If using cultivated roses, try to avoid those treated with harsh pesticides.

Supplies

- ⚜ Stainless-steel pot with lid
- ⚜ Stainless-steel colander
- ⚜ Large heat-resistant glass bowl
- ⚜ Wooden spoon

Ingredients

Petals from 6 roses

Spring water

Directions

- ⚜ Remove the petals gently, and wash if necessary.
- ⚜ Place the petals in the pot, then cover with water so the water is about two inches higher than the petals.
- ⚜ Bring to a boil slowly over medium-high heat, stirring frequently.
- ⚜ Remove from heat, cover, and let rest until cooled.
- ⚜ Strain using the colander into large glass bowl.
- ⚜ Store in sealed jars in a dark, cool place.

After the rose water has cooled, you can add 1 tbsp of vodka or neutral spirit per two cups of water as a preservative. Blend gently. Save the petals, which will still be full of nutrients and magickal properties. Spread on parchment and dry in a 250-degree oven for thirty minutes, or until dried.

Rosemary

Rosemary is a kitchen herb with potent magickal properties. It was used by Hekate's ancient witches to ward off evil, improve memory, and for invigoration. The traditional lore is that, where rosemary grows, the woman of the home will be in charge and well. It is thus not surprising that some husbands ripped the plant from the ground to prevent this from happening. Nowadays, we women can rule the home as witches with rosemary as one of our familiar spirits.

Rosemary is strongly associated with the sea, given its natural habitat along the shores of the Mediterranean, making this a suitable offering to Hekate Einalia, in her role as a goddess of the sea. Rosemary brings clarity to emotions, tempering the saltiness and depths of the deep blue. It is a warming plant that restores our inner fire without causing an inferno. It is suitable for loving remembrance of the departed, but note that rosemary is not a botanical used alone for summoning the departed or spirits. Add sage and mugwort to a bundle for these workings.

Properties and Correspondences

- ♀ *Latin name*: *Salvia Rosmarinus*, formerly *Rosmarinus officinalis*
- ♀ *Genus*: *Salvia*
- ♀ *Classification*: Herb
- ♀ *Spiritual properties*: Cleansing of the spirit, contentment, invigoration, recollection, restoration.
- ♀ *Physiological properties*: Rub sore muscles and joints with rosemary oil, rub on temples to ease headache, drink a tonic to improve sleep and ease nightmares. Since it is so beneficial, it makes an excellent ingredient in a daily infusion. Balances menstrual cycle and eases symptoms.
- ♀ *Magickal properties*: Awareness, banishing, cleansing, comfort, confidence, contentment, focus, loving spirits, memories, renewal, youth.

- ♄ *Part used*: Leaves
- ♄ *Planetary correspondences*: Sun
- ♄ *Elemental correspondences*: Fire
- ♄ *Archetype*: Ergatis (Energizer)
- ♄ *World*: Middle
- ♄ *Zodiac*: Virgo
- ♄ *Color*: Pink
- ♄ *Stone*: Pink quartz
- ♄ *Animal*: Toad

Indications

Generally safe for all. Large quantities may cause stomach upset.

Formulations

- ♄ Rosemary is an essential in a witch's apothecary, for it stands alone as the supreme bringer of loving purification and protection. It's like Hekate's arms, enveloping you in fierce love.
- ♄ Oils, tinctures, infusions, and waters can all be made with rosemary.
- ♄ Rosemary poultices placed on a sad heart will help it mend.
- ♄ It is easy to grow and widely available to purchase fresh, so always keep rosemary on hand.

Pharmakeia

To ensure an untroubled home, free of stress and conducive to health for the occupants, grow rosemary by your main entrance. It's one of my ultimate witch tips. Rosemary grows well without our involvement. Make sure the plant is big enough to be comfortable. Since this proud member of Hekate's Garden is so hearty, my rosemary is a bellweather for our home. If the plant shows signs of distress, I investigate to see who isn't doing well or if there is a problem with the house or land. A bath infused with rosemary lets you soak in protection and contentment.

Home Security System Spell

Walk your rosemary around your home and property and introduce this spirit to each family member, having them touch the botanical. While enchanting the rosemary, focus on a blessed home. Finish the spell by petitioning Hekate Enodia, guardian of the home, to boost rosemary's power. As you are doing the spell, sing a story of exactly what your happy home entails.

Rosemary Nectar

This is a simple syrup infused with rosemary that is excellent when poured over sponge cake as an offering and treat. My favorite way to use this is as an ingredient in mixed drinks. Make a family-friendly beverage by mixing it with lemonade.

INGREDIENTS

   1 cup white sugar

   1 cup water

   3 sprigs rosemary (about ¼ cup chopped)

DIRECTIONS

   ⚜ Bring ingredients to a boil.

   ⚜ Stir until the sugar dissolves, about one minute, then simmer for another minute.

   ⚜ Pour into a glass bowl and let the potion steep for about ten minutes.

   ⚜ Strain off the rosemary while pouring it into a wide-mouthed glass container.

   ⚜ Allow to cool to room temperature.

   ⚜ Store in an airtight glass container in the refrigerator for up to a month.

Fierce Love Potion

This cocktail is certain to get that loving feeling going. It combines the rosemary nectar described above with one of my favorites—Aperol. Drink up when you want to feel that glow of contentment, especially to release stress and unwind. This is great for getting together with your witch squad to celebrate life.

- ✤ 1 part rosemary nectar
- ✤ 1 part Aperol
- ✤ 2 parts sparkling water
- ✤ 2 parts sparkling white wine or prosecco
- ✤ Mix with ice. Add a rosemary garnish

Saffron

Use of saffron in pharmakeia dates back several thousand years, as a remedial tonic, as a ritual spice, and for evoking deities. Saffron is a most sacred botanical that has always been cultivated, since there is no known wild version of the plant, although its close cousin, *Crocus cartwrightianus*, grows naturally in areas around the Mediterranean. Saffron is harvested from the stigmas and styles of the flower. It is an exquisite and exotic spice that has long been known as one of the most expensive. Today, saffron is harvested in areas stretching from Spain to Kashmir.

Power Color

To the ancients, saffron was a color of privilege and power. Robes made by dyeing cloth in saffron were reserved for the most revered. Deities, heroes, and leaders were often described as being "saffron-robed" and illustrated wearing saffron-dyed clothes known as krokotos *to the ancient Greeks and as* crocota vestis *to the Romans. In various ancient sources, Hekate was depicted as wearing saffron. Saffron is the sacred color of Hekate, it's golden-red hue indicative of a rare visitation of her presence.*

Today, clinical research has demonstrated that saffron is an effective treatment for mild to moderate depression. Soothing, restorative and sacred, it evokes the energy of stillness through which we can perceive our wholeness and that of all things. It is generally safe to consume and amenable to all manner of workings, and is an excellent exotic addition to the apothecary.

Properties and Correspondences

- ⚜ *Latin name:* Crocus sativus
- ⚜ *Genus:* Crocus
- ⚜ *Classification:* Spice
- ⚜ *Spiritual properties:* Soothing the mind, connecting to the sacred, embodiment, entrance into the mysteries.
- ⚜ *Physiological properties:* Depression, distress, premenstrual symptoms, sexual desire and performance, relieves breathing problems, cough suppressant.
- ⚜ *Magickal properties:* Abundance, calm, clairvoyance, connection to the divine, desire, dreams, healing, money, passion, sacredness, stimulation, strength, wealth.
- ⚜ *Part used:* Stigma
- ⚜ *Planetary correspondences:* Sun, Moon
- ⚜ *Elemental correspondences:* Fire
- ⚜ *Archetype:* Chrysopis (Golden One)
- ⚜ *World:* Upper
- ⚜ *Zodiac:* Leo
- ⚜ *Color:* Gold, yellow, red, orange
- ⚜ *Stone:* Tiger's eye
- ⚜ *Animal:* Bear

Indications

Generally safe to consume in amounts up to 1.5 grams per day. High doses in pregnancy should be avoided.

Formulations

- ⚜ Coaxing the desired properties from the threads when cooking is an easy, and potentially sneaky, way to add a bit of witchery to all sorts of dishes. Saffron-infused rice is an excellent boost to passion and makes a suitable offering.

- Saffron tea, infused with a pinch of threads per cup of boiled water, provides an excellent base for adding other botanicals, or you can drink it on its own with a bit of honey.

- Make a concentrated infusion with a few of pinches per ¼ cup boiled water to replace part of the liquids in baked goods. I make biscuits (scones) at least once a week, and I replace the cup of milk with ²/₃ milk and ¹/₃ concentrated infusion. Adjust the amount based on your taste and desired coloration.

- To make dye, add 1 pinch at a time to a cup of boiling water in a stainless-steel pot until the desired color is reached. Add unbleached cotton, cheesecloth, baking-grade parchment paper, string, or yarn. Remove from the heat and gently stir, then remove with tongs. Dry on a surface that you don't mind getting stained.

- A couple of pinches in ¹/₃ cup 80-proof alcohol makes an excellent tincture for use in witchery and as a basis for magical cocktails.

- Make saffron oil by adding a couple of pinches to ¹/₃ cup high-quality olive oil.

- Saffron merges readily with other botanicals. My experience is that it is not a high-and-mighty character. Instead, saffron is open to accepting the properties of other botanicals. I usually add saffron at the beginning of a formulation because of this. Saffron is like a very benevolent queen who welcomes all who don't wish her harm.

- Saffron can work as an incense on its own, but I prefer to add botanicals like mugwort and yarrow to get a better burn.

- To use in a diffuser, add the threads to a carrier oil or a suitable botanical oil like jasmine for sacred work or patchouli for passion.

Pharmakeia

Saffron rice, cakes, and tea are appropriate gifts to offer many deities, including Hekate and her companions.

Trance Dance

Saffron does have some mild psychoactive effects when used in large doses, especially when combined with complementary botanicals like mugwort and dittany of Crete. A dense decoction, or reduction of an infusion, will acti-vate the divine within and strengthen connection to the external sacred. This medicine will have you moving and grooving, if you know what I mean. It may also increase libido, so make sure you give saffron specific instructions if you don't want to go *there*. Sacred sex, while amazing, may not be the goal. Personally, I have amazing results using a tincture made of saffron, dittany of Crete, mugwort, and yarrow, which I use as a version of diktamo, especially for sexual healing. See the dittany of Crete monograph above.

Saffron Magickal Paper

One of my favorite uses of saffron is as a base for writing incantations and creat-ing sigils. Regular paper can be infused using the method described above, but I prefer using unbleached parchment. Note that acrylic paint markers work best.

Sage

Sage is an excellent magickal herb for newcomers to the craft, but it is also a stalwart companion for experienced practitioners. A proud member of Hekate's Garden, sage is one of the core botanicals of Hekatean witchcraft.

Sage is easy to get acquainted with, but has hidden depths. It works magick without a huge amount of summoning from us, which partly explains its pop-ularity. But don't dismiss sage for its accessibility. Let it know that you are serious, and it will respond in kind.

Properties and Correspondences

- ⚜ *Latin name*: *Salvia officinalis* (common), *Salvia apiana* (ceremonial)
- ⚜ *Genus*: *Salvia*
- ⚜ *Classification*: Herb
- ⚜ *Spiritual properties*: Passion, protection, cleansing, "opening the way," clarity, fertility, love, well-being.
- ⚜ *Physiological properties*: Stops bleeding, soothes the stomach and joint pain.
- ⚜ *Magickal properties*: Cleansing, protection, openness.
- ⚜ *Part used*: Leaves
- ⚜ *Planetary correspondences*: Jupiter, Venus

- ⚜ *Elemental correspondences*: Air, Earth
- ⚜ *Archetype*: Lampadios (Guardian)
- ⚜ *World*: Lower
- ⚜ *Zodiac*: Aquarius, Pisces, Sagittarius, Taurus
- ⚜ *Color*: Black
- ⚜ *Stone*: Jet
- ⚜ *Animal*: Dog

Indications

It is generally safe to consume both common sage and ceremonial sage in small amounts.

Formulations

- ⚜ Sage can be used in infusions, tinctures, teas, etc. It is commonly burned on its own in "wands," although a better approach is to unbundle the wand and burn only what is needed. The power of the beautiful cleansing smoke of sage cannot be overstated.
- ⚜ Sage can be used fresh or dried to make tinctures, waters, philters, etc.
- ⚜ Common sage and ceremonial sage have comparable properties, although the latter tends to be a more powerful spirit.
- ⚜ There are many varieties of sage, from Greek to Russian. Experiment with the subtle differences in the energetic signatures of the different types.

Pharmakeia

Growing sage as a protective spirit for the home is wonderful. Choose a variety that will thrive in your climate and geography.

To fumigate with sage, break wands down into individual pieces rather than burning the entire bundle at once. Cleanse your body with the smoke, starting with your feet and traveling up to the crown, moving the sage in counter-clockwise circles to release any stress and miasma attached to you. To protect, go from the head down in clockwise motions, drawing the smoke into a shield around you. Use sage in the khernips ritual (see page 16).

Sage Guardian Amulet

Wear a sprig of sage along with a piece of black obsidian in a small glass vial on a black cord around your neck for continued protection and insight.

Seaweed

Living where I do, seaweed is so much a part of everyday life that it can easily be overlooked—like not taking time to notice the grass. This botanical can be used to honor and evoke Hekate in her role as Goddess of the Seas, and I personally connect to Hekate as Einalia every day. She is here along the shore, in the salty winds, and in all the plants along the coast, and she is the water itself. At the edge of her Garden, meet Hekate Einalia, wander with Circe on her island shore, and visit with Medea as she speaks to us of the past. The ocean represents our emotional depths. Seaweed, in particular, is excellent to connect to Hekate as primal source, since it is as ancient as our planet.

Macroalgae is a broad class of oceanic plants, including rockweed, bladder wrack, Irish moss, and kelp, that have somewhat similar uses for the pharmaka. Products made of various seaweeds, like dulse and nori, are also widely available. Seaweed is renowned for its nutritional value and is used as an ingredient in all sorts of cosmetic, food, and health products. The nourishing nature of seaweed makes it excellent for all spells of abundance and health.

Properties and Correspondences

⚜ *Latin name*: Various, including *Ascophyllum* (rockweed), *Fucus vesiculosus* (bladderwrack), *Palmaria palmata* (dulse), and *Pyropia* (used for nori)

⚜ *Genus*: Multiple

⚜ *Classification*: Macroalgae

⚜ *Spiritual properties*: Abundance, nourishment, healing, connecting to the ocean.

⚜ *Physiological properties*: Source of micro- and macronutrients, detoxifying, healing.

⚜ *Magickal properties*: Abundance, blessings, endurance, stability.

⚜ *Part used*: All

⚜ *Planetary correspondences*: Venus, Moon

- *Elemental correspondences*: Water
- *Archetype*: Einalia (Queen of the Deeps)
- *World*: Under
- *Zodiac*: Pisces
- *Color*: Varies by species—green, red, and yellow
- *Stone*: Pearl
- *Animal*: Dolphin

Indications

Commercial preparations are safe to consume.

Formulations

- Different varieties of seaweed, like dulse and nori, can be purchased ready to consume. There are also seaweed teas like Irish Moss, which is used to treat chest congestion, among other ailments.
- Dulse is a particularly nutrient-rich seaweed from my part of the world that is deeply evocative of primal Hekate.
- Wildharvest seaweed for use in spells, but avoid consuming it unless you are certain it is safe. Some is contaminated by pollutants.
- Air-dry wildharvested seaweed or use it fresh in all potions of abundance and healing.
- Use dried seaweed in fires to connect with Hekate Einalia.
- Fertilize your witches' garden with seaweed, nourishing the soil with all its amazing nutrients.

Pharmakeia

The uses of seaweed for abundance workings are many. Create a simple nest of seaweed on which to place anything you wish to manifest, from coins to pictures of loved ones in need of nourishment. One traditional spell is to place the seaweed in a jar of whisky, adding a few coins. Shake daily to bring money your way.

Add edible seaweed to any meal where you want the participants to feel well-nourished, from serving sushi to sprinkling flakes of dulse on salads.

Rockweed Wreath

Bless your home with the nourishing power of seaweed by creating a simple rockweed wreath to place over your home shrine. Add photos of your beloved under the wreath, allowing the spirit of seaweed and Hekate Einalia to cleanse and bless all.

SUPPLIES

- ⚜ Rockweed (harvest rockweed that is longer to make a larger wreath)
- ⚜ Strong cord to bind the rockweed
- ⚜ Any charms you want to add to the wreath

DIRECTIONS

- ⚜ Once the seaweed has dried, pick up one cluster.
- ⚜ While binding the wreath, contemplate all the blessings you have and those which the wreath will bring to your home.
- ⚜ Beginning at one end, pinch the rockweed tight by wrapping the cord around the cluster and then tying it tightly. Wrap the cord, adding additional clusters as you go, forming the circle. Continue to wrap until you have a complete circle.
- ⚜ Add other botanicals like lavender, juniper, and rosemary once the initial circle is complete.

This wreath can be used as a healing grid, adding other botanicals and stones as you feel led. Place a picture of the person receiving the healing in the wreath. Envision them receiving all the nourishment that seaweed has to offer.

Skullcap

The name "skullcap" can be used for two very different botanicals: American skullcap (*Scutellaria lateriflora*) and Chinese skullcap (*Scutellaria baicalensis*). Here, I describe American skullcap. Note that the two are not interchangeable. The skullcap that is native to North America is a traditional plant master for many indigenous peoples. It has long been one of my greatest teachers. In my twenty years of knowing this mighty spirit, I've grown attached to its complex nature.

Skullcap is a binder, first and foremost. It is dual-spirited in the way it binds, bringing clarity to the mind while also drowning what no longer serves. Skullcap is androgynous, in the sense that it is very high in stereotypical masculine and feminine traits. It brings calm, but through an almost aggressive nature. This isn't a botanical of tender embraces, but of steely strength. Skullcap is fantastic when combined with lavender for instant calm, because it works quickly.

Energetically speaking, skullcap entraps whatever is being evoked under its hood. Whatever your intention, and within his range of powers, skullcap will wrap it up tightly, either squeezing it until there is no life left or enclosing it in a nourishing protective manner. Skullcap sounds complex, but is quite easygoing, so I recommend it for intermediate practitioners. It is happy to share, but not everyone will understand its dualistic nature.

Binding is the fundamental skill of witchcraft, from holding the ingredients in our preparations and spells together to attaching to another. Skullcap is unparalleled in its ability to bind and is thus excellent for all commitment rituals, including weddings.

Properties and Correspondences

- ⚥ *Latin name: Scutellaria lateriflora*
- ⚥ *Genus: Scutellaria*
- ⚥ *Classification:* Plant
- ⚥ *Spiritual properties:* Calming and opening the mind, connecting to the Mother, expanding consciousness, drawing forth soul truth, rebirth.
- ⚥ *Physiological properties:* Antioxidant, anxiety reduction, anticonvulsant, protection against neurological complaints, may reduce menstrual cycle troubles.
- ⚥ *Magickal properties:* Binding (all), clarity, commitment, emotional healing, evoking Hekate, fidelity, rebirth.
- ⚥ *Part used:* Leaves
- ⚥ *Planetary correspondences:* Jupiter
- ⚥ *Elemental correspondences:* Water
- ⚥ *Archetype:* Arkyia (Entrapper)
- ⚥ *World:* Under

- ♁ *Zodiac*: Aquarius
- ♁ *Color*: Blue
- ♁ *Stone*: Blue sapphire
- ♁ *Animal*: Spider

Indications

Not recommended for children, pets, or those pregnant. It is safest to consume for short periods of time, and very high doses can cause convulsions.

Skullcap may be contaminated with germander (*Teucrium*), a group of plants known to cause liver problems. This has led to the mistaken belief that skullcap causes liver problems. Ensure that you are purchasing pure American skullcap.

Formulations

- ♁ Skullcap can be purchased in various forms. Make sure you are purchasing pure skullcap. Buying cut and dried leaves is recommended. The capsules can be opened for use in infusions, tinctures, etc.

- ♁ Wildharvesting skullcap is still possible in some areas of North America.

- ♁ Cultivated skullcap plants and seeds are typically of the Chinese variety, so if you are looking to grow your own, be mindful of this.

Pharmakeia

Use skullcap as a tonic to prepare yourself for rebirth work and commitment ceremonies, and as a binding agent in just about any spell.

Binding Poppet

Poppets are amazing for magick that seeks to control the behavior of another. This version is easy to make and highly effective. It is a version of a coffin spell, in which the target is bound and then buried or placed in a container. Effectively, they become dead to you once they are bound.

Supplies

- Black sock
- Black, red, and white string (about 2 feet of each)
- Taglock, an image of target, a lock of hair, etc.
- Paper
- Black pen

Ingredients

Salt

Skullcap

Directions

Keep yourself well-protected before, during, and after this ritual to ensure it doesn't boomerang back on you. Do not put yourself into the spell or you'll be attached to the binding. Begin with the khernips ritual to banish any unnecessary or harmful energies. At minimum, a dish of salt should be placed in the space where you do the spell for protection.

This is a spell of emotional witchery, so get calm before casting to avoid boomeranging and misdirection. Protection is important, since you are calling to mind the harm the target has done to you or others. Use the salt to sever your ties to the energies you conjure while casting, then scrub your hands with it after you've finished creating the poppet. Keep the poppet in a box or wrapped in black cloth, or bury it outside. Personalize the incantation below as much as possible to amplify the power of the spell. Each cord should be wrapped around the sock three times and then tied at the top.

- Place the taglock and skullcap in the sock.
- Hold the black cord in both hands, summon the energy of the emotional damage done, and then pour it into the black cord, feeling it release from you. As you bind the black cord around the sock, direct all the emotions contained in the cord right into the taglock, saying:
  By cord of black,
  Pain, suffering, and despair I do send back.

- ✣ Hold the red cord, summoning the power of the hurtful actions of the target, and pour this energy into the cord. As you bind the red cord around the sock, direct the power of their hurtful actions into the taglock, saying:

  By cord of red,
  All acts of harm done are bound to them.

- ✣ Hold the white cord, summoning the power of the hurtful words of the target, and pour this energy into the cord. As you bind the white cord around the sock, direct the power of their hurtful words into the taglock, saying:

  By cord of white,
  I bind them this night.
  As I weave, so I do claim.
  Dead to me now, in deed and name.

- ✣ Bury or place the sock in a secluded area—the back of a closet, the basement, etc.—in a box or wrapped in black cloth. Don't forget to seal the grave with the salt.

- ✣ Scrub up with the salt.

This spell releases a lot of embodied pain, so be gentle with yourself in the days after. Take a healing ritual bath after. Carry a piece of pink quartz with you to help weave yourself anew without carrying the burden of the harm the target caused.

Thyme

Thyme was such an important herb of fumigation for the ancient Greeks that it shares the same name with the process of purification. Thyme has been associated with the bumblebee since Greek warriors used them both to decorate their battle gear. Place an open dish of thyme by the threshold to keep away all unwanted creatures, material and spiritual. Burn thyme as an incense to cleanse the environment. It is especially useful for rituals evoking Hekate Enodia, the Guide. Thyme brings ambition and courage, two attributes most helpful along our witches' journey.

Thyme is gently warming, an opener of the way for rituals, and a most excellent herb for all sacred rites. It is traditionally used in the khernips ritual.

Thyme is a revealer of truth and is excellent for use in kairos witchcraft—time travel. One modern application of thyme is in spiritual and personal development work, as it encourages self-honesty. It is also recommended for journeys of soul retrieval.

Properties and Correspondences

- ☿ *Latin name*: Thymus vulgaris
- ☿ *Genus*: Lamiaceae
- ☿ *Classification*: Herb
- ☿ *Spiritual properties*: Awareness, cleansing, easing distress, sacredness.
- ☿ *Physiological properties*: Antiseptic, diluted oil is good for muscle and joint aches, taken as a tonic for cough (also rubbed on the chest), reduces severity of colds when taken at onset as a tonic.
- ☿ *Magickal properties*: Ambition, cleansing, courage, growth, happy home, nightmares, strength.
- ☿ *Part used*: Leaves, flowers
- ☿ *Planetary correspondences*: Venus
- ☿ *Elemental correspondences*: Air
- ☿ *Archetype*: Agia (Sacred One)
- ☿ *World*: Upper
- ☿ *Zodiac*: Taurus
- ☿ *Color*: White, mauve
- ☿ *Stone*: Amethyst
- ☿ *Animal*: Cat

Indications

Generally safe to consume and for use on skin. Large amounts may cause dizziness and upset stomach. Cats are often fond of thyme, and it is very safe for them. Avoid excessive amounts of the pure oil on the skin, as it can be irritating, since it is a rubefacient (causes redness).

Formulations

‡ Thyme can be added to recipes to help clear the air. When you're adding it, sing a little song to Thumon, telling him to cleanse all those who consume him.

‡ Thyme can be used dried or fresh. It is relatively easy to grow as a kitchen herb, and is highly recommended for your moon garden.

‡ Infusions, poultices, syrups, and so much more can be made to unleash the spirit of thyme.

Pharmakeia

Fumigating with thyme, either through burning or asperging, clears the environment of miasma quickly and without fuss. It is recommended for moderate levels of gunk—like when your home is messy, but not a disaster. If things are very chaotic, add basil and lavender to make a powerful trio sure to banish all the nastiness. Use in a bundle or in the khernips ritual. The same goes for using a banisher on its own. Thyme is a sustained push more than a swift kick in the pants (like basil).

Thyme is excellent in household cleansers. Add a few drops of the essential oil to 1 part white vinegar and 4 parts spring water. Keep in a glass spray bottle, ready to banish dust and unwelcome spirits. For those afflicted with nightmares, cleanse the room with this spray, including the bedding and especially under the bed.

Of course, thyme is most amenable to opening sacred rites evoking Hekate and her witches. Given that it is a plant of Fire, Medea is particularly fond of it. Offer her, Hekate, and other Fire deities a simple cheese dish that you can eat as well.

Goat Cheese Crescents

These are very easy to prepare, travel well, and taste delish.

INGREDIENTS

1½ cup chevre (soft goat cheese)

½ cup honey

2 tsp dried thyme

Pomegranate seeds

⚜ Crumble the goat cheese in a bowl using a fork, then stir in the honey and thyme until well blended. Shape into two crescent moons, one for an offering and the other for you to eat during the ritual. Serve with crackers or pita bread.

This is also excellent as an appetizer for when your coven gets together. It is certain to cleanse the mind, creating space for magick and mirth.

Vervain

Persephone's flower, vervain, indicated the arrival of spring to the ancients, heralding her return. Vervain symbolizes the steely strength of the beautiful queen reborn. Used by the ancients in sacred rites, vervain represents rejuvenation. It is one of the most important pharmakoi in our apothecary.

Also known as verbena, vervain is one of the most versatile plants in Hekate's Garden. It is very responsive to a witch's touch and has over two hundred different varieties. Common vervain and the blue variety are very similar, and it is to them that this monograph refers.

Hekate Enodia

Hail, Enodia,
She is the Road,
And Guide along my
Earthbound journey.
Shining her torch,
And dangling her keys.
My heart stretches out to hers.
She replies, as always,
"Follow me."

THE
KNOWLEDGE

Blue vervain is widely spread across North America as a native species, but so is common vervain, because it has been naturalized in many places. Apparently, this applies to the end of my driveway, where a small, but determined, cluster grows—yet another sign that my property was destined to have a witch in residence. Most likely, the British settlers of my village planted some, which then spread across the area. But I've yet to find any growing in the wild.

Sometimes known as ironweed, vervain epitomizes strength that appears delicate. The blossoms are incredibly hardy. They are excellent in bouquets and wreaths, and for adorning your hair. Vervain speaks of the onset of summer, bringing the brightness of steely strength.

The fact that vervain was traditionally used in Germany in the forging of steel is further proof of the strength of this botanical. Strength can be movement, but with vervain, the power is in stopping the flow of damage and creating the space for vitality. As such, vervain is excellent for stanching bleeding and healing by ceasing the disease process. It is also useful for ending bad luck or any harmful shade being thrown in your direction, thus improving your life and ensuring a happy home.

For self-work, vervain is great for vanquishing doubt and improving the way you talk to yourself. It also stops egoic shadow problems from interfering in relationships.

Properties and Correspondences

- ⚜ *Latin name:* Verbena officinalis is native to Europe, *verbena hastata* to North America
- ⚜ *Genus:* Verbena
- ⚜ *Classification:* Herb
- ⚜ *Spiritual properties:* Communication, creativity, freedom, healing, the mind, inspiration, learning, optimism, power.
- ⚜ *Physiological properties:* General tonic, antiseptic, bronchial cough, asthma, detoxificant, diuretic, liver cleansing, menstrual problems, stops bleeding.
- ⚜ *Magickal properties:* Divination, dream work, hex-breaking, defensive magick, prophecy, protection, purification, protection against witchcraft.
- ⚜ *Part used:* Plant, leaves, slender stems, branches
- ⚜ *Planetary correspondences:* Mercury, Venus
- ⚜ *Elemental correspondences:* Air, Earth

- ⚜ *Archetype*: Alkimos (Strong One)
- ⚜ *World*: Upper
- ⚜ *Zodiac*: Capricorn, Gemini, Sagittarius
- ⚜ *Color*: Mauve
- ⚜ *Stone*: Blue agate
- ⚜ *Animal*: Goat

Indications

Generally safe for adults, but not for use during pregnancy or when trying to conceive.

Formulations

Vervain is a most agreeable pharmakoi that works well in all types of formulations. It does have a bite to it, so if the goal is to summon its more docile aspects, blend with a calming herb like lavender and add honey. Persephone was much more than a beautiful maiden; she had her own darkness. So goes vervain, making it a wonderful companion and teacher.

Pharmakeia

Blue vervain is a frequent participant in my daily tonic, serving to balance feminine energies while fueling my writing. A vervain bath on the Summer Solstice is an excellent way to celebrate your own sovereignty and that of our Goddesses.

Add to bundles or burn on her own to both banish the profane and welcome in Hekate and her closest friend, Persephone, especially in their brighter forms. It is an herb of summer, flourishing from June to September. Thus it is useful for evoking the energy of brighter days when we're feeling gloomy. Excellent for work around the Summer Solstice.

Circe's Philter

A philter is a blend of different types of herbal preparations. In this philter, a tincture is blended with an infusion and boosted with essential oil, then formulated into a wonderful spray for restoring our sacred witch powers.

This is a blend to remove the cobwebs from your witch powers through the magick of Hekate's oldest daughter, Circe. Use as a body spray before rituals to unleash your inner pharmaka and to cleanse your sacred space and tools. All ingredients can be fresh or dried, with the exception of the clove, which is the oil in this philter.

INGREDIENTS

Vervain

Yarrow

Saffron

Mugwort

Dittany

Wild rose

Clove

DIRECTIONS FOR THE INFUSION

* Mix 1 tbsp vervain, 1 tsp yarrow, and a few saffron threads in 1 cup boiled water.
* Pour the water over the herbs.
* Strain out the herbs when the mixture is completely cooled.

Use this infusion as a general tonic, especially for erasing self-doubt and speaking your truth. Excellent as a bathing wash.

DIRECTIONS FOR THE TINCTURE

* Place ½ cup mugwort, 1 tbsp dried (or a handful of fresh leaves and flowers) dittany of Crete (if not available, substitute damiana), 1 tbsp (or petals of 1 fresh blossom) wild rose (substitute red rose if necessary) in a 1-pint (500 ml) glass jar.
* Pour 1 cup alcohol or glycerol over the herbs and give it a good shake.
* Add the cooled infusion.

Finish with 7 drops of the oil. Keep in a cool, dry place and shake daily for two weeks. This is an excellent philter to make on the Full Moon, initiating use on the Dark Moon. Once ready, drain off the herbs and store in dark-colored spray bottles. Makes a great witchy gift for those wanting to connect to their inner Goddess. Good for headaches as well, especially stress-induced headaches or those brought about by female hormonal changes.

Circe's Restorative Ritual

This ritual maximizes the power of Circe's Philter. Circe herself may show up to give advice and bless your working. It is excellent for use anytime you feel depleted or disconnected, and great to get the spirits moving prior to a heavier rite or spellcasting.

To use for activation, spray your three spirit centers starting at the root (above your pubic bone and at the base of your spine), then your heart center, then your crown (center of forehead upward to the top of the head).

Walnut

Walnut is a proud, wise master of Hekate's Garden. The properties of walnut both attract clarity of mind and expel unwanted attention. Physiologically, walnut banishes harmful entities in the body, from parasites to bad cholesterol. Not surprisingly, modern research has found that eating walnuts may prevent dementia and support long-lasting mental acuity and clarity.

Historically, the use of walnut in offerings and celebrations involving Hekate can be traced back to Galatia in what is now Turkey. It is the bright shooting star moving across the night sky and bringing piercing clarity of mind. Walnut opens the staircase to the heights of our Higher Selves, the unborn essence that is known as the soul. Up we dance with walnut, past the moon to Hekate's Hall, where the mystical knowledge of the ages is stored.

Walnut lends leaves, seeds, and wood to all our witchery involving the Higher Self, from banishing negative self-talk to facilitating communication with the Mother. In sacred rites, you can summon the energy of our ancestors by offering Hekate walnuts while you munch on them. Traditional meals consumed by her Mystai, her sacred priestesses, often included pomegranates, nuts, and cheese. This meal was also offered to Hekate and other temple spirits. Often, a sort of cheesecake made of honey, eggs, and soft cheese was included. While this ancient feast is great fun to recreate, creating our own traditions makes rituals much more meaningful. Include walnut oil and the nuts in your feasts—and maybe even the Dark Goddess Cheesecake described below.

Walnut, with his balanced approach to attracting blessing and banishing bane through wisdom, is truly nourishing. Ultimately, the message of walnut is to know your own value.

Properties and Correspondences

- ⚜ *Latin name: Juglans nigra* (black walnut); *Juglans regia* (common walnut)
- ⚜ *Genus: Juglans*
- ⚜ *Classification:* Tree
- ⚜ *Spiritual properties:* Awareness, acuity, cleansing the mind, clarity, focus, correcting overabundant emotions and too much Under World energy.
- ⚜ *Physiological properties:* Cardiac problems, cholesterol, shells for wound healing, stops diarrhea, regular consumption is helpful for weight management and inflammation.
- ⚜ *Magickal properties:* Activating intentions for intellectual endeavors, opening the Third Eye, connecting to Upper World spirits, inspiration, wisdom.
- ⚜ *Part used:* Nuts, wood, leaves
- ⚜ *Planetary correspondences:* Jupiter
- ⚜ *Elemental correspondences:* Air, Fire
- ⚜ *Archetype:* Noeros (Learned One)
- ⚜ *World:* Upper
- ⚜ *Zodiac:* Gemini, Leo
- ⚜ *Color:* Gold
- ⚜ *Stone:* Moldovite
- ⚜ *Animal:* Eagle

Indications

Can cause allergic reactions. Otherwise, it is very safe and healthy in small amounts.

Formulations

- ⚜ Walnut oil is an excellent base oil for activation of the mind, and for banishing what blocks your mental acuity. If your psychic powers seem murky, cleanse your Third Eye by anointing it with walnut oil.

- Craft a walnut ink for writing incantations for the Higher Self and for evoking Hekate as the Bringer of Light. This epithet is associated with psychic abilities, prophecy, intellectual pursuits, and wisdom.

- Eating walnuts is good for the mind and body. Add a few prior to a ritual to attune to the Starry Road. Consume after Under World emotional workings to balance your energies.

- Shells can be ground for including in Upper World incense.

- Add walnut to fires for excellent scrying, since it opens the way while banishing the profane.

Pharmakeia

One of my personal favorite magickal uses of walnut is for divination as part of my collection of objects I use for "throwing the bones." In the set, the shell represents the Higher Self, mysticism, and wisdom. It's associated with Hekate's intellectual side, known as *Noetikeia*. If the shell lands face up, the indication is to stay in the mind; if it lands face down, it's time to get more emotional. Walnut is excellent for all forms of divination. Create your own set of prophetic lots with Hekatean epithets on them on walnut tiles. You can use walnut in a pendulum as well.

A walnut wand is helpful for attaching to the energy of the Starry Road and chasing away unworthy spirits. Other uses for walnut shells include using them as magickal containers that bring clarity to whatever token is placed inside.

Walnut is an expeller due to the Juglans chemical poisoning most plants that grow too close to it. Use this property to banish unwanted attention. Walnuts are a symbol of plenty, whether regarding the power of the mind or in our bank accounts. They are costly to purchase and rich to consume. They are excellent on their own as an offering to Hekate that you can repurpose afterward. Better yet, incorporate them into your own feast, as in the Dark Goddess Cheesecake.

Food of the Gods

One of the active ingredients in chocolate is theobromine, which translates to "food of the gods," making it a most suitable offering to Hekate. Chocolate is made from the seeds of the cacao tree. Generally, milk, oil, sugar, and other ingredients are added to make the natural bitterness more palatable. Dark chocolate has fewer additives and a higher percentage of cacao. In the regions where cacao grows, the seeds are used in spiritual-healing ceremonies.

Dark Goddess Cheesecake

This is the highlight of Hekate's Feast—a decadent dessert that evokes the presence of the Dark Goddess through chocolate, maple, pomegranate, and walnut. Chocolate is known as the "food of the gods," while maple is associated with abundance, connection, and limitless love, and is a great relationship booster. Thus it is perfect for expressing your affection to Hekate, while enhancing your connection to her.

Walnut attracts the power of the Starry Road and Hekate as the star-walking Light Bringer. This is her most primal aspect. Before Earth was breathed into life, she was the light that ignited the universe.

This is a special cake that is well-suited for Hekate's Feast on one of her sacred nights in August, November, or May. Start making it just after sundown to have it ready for feasting at the following sundown.

Supplies

- ⚜ 12-inch springform pan
- ⚜ Standing mixer
- ⚜ Pastry bag with a narrow tip or a ziplock freezer bag
- ⚜ Parchment paper
- ⚜ Printed strophalos (Hekate's Wheel)
- ⚜ Tape

INGREDIENTS

- 1½ cups graham-cracker crumbs
- 1 cup finely chopped walnut pieces and another cup for garnish
- ⅓ cup melted butter
- 3 8-ounce packages (250 grams) cream cheese, at room temperature
- 1 cup maple syrup
- ¼ cup packed brown sugar
- 2 tbsp all-purpose flour
- 3 eggs
- 1 cup dark chocolate for the filling, about 4 ounces
- 1½ cups semisweet chocolate for the topping, about 6 ounces
- ½ cup coffee cream
- ⅔ cup white chocolate for garnish, about 3 ounces
- 1½ cups pomegranate seeds

DIRECTIONS FOR CRUST

- ⚜ Heat the oven to 350 degrees.
- ⚜ In a small bowl, melt the butter in the microwave, then stir in walnuts and graham-cracker crumbs until well combined.
- ⚜ Press into the bottom and halfway up the sides of the springform pan. Place the parchment paper over the crust as you press it out to minimize sticking. It really makes a difference. The tighter the crust, the less crumbly the cake. That's truly magical.
- ⚜ Bake at 350 degrees for eight to ten minutes, until set.

DIRECTIONS FOR FILLING

- ⚜ Beat the cream cheese in a large bowl at medium speed until smooth and creamy.
- ⚜ Gradually blend in the maple syrup until well incorporated, then stir in the brown sugar.
- ⚜ Mix in the flour gradually.

THE
KNOWLEDGE

- Reduce the mixer to low speed and beat in the eggs one at a time, just until combined.
- Melt 4 ounces of chocolate. Take some of the batter and mix into the chocolate, then pour this combined mixture into the rest of the batter to prevent fractionating the chocolate. Blend until smooth.

Directions for Baking

- Once the crust is ready, reduce the temperature to 325 degrees.
- Pour the filling into the crust.
- Bake for forty-five to fifty-five minutes, or until set. After forty-five minutes, insert a toothpick. If it comes out clean, the cake is done. You want this cake just to set in the oven.
- Cool on a wire rack to room temperature.
- Refrigerate a minimum of six hours.

Directions for Topping

- Print a strophalos (Hekate's Wheel) on plain white paper. Using clear tape, place a piece of parchment over this, sealing all the edges. Place this template on a firm surface that can be refrigerated, like a plate or cutting board. Tape the template to the surface.
- Melt white chocolate and pour into a pastry bag or ziplock freezer bag. If using a freezer bag, cut a ¼-inch diagonal hole in one of the bottom corners.
- Pipe the white chocolate along the white part of the strophalos.
- Chill in fridge for at least three hours.

Finishing the Cake

- Once the cake and the strophalos are well chilled, create the background of the strophalos using the semisweet chocolate.
- Into the barely melted chocolate, stir the cream a little at a time, until you have a slightly runny consistency.
- Remove the cake from the springform pan.

- ⚜ Pour the chocolate mixture over the top, smoothing it over the sides.
- ⚜ Let this cool for about thirty minutes.
- ⚜ Carefully lift the white chocolate part of the strophalos from the parchment and position on top of the cake.
- ⚜ Garnish with pomegranate seeds and crushed walnuts.

Take many pictures of your masterpiece and share them with me so I can delight in your creation. This is truly a cake worthy of Hekate and her witches.

Yarrow

Yarrow is a potent all-heal in the apothecary. Notably, its botanical name comes from the tale of how Achilles was taught by Chiron to use it to stanch bleeding in his wounded soldiers. Milfoil, another name for yarrow, refers to the thousands of tiny leaves characteristic of the plant. The name "yarrow" is believed to be based on "Hieros," reflecting the sacredness of this plant. The all-heal mentioned in *The Argonautica*'s description of Hekate's Garden may well have been yarrow, since this is an ancient folk name for the herb. Yarrow has been used for medicinal and spiritual work for tens of thousands of years in many cultures, from China to the First Nations peoples of North America.

Yarrow is a proud master plant spirit that is as gentle as it is strong. It is a willing companion of Hekatean witches. There are many varieties of the plant that grow wild in many places all over the planet. It's also easy to grow. Delicate mauve yarrow has even taken up residency in the drainage ditch at the end of my driveway. I love to wear these early bloomers in my hair on the Summer Solstice to temper the heat of the celebration, because yarrow offers a cooling healing.

This benevolent spirit can accompany all sorts of healing of body, mind, and spirit. It eases corporeal and spiritual bleeding and is an excellent companion for exploring the divine within and connecting to the sacred. Yarrow is a plant of Venus that is deeply connected to emotional healing, and a sure-footed ally in all manner of sincere devotion. Use it for love spells to summon true, long-lasting affection and love.

In the divination system of the I Ching, bundles of yarrow are used to facilitate interpretation. Burn an incense or drink a tea to help with your tarot and rune readings.

Yarrow has many other names—not surprising, given that it is a powerful healer. They include allheal, angel flower, bad man's plaything, bloodwort, cammock, carpenter's weed, devil's nettle, devil's plaything, dog daisy, gordoloba, green arrow, herbal militaris, hierba de las cortadura, knight's milfoil, milfoil, nosebleed, old man's (the devil's) mustard, old man's pepper, plumajillo, sanguinary, soldier's woundwort, squirrel's tail, stanchgrass, stanchweed, thousand-leaf, thousand weed, and woundwort.

Properties and Correspondences

- *Latin name: Achillea millefolium*
- *Genus: Achillea*
- *Classification:* Herb
- *Spiritual properties:* Divination, emotional healing, gentle guide to the sacred within and without, calmness, meditation.
- *Physiological properties:* General healing, especially emotional, eases inflammation, relieves stress, stops bleeding, and hastens wound healing.
- *Magickal properties:* Blessings, cleansing (emotional, Under World), connecting to spirits and deities, divination, sacred offerings, relationships, releasing, ceasing discord.
- *Part used:* Flowers, sometimes leaves and stems. Look for products containing only the tops.
- *Planetary correspondences:* Venus
- *Elemental correspondences:* Air, Water
- *Archetype:* Paionios (Healer)
- *World:* Under
- *Zodiac:* Gemini
- *Color:* White, yellow, pink
- *Stone:* Jade
- *Animal:* Elephant

Indications

Yarrow has been proven safe to consume in amounts up to 4.5 grams per day. Avoid during pregnancy.

Formulations

⚜ Yarrow can be used in infusions, decoctions, oils, and tinctures. The formulary depends greatly on the purpose. I drink yarrow as the base of my daily tonic, using about 1 tbsp to 2 cups boiled water. I then add botanicals appropriate to my daily needs and let it steep in the teapot for fifteen minutes.

⚜ As incense, yarrow has a slightly sweet scent on its own and blends very well with other botanicals. Burn on a charcoal disk.

⚜ A yarrow poultice on wounds will help them heal without infection and scarring. Applied on the heart center, the poultice will mend spiritual distress.

Pharmakeia

Yarrow can be used in all manner of ways to heal and to connect to the world of spirit.

Yarrow Medicine Bath

This ritual bath is one of my tried-and-true methods for a deep awakening of authenticity and emotional healing. Combine about 1 tbsp yarrow with 1 tsp mugwort and a pinch of ginger for invigoration (leave out for a calm dose of medicine) in 2 cups of boiling water. Let it steep until it reaches room temperature. Add a piece of pink quartz to the mixture and let it rest for another ten minutes or so. Then pour into your bath.

IX. MAGIKEIA

The Spell

I am the spell.
Weaving my soul fire into every thread.
My emotions,
Thoughts,
Actions
Are the strands.
Adding to these,
I stitch in the spirits,
The plants, stones, and animals,
Colors, symbols, and more.
Weaving the magick,
Within and without.
Calling upon my Goddess to guide my hands.
Yes,
I am the spell.

Magikeia is the art, craft, and science of casting spells. All spells consist of one (or more) of three functions: banishing, protecting, and blessing. The khernips ritual is an example of a banishing spell that removes all harm from your environment. It is an excellent method for creating the sacred space necessary for spellcraft and ritual. When you perform protection spells without first banishing the harmful, you run the risk of encapsulating the negative that is already around you. Banish, then protect. Always. The blessing comes in the form of the plant spirits we choose for our spells. We bless ourselves through abundance, creativity, healing, and rebirth.

Sympathetic magick is the process through which an object becomes infused with the qualities of another source. It is binding, the very heart of the practice of witchcraft. Binding itself can be considered a symbol of Hekatean witchcraft, since it is the fundamental action of all our magickal workings. The doctrine of correspondences refers to the inherent natural properties in botanicals and other components used in spells.

Botanicals, on the other hand, are direct magick, because they have inherent properties, as well as physiological components, that work directly to bring about change. When you drink an infusion of lavender and dittany to amplify your personal sovereignty or wash yourself with a glamour potion of fennel and rose, there is no magickal middleman, no need for a talisman to symbolize you in the spell. You literally *are* the spell. If a spell uses sacred smoke that releases the pharmakoi to do your bidding, its impact on the target is direct.

Several years ago, I started doing an annual witch-bottle spell that combines all three functions of spellwork as a master casting to ensure safety and success for the coming year. In a jar, I add botanicals for each of the months. The fixative is chosen based on the overall energy I wish to create—typically an alcohol that is associated with happy memories or a beloved ancestor. I then add animal and stone spirits, and finally color. I weave all this using the sacred number 13, reflecting the number of lunar months in a calendar year.

Next, I breathe the spell into life through intentions and instructions known as an incantation. The pharmaka's voice releases the spell into existence. With each touch, we craft our potions and talismans into being. All pharmakeia is spellcrafting, whether stirring healing energies into a decoction of garlic, fennel, and honey to soothe a beloved's cough, or creating a witch jar for increasing your bank account. Spellcraft is about summoning spirits and giving them instructions to do a specific task. Often, we create a potion or talisman to ensure that these spirits keep on working toward our goal after the initial casting.

The Keys to Spellcraft

Will, wisdom, and work are the three keys of masterful witchcraft. Will is our passion, seen in our enthusiasm, determination, motivation, and persistence. Wisdom is knowledge, intuition, inspiration, and guidance all combined. Work is our actions, the commitment to living our truth. All that we do in our pharmakeia is a combination of these three keys. What we live is what we breathe into our spells.

The intentional summoning of energies and then directing them to achieve a goal is the most basic definition of spellcraft. A spell is our intention and energy combined with external forces. A spell uses words of power, through declarations and incantations. We may petition Hekate and her daughters, as well as our other deities and guides, for their assistance. Spells create entities that work independently of us according to our directions, in the form of our potions and talismans. That is the heart of witchcraft: summoning and then commanding spirits, whether they be botanicals, colors, or lower-order spirits like elementals and some daimons. These are then crafted into a new spirit in the form of a potion, talisman, sigil, or poppet. This is very different from a ritual, in which we may feel the impacts long after the ritual ends, but no spirit is created to do our work.

An intention is the focus of a spell. It's a sort of mission statement that focuses in strategically on the goal. When commanding botanicals, as with all spellcraft, it is necessary to speak as if the task is already accomplished. All spirits respect confidence. It keeps the harmful ones away and draws your allies closer. Beginning all workings in this way sets the tone for success.

Depending on the spirits summoned, you may petition their favor or you may command their services. Generally, I petition higher-order spirits and deities. For summoning Hekate herself, I always petition. For commanding her seven sacred forces, I instruct and direct, but don't ask. The energies of the worlds and elements as master currents are omnipresent and available for our use without seeking approval. That doesn't mean I don't express gratitude for their support, however. Gratitude is an essential part of any effective spell. Higher-order spirits and deities are best petitioned rather than being told what to do.

Blessing and Bane

Pharmakeia, like all true witchcraft, is about both blessing and bane. As reflections of the universe, we are both dark and light. Our practice resides in the shadows, the space between bright and night. We reside at the crossroads between the spiritual splendor of Hekate's Garden and the material world. Here in this place, we listen to the teachings of the plant masters and our Goddesses, who tell us that witchcraft knows no right or wrong, no black or white. It simply *is*.

THE
SPELL

There are times when our spells are those of attraction, bringing us healing, financial benefits, new jobs, and entrance to the mysteries. At others, our workings are necessarily baneful—banishing illness, binding a toxic person unto themselves, and protecting ourselves from harmful spirits. The pharmaka speaks her truth through her spells and accepts full responsibility for all that she does.

I don't often do baneful workings on another person. My focus is on my own path, success, and health. However, if I need to deceive to protect myself or my beloveds, I don't hesitate. Witchcraft is about persuasion—of the spirits to do our bidding, of the gods for their favor, and of the correspondences for getting the job done. That is what spellcrafting is.

I have a Black Jar of Secrets in which I keep what I don't want revealed. I have poppets who are taglocked to others that I dig out on rare occasions when my magickal powers of persuasion don't yield the results I need. I weave sigils into documents so the outcome goes my way without telling the others involved. I've banished my enemies without asking their permission. Trust in yourself to determine the best course of action for your spellwork.

The Role of Binding

The basic technique for binding ingredients into a spell is done through the instructions we give the spirits we are working with. Some botanicals are easier to direct than others. There are specialist pharmakoi who are excellent at binding other spell ingredients together, like birch and skullcap. As you develop your spells, consider how you will achieve the coagulation—the binding together—of the various components. How will the botanicals be synergistically merged?

We often seek to bind others in our spells, in the same way we use our directions to control the ingredients in them. Binding is about combining and control. There are many applications for binding spells, from attaching a spirit ally to us to entrapping a horrible person's energy onto themselves. For instance, this binding torch spell can be adapted for any purpose, from binding money to you, to resolving legal issues, to controlling the actions of another. It combines three different techniques—torch, taglock, and cord—giving it added strength.

The Power of Three

A torch spell is one wherein a talisman is burned to release its power. A binding spell traps the energy onto a target using a symbolic representation of the person or object to create a tether, known as a taglock. A cord spell is activated by braiding and/or knotting a cord while reciting an incantation. Each of these techniques on its own can be highly effective. Together, they are unstoppable.

The spell requires three cords—black, white, and red—each about ten inches long—and an image of the binding target. The black cord is for emotions, the red for actions, and the white for thoughts. The three cords can be soaked in a birch or skullcap potion in advance and these can be burned as incense. Add a protective botanical like oak to the incense, but not to the potion, to eliminate the risk of spell blowback. Add other botanicals suited for your needs.

Directions

⚜ Keep yourself well protected before, during, and after this ritual to ensure it doesn't boomerang back on you. Do not put yourself into the spell or you'll be attached to the binding.

⚜ Begin with the khernips ritual if you need to. At minimum, a dish of salt should be placed in the space where you do the spell for protection. This is a spell of emotional witchery, so get calm before casting to avoid boomeranging and misdirection. Protection is important, since you are calling to mind the harm the target has done to you or others.

⚜ Create a binding cord by braiding the cords together while reciting this incantation:
By cord of black,
_____ *I do send back.*
By cord of red,
All acts of _____ *are bound to them/me/etc.*
By cord of white,
I bind this _____, *as is my right.*

- Tie the cord around the taglock, the image used. This makes a scroll into which you can place the botanicals. You may need to wrap them in parchment paper first, twisting both ends and then sliding it in. This is your torch.

- Once the torch is assembled, burn it to release the spell onto the target. As the torch burns, summon the energy of the element of Fire to activate the spell and then summon the element of Air to carry the spell to the target. Burn both ends of the torch, then bury or otherwise dispose of it. I have a cave where I stash spells like this one.

- Once the braid is complete, wrap it around the taglock three times, while envisioning the person being wrapped in the cord, with all their harmful thoughts, deeds, and feelings bound to them. You can add a piece of birch bark around the rolled image before wrapping the cord around the taglock. Tie three knots in the cord once it's around the picture.

- Light both ends of the torch. Recite the incantation above until the flames extinguish themselves. Direct the smoke to the target, wrapping the smoke around them until they are completely bound.

- Finish by petitioning your chosen spirits and deities to amplify the spell.

- Sprinkle the salt around the talisman to contain it, then rub it in your own hands to separate fully from the working. Don't ever untie the cord.

The Witch's Voice

By going through the process of thinking about what we hope to achieve, we can narrow our focus to exactly what we want. The more precise an intention, the more effective the spell. You shift from intending to manifest, to claiming that it is already manifested.

Thus, a great intention brings into alignment our magic, actions, feelings, and thoughts as they relate to the goal of our spell. Taking the time to write a great intention makes all the difference. Keep it short and precise. Use strong verbs that will truly activate your chosen botanicals.

Speaking to the forces we are petitioning adds embodied energy, as do ecstatic practices like hand signals and dance. Hekate's ancient witches practiced in this way. They danced, tranced, recited incantations, and sang spirit into their pharmakoi. Follow the dance steps of Circe and Medea, moving and singing your spells into life.

Singing and dancing our spells adds the vibrational power of the Middle Self to any working, both through the actual energy of the tone and words, and through further sharpening our focus. You don't need to be a skilled singer—recall that Circe had a human voice that was unbearable to the gods. She sang anyway and found her plants and animals were pleased to hear her. Rhyming and other structural features of what you say or sing also add power to the spell.

Anatomy of a Spell

The best way to understand the structure of a well-cast spell is by working through an example. You are welcome to cast this witch-bottle spell exactly as I have written it, using correspondences and spirits suited to you and your goal, or be inspired by it to create your own unique working.

My intention for this spell was:

Keeping Her Keys will be protected from all harm, with steady healthy growth that leads to success that supports my community and creates financial security.

There's a lot that went into developing that intention. Protection includes many concepts, from banishing haters to ensuring that my health stays good. Growth that's steady and sustainable is my goal, not a wild roller-coaster ride of ups and downs. Success, to me, includes providing content that benefits my community as well as my own personal prosperity. If there's one thing I've learned, it is that taking my time in developing my intention is vital for effective spells. Avoid rushing into one. Desperate witchcraft rarely goes well.

The magickal creation that will contain the energy of a spell is known as *magikeia*. This can be a potion, a talisman, a sigil, a poppet, or even an altar. One of my favorite forms of magikeia is to create an altar with a candle, a card, and a botanical. This incorporates the sacred Triformis energy of the Triple Goddesses, representing wholeness and creation. The three-part spell can consist of correspondences that are additive or complementary. Additive correpondences are botanicals (and other spirits) that have similar properties evoked

into the spell so that they amplify the overall power because of their homogeneity. Complementary correspondences are those that have disparate abilities that we combine into a whole spell.

I chose a witch bottle with a talisman for this spell, because both are excellent for long-lasting spells. Layering, blending, and merging of the correspondences ensure that the spell will work for an entire year.

Depending on the spirits summoned, you may petition their favor, or you may command their services. Generally, I petition higher-order spirits and deities. For summoning Hekate herself, I always petition. My experience with Circe is that she is easily summoned whenever there is witchcraft happening. Medea tends to demand more from us with our petitions. For commanding her Septem Novum, the seven sacred forces, I instruct and direct, but don't ask. The energies of the worlds and elements as master currents are omnipresent and available for our use without seeking approval. That doesn't mean that I don't express gratitude for their support, however. Gratitude is an essential part of any effective spell.

Correspondences and Spirits

Although this book focuses exclusively on plant spirit witchcraft, pharmakeia involves evoking, blending, and merging spirits of all the kingdoms of the natural world. Incorporating botanicals, animals, and stones in spells is the foundational layer of all Hekatean withcraft. In this spell, I use an owl charm and botanicals, braiding them into the spell using a potion and a charm that I tie onto the bottle.

I take a simple approach by blending my chosen botanicals in the direction suited for their purpose, while focusing my attention on their properties being evoked. Banishing herbs are blended counter-clockwise, for example. In this spell, I focus purely on attracting protection, growth, and success, so I blend clockwise while drawing the New Moon into them. It's a lot of mind work, but, with practice, it gets much easier. In this spell, there are nine major parts, with a botanical to represent each one. I always weave the number of ingredients into the spell as well. Nine is associated with accomplishment, inspiration, protection, and moon magic, so it makes perfect sense to have this number of ingredients for a spell of protection, growth, and success.

In this spell, I call upon Owl to be my ally as the spell works. I make a talisman out of the owl charm, black, red, and white cord, and objects to represent the nine key parts of the spell.

Next, I select Hekatean currents and archetypes for the spell. (Refer to the individual botanical monographs for the corresponding archetypes.) Petition Hekate and her daughters using those of their archetypes that are relevant to your spell. Generally, a Hekatean spell has three layers of spirits, with one always being a botanical.

Use your intention to guide your selection. Narrow down the characteristics of each correspondent and spirit. Contemplate how each goes together, but also how each works independently. Weave a web—drawing it often helps. Honestly, I use an Excel spreadsheet for my major spells. Keep in mind that all spirits, from plant to Goddess, have their own free will and personality. Sometimes you may not be able to work with them. The process can take time, but it's well worth it.

Be sure to make your spell personal. I never cast a spell without including material representations of people and places involved with the outcome, especially the people and objects involved. Blood, hair, nail clippings, skin, and even urine can be used. As you add these bits, envision your energy as it will be when the spell is successful, pouring into it and mingling with the other spirits engaged. Inserting sigils, words, and other representations of your focus on paper works extremely well. As the liquid breaks them down, they become part of the energetic currents emanating from the witch bottle. Add your personal sigils and symbols, too. Pictures and written names can be used as well, but they usually aren't as effective.

Incantation

Once you've chosen your spirits and correspondences, it's time to write an incantation activating all their energies. The incantation directs the spirits summoned into the spell.

Incantations can include words, actions, and feelings. The more energy given to the direction being given, the more likely the spirit will be to do as instructed. Once the spirits have been chosen (or have appeared on their own), craft the incantation so that each one is specifically called upon. In addition, add sections where you describe your overall mission. I share the incantation for my protection, growth, and success spell below as an example.

I always write an incantation that rhymes, drawing on the energy of the rhythm in addition to the power of the spoken words. My rhymes will never win a poetry slam, but they get the job done. When writing your own

incantations, use a structure that feels right for you. If you can't say the incantation with authority and confidence, your spirits will get concerned about your sincerity.

Incantative actions include the methods used with correspondences and spirits, such as blending botanicals in a specific manner. Summoning the emotions associated with achieving your goal is also helpful. If I am petitioning Hekate, I usually begin with this process, then move on to lower deities, then spirits, then the pharmakoi, etc.

Casting

Depending on the environment in which you are casting the spell, cleansing may be in order, and you may need to cast a circle if there is discord, disarray, or distress where you'll be doing the work. I use a black candle in this spell.

Next, I recite the incantation while blending the botanicals and creating the owl-ally charm. I also add a few drops of my blood. The charm bonds me to owl so that she becomes a fetch of sorts, carrying out the work of the spell for me and helping me along my way toward achieving my goals. Once all the components are ready, I craft the bottle, again saying the incantation. Holding the vision of what will be achieved through the spell while creating the bottle is key.

Creating the Witch Bottle

Always use a clean clear bottle or jar with a tight lid for a spell of attraction like this one. Sometimes the lid traps the spell, as with a banishing, but for this spell, it's about keeping the ingredients free of contaminants. Sealing the jar with wax and/or fabric is also helpful. Don't worry about the spell not being able to escape the bottle. The spirits within know how to travel through space and time.

The liquid in a witch bottle can be water, alcohol, or even urine. Moon water, captured during an appropriate moon phase, is easy to work with. Several types of alcohol also have different spirits (pun intended), so use your intuition and consult standard interpretations to make the wisest choice. You may have a personal type of alcohol that truly speaks to your soul. I certainly do, so I often use bourbon, as I do in this spell. Alcohol is good for longer-duration spells. Vinegar is great as well, especially for banishing and cleansing witch bottles.

Note that, for a long spell like this, you may get some mold buildup. Don't throw out a spell when this happens. In an attraction spell like this one, that's a good sign—unless it stinks. For repulsion spells, like banishings or removal of barriers, smelling bad means the spell is working.

While I use a witch bottle in this spell, the same process can be followed for other types of spells, including sigils, paquets, and poppets.

My incantation runs like this:

I cast this spell when the moon is new,
Great Selene, now I summon you.
Pour your fresh light into my claim,
I call you down in Hekate's name.
Into these plants, your energy flows,
With each drop, my spell so grows.
Hail to you, Pharmakoi Kyrios,
Know your time has come at last.
Join with my spell, your rest has passed.
Heed my words, I command you.
Make this spell strong and true.
Sage, first to you I call,
Lend your strength and purify all.
Juniper, grant me knowledge of those of ill intent,
Boundaries enforced; enemies are far sent.
Foxglove, your powers I now rend,
Healing and harmony into my blend,
My pretty, poisonous witches' friend.
Benzoin, resin from far away,
Add your focus and calm starting this day.
Birch, creativity and growth from you I take,
Add your wisdom to this spell I make.
Mugwort, most potent plant,
Powerful growth you now grant.
Bay leaves I add for blessings and more,
Send truth and kindness to you I implore.
Rose, fairest flower, I ask you to share
Support and blessings, all you can spare,

Not only to myself, but to all those who enter here.
Oak, grant security and success from now on,
Mighty tree of magick I now call on.
Great plants, I stir and bind,
Mixing your spirits, the moon's and mine.
My spirit companions and eager friends,
I praise you for all that you lend.
Fairest moon, send this spell aflight,
Releasing it through your eternal light.
This spell has been cast,
The work is done,
What is bound cannot be undone!

Types of Spells

In general, spells are either blessings—drawing things to us—or banishings—sending things away from us. The focus of the spell is the overarching energy. Most spells can be adapted to be a blessing or a banishing. Cleansing and purification, as with the khernips ritual, is a banishing spell for removing all miasma. Banishing that which harms should always be done before engaging in any type of blessing. We always want to rid ourselves of the baneful while welcoming the beautiful, however we define these things.

Here are some of the more common types of spells:

⚶ *Abundance:* Prosperity is a very personal concept; what represents plenty to me may feel like poverty to you. An olive-oil base, with additional botanicals correspondent to your needs, makes a super attractor of abundance. Place an open bowl in the heart of your home.

⚶ *Attraction:* Spells of attraction can include anything we want to draw to us, from a romantic partner to a new job. Bay laurel can be used for just about any attraction spell. Write your focus on a leaf, and wear it on a cord around your neck or carry it in your pocket. Bay laurel close to the heart works exceptionally well.

⚶ *Binding:* Birch and skullcap are excellent binders. Adding them to any spell of restriction—because that is what binding is—will ensure success.

- *Growth:* Whether you want to grow a business or a personal attribute like sovereignty, growth spells are designed to nourish whatever it is. Thyme, along with botanicals specific to your goal, is fantastic for growth. Anoint a candle with thyme and olive oil and light daily while focusing on your goal.

- *Hastening:* Patience may be a virtue, but there are times when we need to speed things up. Fennel seeds placed in a circle on an image of whatever it is that needs to happen fast work well.

- *Healing:* Healing is complex. We may need to banish or bless, or both, depending on the problem. Some botanicals, like garlic and yarrow, work for all manner of healing.

- *Manifestation:* Creating something out of nothing is pure magick. Manifesting spells can include a variety of purposes, from finding lost things to feeling grateful when things are in chaos. Rose and agrimony are good all-purpose manifesters.

- *Mediumship:* Communicating with the Other Side, specifically speaking with the spirits of the departed, can be augmented through spells that enhance our skills in this aspect of deathwalking. Dittany and lavender are especially useful (see the Crossing the Veil Tea in the mint monograph).

- *Protection:* Banishing is about removing the harmful, while protection is about continually keeping it at bay. General protection botanicals include sage and most strong poisons, like American mandrake and foxglove. Fumigation of the environment and the body that encircles and binds the properties of the protective pharmakoi using their sacred smoke while describing the protection being enacted works very well.

- *Psychic abilities:* Many botanicals work to strengthen our Third Eye. If yours is feeling blocked, create a mugwort poultice talisman by soaking fabric in a strong decoction, then placing it on the middle of the forehead for about twenty minutes while lying on your back with your knees raised.

- *Removal:* These spells involve all types of banishing of the unwanted. Mint can be used for just about any removal working. Place an image of what needs to be banished at the bottom of a small black box, then cover it with mint while envisioning the target being removed from your life. Seal the box and then dispose of it.

THE
SPELL

224

- *Reversal:* This technique is used whenever we need to change the course of events, modify our feelings, or undo our actions. Fill a small black bowl with botanicals suited to your purpose. Using the index finger of your left hand, draw a reverse (counter-clockwise) spiral while stating your intention. If possible, burn the botanicals; if not, discard them.

- *Transmutation:* There are times when we have an abundance of something that we need to transform into something else. If someone is being hateful toward you, for example, turn their vitriol into affection by giving them a gift comprised of loving botanicals like aster or rose. Of course, you'll have enchanted this gift with instructions on exactly how this person's emotions and actions will be transmuted. Works like a charm.

Botanical Candle Magick

The process of infusing botanical spirits into candles (*pharmakeia lucerna*) is one of the most versatile forms of spellcraft. You can use scented candles, as long as they contain actual botanical essences, to evoke the spirits and direct them into your spell. More effective is to add the botanicals you chose for the spell to the candle. The simplest technique is to place the botanicals around the base of the candle, drawing out their properties and then merging them with the candle through your intentional directions.

Candles in the elemental colors are excellent choices, for you can summon the corresponding elemental spirit in addition to Fire. Choose a candle that matches the method. If you are doing a one-off spell, use candles that have a short burn time, like a tea light or a small taper. You can also cut larger tapers.

Dressing Candles

Begin by cleansing the candle from miasma, if necessary, by rubbing it with salt or soil. Then attune the candle for pharmakeia by using a fixative like olive oil, concentrating on adding the powers of the fixative to the candle as you rub. Use a clockwise circular motion for attraction workings, a counter-clockwise motion for removals, and alternate between the two for spells that are a combination.

Cover the candle in your chosen botanicals, ensuring that the blend is ground small. Larger pieces can flare up when the candle is burning, especially if it is a narrow taper. Spread the blend on a piece of parchment and mix in a bit of the fixative, just barely coating the botanicals. Roll the candle back and forth across the blend, concentrating on activating the powers of the plant spirits and directing them into the candle. Then wrap the candle tightly in the parchment and roll some more. With pillar candles, you can apply more force, so that the botanicals really merge into the candle. Once you are happy with the appearance, wrap the candle again until it's time to use it. You can add a protective black cloth as well.

Infusing Candles

To infuse the botanicals into a candle, gently warm the candle in the oven. This is tricky with slender tapers, but works well with candles that are at least two inches in diameter. Heat the oven to 300 degrees and follow the dressing protocol. Once you are happy with the appearance, wrap the candle very tightly in the parchment and then with foil. Be sure to seal each end by twisting it tightly.

Heating times will vary, so set a timer for five minutes and then check every minute or so, turning the candle frequently if you have it lying down. When the candle is slightly soft to the touch, be sure to rotate it. You can set up a bed of foil as a nest to hold the candle in place. When the candle is slightly soft all over, remove it from oven and roll it some more. Unwrap it from the foil and roll it a few more times, then open the parchment and make any final adjustments so you are pleased with the appearance. Add sigils, charms, stones, etc. as you like. Stand the candle to cool completely. Once cooled, you can wrap it in fresh parchment and/or black cloth to store until you are ready to use it.

Simple No-Fail Candles

These candles are great on their own, but adding a botanical blend suited for your purpose is fantastic. To create black candles, add about ½ tsp activated food-grade charcoal to the melted wax. A few drops of rose water or pomegranate concentrate can be added for pink/red candles. Experiment with other natural dyes for other colors, like blueberry (purple), saffron (yellow), and chlorophyll (green).

SUPPLIES

- Small covered metal tins, silicone mold, or heat-proof glass jars (1 inch or more deep)
- Tea lights (about a dozen) and/or beeswax pellets

DIRECTIONS

- Prepare your blend using essential oils and dried botanicals that are ground to small pieces.
- Preheat the oven to 250 degrees and line a baking sheet with parchment.
- Create your sacred workspace by lighting a protection candle, cleansing the space, etc. Working on a black cloth is always a good idea.
- Remove the tea lights from their foil containers and cut them into pieces, saving the wicks.
- Arrange the cut tea lights and/or beeswax (I use about $^2/_3$ beeswax, $^1/_3$ tea light) in the heat-proof container. If you use soy chips instead of tea lights, a blend of 1 part beeswax to 1 part soy works well.
- Place in the oven. (There are many other ways to melt wax, but this is the easiest.)
- Once the wax has melted, remove it from oven and stir in your botanicals using a wooden skewer.
- Add a wick in the center. You can also use multiple wicks.
- Let cool for a few minutes. I usually use this time to put the finishing touches on the herbal that will go into the candles. As soon as the wax starts to form a skim on the top, place a bit of the dried blend on it.
- Let cool completely and cover.
- These are great for spells, sacred rites, and daily devotional work. Can also be used in place of incense.

If you can't burn candles, make melting disks using the tins or a silicone mold (there are so many amazing shapes available) following the same procedure above, but omitting the wicks. Melt the disks by heating, such as in a specially designed vessel or even on a heating pad. The released vapor works in the same way as the smoke.

To make dipped candles, or for using non-heat-resistant containers, use the bain-marie technique outlined on page 64 to melt the wax, then add the botanicals. Either dip the length of wick desired into the wax repeatedly, until you have your appropriate thickness, or pour the wax into glass containers like mason jars.

Casting a Candle Spell

Candle spells, like all others, begin with a great intention. Then summon Fire and direct it into your spell, releasing the energy on the wave of the fiery element, adding in the power of Air through smoke. The correspondences you choose will ride along this current—the color of the candle, the botanical properties, and the sigils and symbols you add. These spirits are combined and directed through an incantation.

Once you have your candle and intention or incantation ready, cleanse the space if necessary using the khernips ritual, then relax into the purified environment. If necessary, burn a protective botanical to keep harmful energies at bay. Now light the candle. As you watch the flame, concentrate on your intention, incantation, or petition. If you are evoking deities like the Triple Goddesses, or other energetics like the moon or elements, call upon them now.

- ⚜ Start with deities, then spirits, then astrological forces (e.g., the moon, Mercury), then earthbound spirits. Always summon the element of Fire, connecting it to the burning candle. Say: *Candle, candle, burning bright, grant this spell I speak tonight.*

- ⚜ Explain to each of your chosen pharmakoi the task you have for them. Sit quietly, contemplating the goal of your spell. Project strong images in your mind about what you are manifesting into the candle. Think about exactly how the intention will be manifested in your life.

- ⚜ Focus on the images, feelings, and actions associated with manifesting your spell while staring at the flame. As you stare into the flame, place your hands gently on either side of the candle so that your palms are flat or cupped around it. Begin to transfer your ener-

gies through your body, into your hands, and then into the candle itself. This transfer of energy will ensure that the candle is attuned to you.

⚜ If this is a one-off spell, continue this process until the candle is burned down. As part of a longer spell, about five minutes a day is usually enough.

⚜ Once your spell is cast, begin to study the flame, smoke, and wax. Relax into the flame, inhaling the scents of the botanicals, allowing messages to come forward. Be calm, but aware.

⚜ Study the direction of the smoke and its composition. The smoke should be directional, indicating that it is going into the currents used in the spell. If it is just floating around, work to direct it.

⚜ The direction, size, and consistency of the flame also provide messages from spirits and reveal the strength of the spell.

* If the candle goes out on its own, relight it while placing your intention energy back into it.

* If the candle burns quickly, the energy you placed into the candle is being released faster and the spell will work quickly.

* If the candle burns slowly, the energy is being released slowly and evenly and will come back around to you gently and over time.

Whether to discard or keep the remains of a spent candle depends on the nature of the spell. Candles used in removal magicks should be disposed of immediately. For spells of attraction, like love and prosperity, you can place the remains on the altar until the goal is manifested.

Botanical Poppets

Poppets are best used when you want to have control over a distinct other, whether human or spirit. For this magick, you must maintain a clear focus for the control. Cursing someone to experience all the harm they inflicted on others is one example. If you are creating a healing poppet, include symbols and taglocks of the focus—for instance, smear a drop of the target's blood onto the "heart" of the effigy with a healing incantation to ease someone suffering from cardiac distress. Of course, that same drop of blood can be used to inflict cardiac troubles. Be careful. Magick is magick. Intentions are what tells the magick what to do.

With poppets, you need to list the aspects of the target that you are going to control. These can be additive—pushing the target into new thoughts, feelings, and actions—or subtractive—stopping specific habits. Consider how these controls will complement the existing nature of the person or spirit. For example, when creating a curse poppet, the intention can be that the person no longer engages in harmful behaviors (subtractive) and bears the weight of the harm they've previously caused (additive). A complementary aspect would be to include that the person's anger (already existing) becomes directed inward.

A spirit poppet that is intended to fully contain an entity should clearly include wording in the intention that indicates that, otherwise remnants of it will still wander free. This approach is particularly useful for harmful spirits like shades and malevolent ghosts. For instance, you can use words like:

> *To the spirit who haunts me, I cast you into this poppet, no more are you free to roam. Into the poppet you go, and I control you from now on.*

The poppet is a spirit trap. To harness the energy of a spirit while letting it retain its own free will requires ensouling part of it while leaving it whole. The intention should be worded to reflect this—for instance:

> *I cast into this poppet the spirit of mugwort, binding it to my magick.*

Using a poppet to harness the powers of a spirit or deity so that they are always within your control is another intention suitable for a poppet. For this, use an intention like this:

> *I bind the powers of Medea's poison magick into this poppet, claiming them as my own.*

Designing a Poppet

Poppets can be incredibly simple or very complex in their design. The simplest poppet is basically any media that is activated for your purpose. A bar of glycerin soap can be carved with symbols. A square of fabric, known as a paquet, can be used by wrapping it around a taglock and tying it.

Usually, a poppet takes on the basic physical appearance of the target, such as a human body. A simple technique is to shape a head, fill it with a nut (e.g.,

walnut for mind or spirit work) and then tie it off and bind it to the person or spirit.

Fabric, clay, and wax are easily worked with. Consider the nature of the target. Fabric and clay are great for enduring poppets. Wax is excellent for a temporary one, or for a poppet that will be destroyed. Keeping in mind the nature of the target and your intention, choose correspondences that will augment the power of your spell.

- ⚜ *Fabric:* Black for cursing, protection, banishings, bindings, and most types of witchcraft. White for purity and revelation. Green for abundance. Pink for compassion. Blue for communication. Yellow for illumination. Purple for sovereignty and personal power. The fabric can be the taglock—using an old t-shirt or sock are two examples. The thread and string used should also match the intention.

- ⚜ *Botanicals:* Choose ones that are likely to last for as long as the spell needs to. Fresh ones will shrink as they dehydrate, so dried is best to maintain the integrity of the poppet. Cut, dried roots like black cohosh (divine feminine, easing female issues, binding to a woman) work well. An entire root from mayapple, wild carrot, yellow dock, and others can be used as well. Carve symbols into it and add the taglock. Vegetables like potatoes and carrots can also be used for short-term poppets. Botanicals may include mugwort (protection, all witchcraft), yarrow (healing, prophecy), rose hips (love, protection, detoxification), birch bark (sovereignty, binding), and pine cones (prosperity). Nuts and seeds that suit the intention can be used as well.

- ⚜ *Stones:* These can represent the mind, the heart, and physical organs. Choose ones that work with your intention: blue agate for communication, soothing the mind, controlling another's mind; pink quartz for creating love energy, either to persuade your target in your direction or to create feelings of self-love in them; black obsidian, jet, charcoal, or coal for removal magick of all sorts, from protection to cursing.

- ⚜ *Symbols:* These can be drawn, stitched, or carved into the poppet. They may include astrological signs, numbers, sacred geometry, etc.

- ⚘ *Stuffing:* The botanicals used to stuff cloth poppets can be augmented with extra bits of the fabric used to make it. Cotton wool, rice, and beans can also be used.

- ⚘ *Features:* Make the poppet resemble the target as much as possible. Are they short or tall? Thin or thick? Use a hair taglock for the hair. Draw features that are similar to the target. Use buttons that match the person's eye color.

- ⚘ *Clothing:* Dressing the poppet to resemble the target is another way to ensure its efficacy. Strips of cloth can be used for the binding process. Recite your intention as you wrap the poppet. Choose an appropriate type of fabric and color.

Once the intention and design are set, choose the hour and date that work best for you, considering astrological influences and date significances (e.g., Friday is Venus' day, well-suited for poppets that are love spells). Then assemble your materials and written intention. I like to insert a miniature version of the intention as the heart of the poppet.

As you create the poppet, envision the results of your witchery. How will your target heal or suffer? How will the spirits being bound work for you?

Activating a Poppet

Once completed, activate the poppet with words of power that give life to it. Write an incantation that is firm and directive. Use strong verbs and short sentences. The poppet must be well controlled by you for it to work. Here is an example:

> *Now complete, this poppet now comes to life, bound to that which is my target. Firmly under my control. As I speak it, it is so.*

The poppet can be anointed with appropriate oils or waters, or even baptized.

Poppets are meant to be manipulated by their owners, unless the point is to bind a target completely to itself. At minimum, you should hold the poppet while activating its powers and whenever the target requires attention, or when you wish to harness the power of the poppet. Rubbing the eyes to help another gain clarity, anointing the crown to encourage wisdom or soothe the mind or piercing the heart to inflict pain can also help.

The poppet can be destroyed to sever your connection to the target completely or to bring about its demise, whether regarding a specific action or

otherwise. The poppet can be locked up in a coffin/box to prevent the target from acting. This sort of spirit trap is good for problem entities. Burying this type of poppet works well.

For long-term control of a target, the poppet needs regular use and may require energetic boosts by anointing or spraying with an appropriate botanical. Keep it in a dry place out of sunlight. If the poppet is performing a specific function like protecting magickal objects or watching over a child, keep it nearby.

Botanical Spirit Poppet

This poppet is made by stuffing fabric with your chosen botanical. It creates a servitor spirit that is derived purely from the deva (archetypal soul) of the plant. This is best suited for botanicals that have strong personalities and is most useful for plants that you can't grow in your immediate environment.

Mr. Philip Mandrake

*My personal poppet is Mr. Philip Mandrake, who guards my most treasured
magickal objects. He resides with them, keeping them safe and charged.
I talk to him regularly. Mandrake is a most willful plant that needs
strict management, but is most useful as a spirit to watch over witchery.*

DIRECTIONS

⚜ Choose a pharmakoi that speaks to you and/or represents energy you wish to control at will.

⚜ Decide if this poppet will be a constant companion or for use only on specific occasions. Poppets can be friends and guides that we interact with daily, or restricted to limited use.

⚜ Research the properties and use your intuition in selecting one. Once your intention and design are ready, create the poppet.

⚜ As you stuff the poppet with the plant, animate it into a conscious ensouled spirit, but one lacking free will (unless you want it to act independently). Envision the plant clippings combining into a living entity, merging with the fabric and symbols. Be directive throughout this process, lest the poppet become too willful to manage.

☙ Once finished, command the poppet to perform its function.

☙ Regularly use the poppet to remind it of its function.

☙ Destroy the poppet when the mission is accomplished, if it becomes too weak to reanimate, or if it is too willful. Burning it is best.

X. SIBYLIKA

The Prophecy

Mistress, I call forth your Sibyls.
Grant me their companionship now.
Accept my gratitude for welcoming me into their fold.
To the Sibyl of the Ground, Keeper of the Key of Visions of Earth, I summon
*   you now.*
To the Sibyl of the Breath, Keeper of the Key of Visions of Air, I summon you now.
To the Sibyl of the Flame, Keeper of the Key of Visions of Fire, I summon you now.
To the Sibyl of the Depths, Keeper of the Key of Visions of Water, I summon you now.
To the Sibyl of the Cave, Keeper of the Key of Visions of the Under World, I
*   summon you now.*
To the Sibyl of the Garden, Keeper of the Key of Visions of the Middle World, I
*   summon you now.*
To the Sibyl of the Starry Road, Keeper of the Key of Visions of the Upper World,
*   I summon you now.*
I claim my place among you.
Show me the mysteries, guide me toward deeper understanding, teach me your ways.

Hekate is the Spinner of Fate. She spins her Wheel according to her laws, sharing her wisdom with her witches who seek the powers of the mystical in earnest. Her priestess-prophets from ancient times have been known as the Sibyls. When we embrace our psychic powers, we enter the Wheel, seeking to know the unknown through prophecy, and claim our place among the Sibyllae. Like the Sibyls of old, we experience visions through both direct communication with Hekate and the spirits, and through the sympathetic magick of our chosen tools, like the cards.

Oracular workings, the profound revelations of possible futures, can be overwhelming when experienced. There is a cost to these gifts of Hekate that is often felt as a type of temporary madness, a feeling of being incredibly drained or of being connected to all things. It can even manifest as physical illness. The Sibyls knew this madness well. Seek their counsel to help you deal with symptoms of deepening psychic powers. Heed their warnings about going too deep and too far. Intense oracular work should be reserved for rare occasions.

Bay laurel is amazing as a boost to psychic work, but it can be amplified by anointing the leaves (dried or fresh) with lavender and frankincense essential oil. Dried leaves thus dressed can be burned as incense. Wear an anointed dried leaf as a talisman on a red cord around your neck, activating it with psychic sigils and symbols.

Oil of the Fates

Make this oil by blending 7 drops frankincense, 7 drops lavender, and 3 bay laurel leaves in about ½ cup olive oil. Let the oils merge and activate under the Full Moon as it waxes for a week. Anoint your Third Eye with it prior to any psychic work. You can also use this to create a Sibyllic patch by soaking a piece of cloth in the oil, or use it to anoint all your prophetic tools, from cards to crystals.

Psychic Medicine Bath

Make a ritual bath for inducing prophetic trance by adding 7 bay leaves to the water, along with 7 drops each of lavender and frankincense essential oil. Drink some Crossing the Veil Tea (see page 163) prior to the bath to further augment your trance experience.

Reading the Leaves

Reading botanicals for their prophetic messages is practiced in many forms within Hekatean witchcraft. The residue of preparations remaining at the bottom of a cup can be used to connect with the Triple Goddesses and with the Other Side. The Crossing the Veil tea is excellent for this practice. Drink a cup and then allow your Third Eye to focus on what remains at the bottom.

The ancient Sibyls were known for using bay leaves to divine the future. They cast them as lots, known as the practice of cleromantica, using them as a connector to the wisdom of the Goddess. Then they wrote the received messages on the leaves and left them for the recipient at the entrance to their sacred caves.

Adapt this practice by inscribing leaves with words, sigils, and symbols. Keep the leaves in a black bag and draw from it while concentrating on your query.

You can evoke Hekate's many archetypes, her *nobilis coterie*, by infusing bay leaves with her mysteries:

- *Hekate Astrodia* represents the Upper World, with messages of wisdom, mysticism, contemplation, purpose, and sacred rites. She speaks to the future, revealing her mysteries as the Mistress of Fate.

- *Hekate Enodia* represents the energy of the Middle World of material possessions, career, relationships, and action. She speaks to the present.

- *Hekate Chthonia* represents the Under World and transmissions regarding emotions, healing, witchcraft, intuition, and rebirth. She speaks to the past.

- *Hekate Kleidoukhos*, as Keeper of the Keys, represents the element of Air and speaks to the mind, communication, education, knowledge, and transformation.

- *Hekate Lampadios*, as the Torchbearer, represents the element of Fire and carries messages relating to sovereignty, power, change, growth, creation, destruction, and guidance.

- *Hekate Alkimos*, the Strong One, represents the element of Earth and speaks to acceptance, courage, effort, endurance, and strength.

- *Hekate Einalia*, Queen of the Deeps, represents the element of Water, bringing transmissions regarding assertiveness, betrayal, the shadow self, root causes, and secrets.

Hekate Astrodia

Dear Astrodia,
Star Walking,
Moon Mother.
Mysterious Majesty,
How can I ever behold you
with my humble mind?

Assembling Your Own Spirit Coterie

Assembling a set of botanical spirits that speak prophecy to you is incredibly rewarding. This can be an intuitive process, where the meaning of the botanical is assigned purely as it speaks to you, or it can be based on its standard properties. My set is a mixture of both. Seeds, nuts, tiny branches, bits of roots, and hardy leaves are excellent for including in the coterie. Examples of pharmakoi suitable for a coterie with their dominant energies for divination include:

- *Acorn*: Authority, confidence, independence
- *American mandrake*: Fertility, revelation, secrets
- *Benzoin pellets*: Balance, correction, reparations
- *Birch bark*: Growth, purpose, tranquility
- *Black cohosh*: Femininity, Goddess, love
- *Foxglove seeds*: Cleverness, the past, time travel
- *Juniper berries*: Banishing, clarity, strength
- *Pine cone*: Creativity, harmony, reconciliation
- *Pomegranate seeds*: Afterlife, destruction, forgiveness
- *Poppy seeds*: Dreams, sex, visions
- *Walnut*: Clarity, fertility, spirits, the mind

In ancient Hekatean witchcraft, a collection of objects like these that were used in divination were called *cleromantica* and were used in the practice of casting lots to reveal the future. This practice, more popularly known as "throwing the bones," was often used at oracles and by the Sibyls to connect with the gods and petition the Fates to reveal their secrets.

Smoke Scrying

There's nothing more Hekatean than relaxing into the flames of a huge bonfire and opening up to the messages of our Mother. Candle scrying, focusing on the burning flame as a conduit of connection with the spirits, is one technique that frees us from the constrictions of more structured methods of divination, like the tarot. The trick is to sink into the spirit of the flame and allow your thoughts to come and go so you can connect to the spirits and Goddesses.

Capnomancy, scrying using smoke, is an another excellent practice for opening up to the Goddesses when burning botanicals. Select ones that speak to your intention, whether it's for guidance about finding a new job or for repairing a damaged romantic relationship. Burn fennel seeds with mugwort for the former and rose petals with skullcap for the latter. The Hieros Pyr Incense (see page 74) is excellent for all types of smoke scrying.

Oracular and Tarot Cards

The spirits of the pharmakoi can be summoned using the many beautiful botanical oracle decks available. This technique is called *cartomantica*. Use these cards in spells as you would their corresponding botanicals. Carry one card as a charm or bind them together into a talisman. Study the cards and connect to the spirit of the pharmakoi by contemplating specific cards.

Many cards in tarot decks feature specific botanicals. Reading the book that came with your deck will provide insight. Charge your decks of cards by placing them in a black bag and then adding the Hieros Pyr Incense (see page 74).

XI. AGIA

The Sacred

My feet touching the earth,
Feeling your pulse with each step.
The blood-fire of your womb
That birthed the universe.
Awakening your sacred Horde,
Both beast and botanical.
The spirits of flesh and ether
That walk the world on this darkest of nights.
So does yout blood-fire call to your witches
On this darkest of nights,
Offering nourishment.
The Mother speaks:
"Drink from my cup,
Dine at my feast."
And I do.

We restore our sacredness through the nourishment provided by our altars and rites, entering into the delights of Hekate's Feast. The spiritual sustenance offered through the Witch Mother can be augmented by celebrating a feast that also feeds the body, our *corpus sacris*. Such feasts can also be offered to Hekate, Circe, and Medea. We share in the reciprocal bounty of the sacred feast that blesses soul, mind, and body. The Triple Goddesses are well pleased by our offerings made from their Garden. What favors them most is when our offerings are sincere—whether an elaborate cheesecake or a simple sharing of our favorite chocolate bar. We are their descendants; their spirits live in us. By partaking of a shared feast, we celebrate our blessed connection with them and their gifts.

In ancient times, households in certain parts of Greece took a meal to Hekate at the crossroads on nights when the moon was dark. Modern Hekateans often observe this practice, known as the *Deipnon*. The meal offering was left after a purification ritual, perhaps similar to the khernips ritual, was performed. Once the miasma was removed from the home, the protection of Hekate was sought by leaving her a lovely meal. Any offerings left at a crossroads should be considerate of those who frequent the location, especially animals.

When I chose which recipes to include in the monographs, I included the ones that I most love for celebrating Hekate's Feast, from the Goat Cheese Crescents to that unforgettable Dark Goddess Cheesecake. Add your own protein—a local species of fish is most traditional—and you will truly be dining with the Queens. Set their places at your table and welcome them in. Alternatively, a simple tea ritual with the Crossing the Veil blend and a plate of biscuits, coupled with a lovely incense, is sure to welcome them.

The Crossroads

For those of us who belong to her Horde, our offerings are made in gratitude. We meet her at the crossroads to stand in our power, while banishing those who would harm us out of fear. Juniper is an ideal botanical ally for connecting with Hekate at her sacred crossroads. It opens the way by banishing harmful energies, cleansing the soul, evoking our Mother's presence, and instilling calm clarity. How useful the ubiquitous juniper is for mind, body, and soul.

Juniper is perfect for entering the crossroads, that portal where the veil between the material world and the Other World can be transcended. Medea used juniper in her spells—for instance, when she tamed a fierce snake by placing sprigs over its eyes while dousing it with other herbs and singing her incantation. Ancient statues of Hekate sculpted from juniper have been found. It was also special to Circe, who burned it as an incense. Hail to the original witch for her use of juniper. Heed her practice: snip a sprig and burn it—fresh or dried. The smoke is a lovely white and the smell speaks of comfort, clarity, and clairvoyance.

As a pharmaka, explore the botanicals at the crossroads. You'll find different species than in other nearby places. Keep in mind that the crossroads extend to all junctures of sea, land, and sky, as well as the meeting point of roads and paths. Bogs, ponds, and swamps open the way to the Other Side as they combine the reflected energy of the sky with their often plentiful botanicals and the murkiness of their depths. A spot in the forest that may feel like a portal to the Other Side is probably a crossroad.

The Altar

Altars are portals of power that connect us to the spirits evoked within their contents. Think of them as a synergistic grid that becomes a unified force for evoking the spirits you seek. If you follow my blog, you'll know that I have a thing for elaborate altars, full of many botanicals, statues, bones, stones, and other relics. What you don't see are the private altars that I have around my home, with bits of botanicals, found stones, and deeply personal objects. There is no right way to create an altar or to incorporate the pharmakoi into it. Use the monographs to guide you in choosing the right objects for your altar's purpose, and then let your intuition guide you as you create a sacred space that can be incredibly nourishing.

Create your own crossroads altar by combining branches and twigs from birch, pine, juniper, or oak into a tripod and placing icons of the Triple Goddess inside the three legs. Hang charms, bones, ribbons, and other relics on the branches. Another way to create a crossroads altar is by taking one botanical from each of the three archetypes (Chthonia, Enodia, and Astrodia) and forming a six-rayed star, like the center of Hekate's Wheel.

Altars can be just about anything that speaks of the sacred to you. Arranging dandelions in a circle around your favorite crystals and adding a white candle creates a lovely healing altar. Place talismans of those for whom you are creating blessings in the circle.

The Ritual

Our rituals are our expressions of the sacred through our words and movements. We can speak to the spirits, hold silent space, or dance in delight. A ritual can be a moment of quiet gratitude or as intense as the Triple Goddesses rite. Rituals create stillness within us, even when we are moving about, which is a sign that we've transcended the mundane to enter the sacred. Time slips away as we are in this state of flow. Many botanicals are masterful for helping us achieve this energy. Resins like benzoin, frankincense, and myrrh always evoke the spirit of sacred rites and activate our inner divine. Basil, sage, and thyme are also excellent for encouraging the creation and performance of rituals.

In general, a ritual begins with a call to the spirits sought, whether they are the Septem Novum or the Triple Goddesses. This evocation is accompanied by an offering, after which the petition, or the purpose of the rite, is expressed to the spirit in attendance. We then spend time in their presence, communicating with them and experiencing their sacredness. We end our rituals by expressing gratitude to higher-order spirits and our Goddesses and releasing the energies of lower-order ones. In general, treat the pharmakoi, when they are evoked as spirits, as higher-order beings and their physical *materia* as lower-order. As with any relationship, the more you approach the entities with respect, the more they'll let you know how they wish to be treated.

Triformis Ritual

The three fundamental parts of any sacred rite are banishing, protection, and blessing. We banish the harmful, protect from further trouble, and bless ourselves, our beloveds, our spaces, and our goddesses and spirits. We call upon the magick, medicine, and mystery of plant spirits to accomplish these three aspects of any sacred rite. The name of this ritual is an ancient term meaning "of three faces." The term thus also applies to the Triple Goddesses and reflects the three parts of plant spirit witchcraft: magick, medicine, and mystery.

Begin with the khernips ritual, then protect your space using the sacred fire by lighting a dressed candle and encircling your immediate environment to create a closed sacred space. This is the flame that protects and nourishes, creating the environment for activating the blessing. For the blessing, choose botanicals appropriate for your focus. An incense made of bay, mugwort, and sage is an excellent all-purpose blesser. Inhale the smoke and use a feather to direct it outward toward all those you are blessing.

You can do this ritual as is and also to start all sacred rites. You can adapt it for the various stages of the life cycle as well. For celebrating the birth of a child, anoint the baby with the *aqua sacris* created during the khernips process, surround the infant with an anointed candle, and bless it with a blend of lavender, rosemary, and yarrow. For adolescents embarking on the journey to adulthood, anoint them with the sacred water, protect them with the candle, and bless them with a blend of appropriate plant spirits—oak for masculinity and black cohosh for femininity.

Hekate teaches that, without death, there is no life. Perform this ritual for the departed using botanicals that will ease their transition to the spirit world, like a blend of lavender, poppy, and sage. Perform it for marriages with a suitable blend tailored to the couple. Aster, dandelion, and lavender with bay and skullcap will ensure an enduring happiness. The ritual done as part of a birthday celebration is an excellent sacred addition to the festivities.

This ritual can be adapted to other momentous occasions as well, like blessing a new home, starting at a new school or job, or even the new beginning that comes after a divorce or breakup. For a home ritual, perform each segment in each of the rooms and then do it around the perimeter. Bay, juniper, and yarrow are excellent for this. Fennel is perfect for school and work. After a breakup or other emotional loss, use dittany of Crete, lavender, rose, and yarrow. Perform the ritual for your beloved pets as well, whether to welcome a new kitten or to say farewell to an old friend. The ritual can also be used for major acquisitions and purchases, from new cars to furniture.

In this ritual, you communicate with a pharmakoi in order to receive its magick and medicine and glimpse the mysteries of the deeper world. Approach the botanical with caution and respect. Sit with the plant spirit. Don't expect immediate contact. Consider this as no different from connecting with Hekate or even other humans. This takes time and practice. You'll know you're connected when you feel a tug on your outstretched cord from the plant. The green cord will stretch out toward you, bringing you the medicine you need.

Pharamakoi can be invoked into our beings through blending and merging. It is entirely up to you how open you are to letting the plant possess you to deliver its medicine. Go cautiously with the more powerful plant teachers, especially those in Hekate's Poison Garden.

Offer your thanks to the spirit for opening to you. Tell the botanical of your intention for the ritual. Ask the plant spirit what is there for you to know about it. Listen to any messages. Record any specific information in your Book of Life. Then thank the plant for lending its energies to your working and gently disconnect your power cord.

When you are doing this ritual, you may find that you are being pulled to a deeper connection to the botanical. There are several plant spirits with whom I have a relationship—from my close spiritual connection with rose to my household love for sage. These are my personal pharmakoi.

DIRECTIONS

Let the interaction flow naturally, while maintaining your boundaries. Only go as deep as you want to.

- ⚜ Begin by connecting to the emotional wisdom, letting it come through the Lower Self. This is a reciprocal interaction. When the pharmakoi shows you an image, respond by sharing your immediate reactions.

- ⚜ Try to avoid applying words to the experience.

- ⚜ See colors; feel emotions.

- ⚜ Ask the spirit to share gnosis with your embodied being from theirs (the Middle Self).

- ⚜ Feel the sensations that the plant shares and respond in kind.

- ⚜ Finally, connect with the intellect and mystical abilities of the botanical spirit and share your reactions (the Higher Self).

Magickal Objects

Statues, images, symbols, and other representations of deities are beautiful, but their power is much more than aesthetic. These objects are beacons that connect us with the gods and Goddesses. Properly activated, they serve as a portal to communicate with the deity. Offerings are often left in the form of icons as a sign of veneration. Dressing statues and images is another way to honor your deities. Placing botanicals, ribbons, bones, charms, and more on icons is a form of veneration.

Through the process of vivification, magickal objects become attuned to the energy of the deity. In some traditions, part of the deities' energy becomes ensouled within the object, while in other approaches, the representation serves as a conduit. These objects should be cleansed, protected, and activated. In general, I recommend using a wash that is specific for sacred work. The khernips ritual can be adapted for this use, with two wash basins being used.

Vivification is the process of activating a representation or magickal object and linking it to your chosen deity. It includes petitioning the deity to bless both the object and its owner, and to activate it as a means for connecting to her. Ensouling a statue or other object directs the energy of the spirit into it. When petitioning the chosen god or Goddess to deify an object, it's likely they will leave their imprint on it, creating a portal for connecting with them.

- ⚜ Prepare an appropriate offering to make as you petition the blessing of the object.

- ☙ Anoint the object, usually with oil, although dirt and smoke can be used for objects not amenable to liquid anointing. Gods and goddesses can have different requirements. Representations of chthonic deities like Hekate, Persephone, and Hermes should be anointed working from the head down, finishing with the Under World that is their principle domain.

- ☙ Your anointing oil should be made of a fixative (base oil) and botanicals that are sacred to your chosen deity. Chthonic deities, for example, are amenable to deathwalking oil, but all deities will accept the sovereignty oil, as it acknowledges their power and your own.

- ☙ Anoint three times: once for protection, once for their blessing, and once for activation. You can revivify an existing object or use a new one. You can recite something like the following, as you do each of the three rounds.

Hail, _____,
I honor you with this _____.
Attend me now,
Protect this _____.
Bless it with your _____.
Pour your spirit into it,
Rendering a connection between me and you.
I pledge to honor you.
Hail, _____,
I give you this offering as a token of my sincerity.
I am grateful for your powers bestowed in this _____.

Magickal objects that become depleted of their power can be re-cleansed and recharged following the steps above.

XII. SOPHIA

The Wisdom

I crave the depths,
The darkness,
The unknown,
The deepest places inside of me
That are infinite and pure.
I long for the heights,
The fire,
The mysteries,
The ascent into countless possibilities.
I stand at the crossroads,
The threshold,
The in-between,
And I am stillness.

The journey to wisdom—*sophia*—takes place one step at a time as we go deep within and transcend to the forces beyond. This occurs when we dance within ourselves, uniting the shadow and soul. As practitioners of botanical witchcraft, we turn to our beloved pharmakoi to partner us in this eternal dance. Entering expanded consciousness is where we truly go deep into this dance to encounter the ecstasy.

As spiritual medicine, botanicals work on our physiological being to alter certain neurochemicals so that our ability to experience the mysteries within and without is enhanced. They also work directly on our spiritual DNA to broaden our connection to the etheric realms. When we drink, anoint, or inhale their spirits, we activate our attunement to all that exists outside of regular consciousness. They assist us in our expansion undertakings so that we may go further on the journey of the soul, as we work toward ascending beyond the need for corporeal bodies. They, too, are progressing, with many presenting to us as pure spirits, no longer constricted by physical encasement.

Dancing Partners

Many of the pharmakoi are our able partners in opening the way, expanding our dance floor to uncharted spiritual territory. Through inhaling their sacred smoke, consuming their potions, anointing with their spirits, and even being in their presence, we can travel deep into ourselves and then outward to the unseen worlds. I've offered many techniques, including Medea's Flying Ointment (see page 156), the Mugwort Medicine Patch (see page 154), and the Crossing the Veil tea (see page 163), that will help open you to the deeper world.

The Mother and her daughters are our guides as we cross the threshold into the etheric, leaving the corporeal behind. At times, we enter this space when we perform our rituals and spells, but it is often through ecstatic practices like journeying and trance ceremonies that we truly cross over to the Other Side.

Chronos and Kairos

The Green World follows a rhythm of life-death-rebirth that is cyclical rather than linear. Hekate's Wheel is this circle, always spinning. The Goddesses and all spirits function on this circular time, kairos, rather than human chronological time. When we enter into the world of spirits, we step into the kairos. As such, our interactions may not proceed according to the linear restrictions we impose on ourselves. We may have a profound experience, feel nothing special, or even fall asleep. Days after, we may suddenly receive a profound transmission in waking life or the dream world. Signs will appear. Be open to them. Pay attention to unusual occurrences.

Two stories from my students may help you to understand how the Goddesses come to us. In the first, a woman kept encountering the same man, totally unknown to her, at her workplace every day. No matter what time she arrived for work, he was leaving the building and held the door for her. She got a certain vibe from him that he was an *angelos*—a messenger—from Hekate. She was going through a very difficult time and, each time they passed, she felt as if she were in the presence of the divine. She felt calm after each brief encounter. This woman was open to the Goddess speaking to her as she willed it, trusting that Hekate would know how best to offer her comfort. She was *paying* attention instead of *seeking* attention.

In the second story, a mentor was in deep study of a coven ritual, practicing the hand movements and verses quite intensely. When he finally did the ritual with another coven member, he was disappointed that his experience was lackluster. Two days later, he happened to glance in the mirror and was immediately pulled into kairos to experience a profound soul retrieval.

Meditation

Meditation is the shifting of awareness to being present within ourselves; it creates the dance floor where we explore our twin flame. It moves our vantage point from the sense of self to our *true* self—from having thoughts to being *aware* of having thoughts. It shifts us from being an actor to the director. This is why meditation is so vital to us on our journey, because it is the micro-act of power that becomes the macro-experience of sovereignty—the experience of wholeness.

The ability to transcend through ecstatic trance is strengthened through the regular practice of expanding our conscious mind through meditation. When we rush too fast to experience the deeper world, we run the risk of "spiritual bypassing," which is experienced as physical, psychological, and spiritual distress. This can be avoided by regularly doing the dance of the shadow and soul that meditation brings.

When we become aware of our thoughts through contemplation (which is the beginning of meditation), we create unity within. We understand that we are both actor *and* director. I think common misperceptions about meditation make the practice seem so intimidating. Meditation is not emptying the mind; it's mindfulness. It's sitting with yourself; it's seeing thoughts as within your control. It's consciously shifting your attention to a mantra, mental imagery, or music so that their vibrations can attune you further toward wholeness.

Meditation can open the door to trance, where we experience a connection to the deeper world—where we explore the mysteries within and in the

cosmos, and receive messages from the divine of our understanding and our spirit guides.

Three-Selves Meditation

Shifting our awareness to our spiritual power centers encourages us to experience the wholeness within us and permits connection to the universal flow. We are beautiful creations of the Garden of the Goddess, consisting of roots—the Lower Self—trunk—the Middle Self—and branches—the Upper Self. At times, we are so preoccupied with life that we lose our connection to our sacredness within, in the same way that we forget we are part of the Green World. This meditation, also known as the *Meditatio Corpus Pharmaka*, unifies the root, which is the seat of emotions, with the trunk, which is the unifying force that joins the Lower to the Higher Self, which is reflected in our branches. This is the meditation of plant spirit witches that reconnects us within to empower our own magick, medicine, and mystery.

It is important, when performing this meditation, that there be no unwanted energy present in your meditation space. Burn juniper or sage to get rid of any miasma lurking around. A bowl of salt will also work. Performing the khernips ritual is a powerful way to start any meditation. Remove unnecessary electronics from the space.

If you are feeling distracted, begin by counting down from 13, seeing each number on the screen of your mind. Expand this meditation by envisioning yourself as a specific botanical. Are you a beautiful, yet thorny rose? Perhaps a super-healing yarrow?

THE ROOTS

The Lower Self represents magick. Its center is located at the root, within your pelvis. Begin there. Stretching your roots deep into the soil of the garden, connect with the roots deep down in the earth. Release all that blocks and binds you to where it will be reborn.

⚜ Begin with your current feelings. Are you stressed or at peace? Whatever emotions are within you, acknowledge them and sink deeper into them, as they become one unified experience of wholeness. Now explore the state of your physical being. Allow your root, through your sitting bones and feet, to become rooted to the earth beneath.

- Where are you holding tension? Release that gently down through your body, letting it dissolve into the ground beneath you.

- Feel the earth beneath you restore your magick, drawing it up through your roots.

The Trunk

The Middle Self is the power seat for medicine. Its center is located at the heart. It represents the combination of the external material world with your body and inner life, adding the power of the sacred unseen world. This all comes together at the crossroads of the heart center.

- Breathe into your heart center, feeling the beautiful fire within you, allowing it to spread through your body.

- Stretch out this fire so that it nourishes all that is blessing to you and burns away all that harms. See this fire of yours connected to all the world around you. This is the medicine of the trunk.

The Branches

The Higher Self center is located at the crown. These are our branches, stretching up, up into the mysteries.

- Become aware of your thoughts, feelings, and embodied state. See your thoughts as fleeting images on your mind-screen. Coming and going. You aren't attached to any of them. None are right or wrong; they just are. Non-judgment is the practice at this stage of meditation. You stretch up toward the Starry Road, becoming attuned to the mystical energy above.

- Rest here in this space, allowing thoughts and feelings to come and go. Slowly allow yourself to go deeper within, until you find stillness. Be in this place where your Goddesses and spirits can speak freely with you. This is the mystery.

- When you are finished, release your connection to the Starry Road, gently pulling your energy back into your crown.

- Separate from the world around you by pulling your energy back into your heart center.

THE
WISDOM

- ✢ Disconnect from the ground by pulling up your energetic roots.

- ✢ Count back up to 12, leaving that one bit of connection to your energetic self and the deeper world.

Fire Dancing

Within each of us burns the eternal Wheel of Fire, symbol of Hekate's power that fuels all of the natural world. This fire-dancing ritual, *Animarum Pyriphoitos*, is a kinetic ecstatic ritual in which you will enter the Wheel of Fire through actions as well as words. Play music that gets your wheel of fire going to help you ease into the dance. Hekate's Wheel of Fire burns bright, shining the way, nourishing us; but it also destroys all that no longer serves. The fire illuminates the way to wholeness within and to deeper wisdom. You will experience the pharmakoi as they are strengthened by the flames, releasing their sacred smoke, covering you with their ash, and blessing you with their wisdom.

DIRECTIONS

- ✢ Blend equal parts benzoin, mugwort, and American mandrake well with a mortar and pestle. Crush the benzoin first, then gently macerate the mandrake, and finally incorporate the mugwort.

- ✢ Burn as incense during the ritual to experience the flames fully. The mixture can also be used in an oil for anointing the Septem Novum on the body. Combine about $1/3$ cup of olive oil with $1/4$ tsp of mandrake, 1 tsp of mugwort, and 1 crushed fingernail-sized knob of benzoin. Cap well and keep in a cool, dry, dark place. Gently shake each day. I recommend that you set this blend on the New Moon for use during the Full Moon. I find that anointing my feet, wrists, crown, heart center, and lower belly (not too close to sensitive bits) with this oil works well for inducing fire dancing, especially with the incense burning. If you're new to mandrake, test a drop of the oil on the inside of your right elbow.

- ✢ Construct an altar with fiery symbolism and dress to bring out the fire dancer in you. As with all rituals, perform the khernips ritual if the space is unclean.

EVOCATION

❦ Envision the Wheel of Fire spinning deep within you at your heart center. As you move your hips, you swirl it into motion, spreading the fire.

❦ See this fire spreading out from you, stretching out to all the natural world, connecting your fire to theirs, forming the Wheel of Fire.

❦ When you are ready, call out to Hekate:
I call to you, Terrible Queen of the Hieros Pyr,
Your fire reigns.
Your flames fuel all that is.
Hail, Hieros Pyr, Keeper of the Wheel of Fire.

PETITION

Customize this as you feel led or speak as is. Pause after the evocation to connect fully.

❦ Steady your breathing and continue to dance.

❦ Allow messages to come forward.

❦ Plant your feet firmly to the ground before petitioning to enter the Wheel of Fire. Say:
Grant me access to your Wheel of Fire!
Reveal to me the mysteries therein.

❦ You'll feel the connection here if access is granted. Say:
I enter your Hieros Pyr,
I walk your Wheel of Fire,
Dancing in the flames.

ENTRANCE

❦ Resume your physical dancing if you have stopped.

❦ Embrace the flames as you move.

❦ When you are ready, continue with the petition:
Let me drink your fire,
Fueling my power,
Let me carry your fire,
Burning all that which no longer serves,

Igniting what must be born this moment,
Revealing to me the mysteries of your Wheel of Fire!

- ⚷ Remain in the Wheel, continuing to dance and experience the power.

- ⚷ Take your time disconnecting from the Wheel of Fire. You may have been given a symbol of your unique fire.

- ⚷ Steady your breath. When you are ready, finish the ritual with the benediction:
  For your fire is without end or beginning,
  The flame burns and gives birth,
  The smoke spreads your power,
  And I rise from the ashes
  In gratitude,
  I take my leave now.

The firewalking trance can leave you depleted or invigorated. An excess of either is a sign that you need to pull yourself back to the Middle World using centering. You can also use the sensory grounding technique by connecting with taste, smell, touch, and sight. Emotions may surface as you do the ritual and in the hours after, because you have shone the light deep within your spirit-self. Connect with a trusted friend to share your experiences. You can always reach out to me. After you disconnect from the fire, you may become very chilled. Prevent this by wrapping up in a blanket as soon as the ritual is complete. Make sure you eat a carb-rich snack while processing the wisdom received.

Journeying to the Garden

Hekate's Garden is our entire universe—corporeal and etheric. Her Anima Mundi infuses all there is. However, there is an epicenter of the Garden, an innermost chamber which all the master spirits inhabit. These spirits can wander through the rest of the etheric/physical Middle Worlds as well. We may meet them when we hunt the wild pharmakoi. They can visit us in our dreams, and we can intentionally seek them out through trance. Unlike fire dancing, this journey is one of calm awareness. It provides a counterpoint to the heat of the Wheel of Fire. This journey can be done at any point in the lunar cycle. Take note of the lunar phase and astrological considerations for your chosen date in your Book of Life, then include these possible influences when processing your experiences.

You can prepare for this journey by working with bay laurel, mugwort, and sage. Create this incense, make a psychic patch or flying ointment, or collect living plants to arrange on your altar. If you don't have access to the material forms of these spirits, purchase or make plant spirit cards of them. Arrange your altar honoring these spirits. To augment the journeying experience, you can use a patch or an ointment, or consume an infusion.

I recommend using the khernips ritual of purification before beginning the journey and burning the Three Keys as an incense or heating of an oil made of it in a diffuser.

The Journey

Begin with the Three-Selves Meditation (see page 250). Once you are unified, turn your attention inward, going deep into yourself. You find yourself in your Inner Temple, your sacred center. Once inside, tend your fire, greet anyone in residence, and notice the surroundings. You notice a door at the back of your temple. Open it, noticing the appearance, the symbols, the energy. Step through.

Once through the door, you are surrounded by the verdant world. Illuminated with the essence of the Anima Mundi, it glows. Enlivened by the Anima Mundi, its vibrations create a vibrant hum. At your feet, sprites and pixies scamper. You greet your animal companions. Your path is made of your stone spirit allies—amethyst, quartz, obsidian, red jasper, and others known only to you.

You experience a familiarity, a reconnection, a dissolution of the false separation between you and the spirit world. Your three souls sing in harmony with each other and the place. You have come home to Hekate's Garden. You are not here to wander, but are full of purpose, to meet the Pharmakoi Kyrios—Salvia, Artemisia, and Nobilis.

Your protectors, guides, and teachers watch over you. There is a charge in the air—a power, a sense of royalty being present. Looking ahead, you see three beings seated on thrones. You approach them, knowing that you are in the presence of the supreme plant spirits.

Their size is substantial; the thrones are living creations, as are they. The air is permeated with their energy, the smells of bay, mugwort, and sage. It is like a gentle mist, coating you, seeping into your pores. There are smaller

pharmakoi milling about in this place, which you now realize is a natural throne room that is home to many spirits. There are animals, birds, and other creatures. The river running through is rife with watery creatures and spirits.

The plant spirits descend from their thrones, coming toward you. As they approach, their form becomes more similar in appearance and size to you. There is deep comfort, power, and connection between them, which they extend to you, stretching out their branches and tendrils. They stand before you, joined, and wrap you in their shared embrace. Their tenderness and power run through you.

You instinctively know their names. Salvia wraps you with protection and inner work, and empowers your witchcraft. Artemisia's embrace brings clarity, visions, a strengthening of your psychic power, and the gift of integrity. Nobilis gifts you with kindness, a strength of will, and support for others that creates true prosperity.

Joined in this circle, you merge your own tendrils, branches, and roots with theirs, sharing your experiences, talents, and desires. You communicate through words and feelings, through the movement of your circle. You receive their wisdom.

They slowly begin to detach from you, gently releasing their tendrils, branches, and roots, returning to their chosen appearance and stature. Mighty giants once more. You look down at your hands to find the symbols given to you. Thank them for their protection, guidance, and wisdom. Watch them ascend their thrones.

You bid them farewell, knowing that you can return to Hekate's Garden whenever you wish to explore deeper. Walk through the red door back to the liminal space between the energetic realms and your Inner Temple. Close the door, again confident that, now that you have opened this world, you can return anytime.

Cross back into your Inner Temple, spending time here as you wish to communicate with those in residence, sharing your experience. Perhaps spend some time on your throne contemplating what you encountered.

When you are ready, leave your temple, walking up the path to your physical self once again. Begin to return to embodiment, counting your steps, noticing how they become heavier with the weight of your physical being as you are reunited.

Bring back with you the wholeness in your soul, your spirit self united within and without. This unison spreads to your Three Selves. Indeed, your body vibrates with the feeling of wholeness. Spend some time here relishing the experience, imprinting deep into your physical being, reconnecting and activating. This is a calm wholeness—confident, full of the wisdom you've gained, healed from the illusion of separation. Merging souls and selves, intuition and intellect, meeting at the heart center that joins us to the external world.

Returning now to the corporeal Middle Self, let your attention turn to your physical being. Begin with your breath, expanding and releasing natural deep breaths, sending out your essence back into your surroundings. Feel your neck, shoulders, arms, hands. Turn your attention down through your torso, into your root and legs. Breathe in and out, using the breath to shift back into your physical being. Release your tether to the earth beneath, fully restored to your body now. Spend some time in this space, consolidating the wisdom and experience you have gained.

THE
WISDOM

XIII. INITIO

The Mystery

I claim my rightful place
Among my kindred
In the Garden of the Goddess.

Initiation (*Initio*) is the greatest of mysteries, for with it comes the final destruction of the illusion of separation. The wisdom gained through pursuing the majesty of the Anima Mundi, by dancing in her sacred fire, has shown me that the things that brought me the most pain are my greatest blessings. These trials, bestowed by the Witch Mother herself, are necessary tests as we move deeper into initiation. As she gave her ancient daughters challenges to prove their mettle, she grants me these blessings disguised as banes. Initiation can be finalized through a beautiful ritual, but true initiation comes when we stand before the Mother in our brokenness. We are called to the practice of pharmakeia by the Mother, for she knows that, through her path of plant spirit witchcraft, we can find our wholeness. Our cry of desperation in the night opens the gates to our own depths, which allows us to be embraced by Hekate.

Our culture avoids the darkness. We fear our shadows. But true initiation resides only in the depths. We are initiated into our wholeness through spiritual dismemberment and death. The wisdom of the pharmaka is this: All things must die to be reborn. That is the experience of initiation—to allow to die, creating space for deepening our connections with the verdancy and the Triple Goddesses. We level up in the messages we receive from our allies, our spells become stronger, and we journey deeper into the spiritual Garden that is all of the cosmos. Like Circe and Medea, we find wholeness through this dance between the spirit and the corporeal worlds. We are marked long before birth into this particular life—wild witches dancing within the gates of

Hekate's Garden. This is the dance of wholeness between the shadow and the soul. Our practice of pharmakeia is the tune to which we move. Initiation is the reconnection to our source.

When we experience this reconnection, known as merging, our connection to the Goddesses and to all spirits greatly expands. We can open ourselves up to welcoming them into our space through evocation in ways that truly reveal the enormity of their presence. This is different from when we connect to them through our minds. It is a visceral experience. We feel their touch on our skin; we hear their breath; they stand with us. We can expand this further by allowing them to interact within our beings through invocation. The process of invoking involves dancing with the spirits in the same way that we do with our shadow selves. This experience permits the spirits to speak directly to us, as though they were in our minds rather than as external entities.

Blending goes deeper yet. It is the sensation that the spirit is actually interacting with us at the cellular level. Aspecting, or trance possession, occurs when we permit the spirit to use our physical selves as vessels through which they can speak or act. The lack of sense of self that we experience in aspecting is similar to what occurs in all forms of invoking, but aspecting often brings a complete removal of the conscious mind. This should be reserved for rare occasions.

The beautiful experience of invoking the Goddesses and other spirits and becoming viscerally connected with them is one of the rightful practices of plant spirit witchcraft. With initiation comes invocation, through our claim as practitioners of pharmakeia. As Hekatean witches, we gain the power to commune more deeply with the Goddesses and the pharmakoi.

In the initiation below, you allow the presence of Hekate, Medea, and Circe to permeate your space and, if you are comfortable doing so, draw them into your being. Give them space within you so that you can experience wholeness as a Hekatean witch. Feel their spirits coursing through your veins, communicate with them from within your mind, and dance with them as a unified whole if you are so inclined. This ritual is a celebration of your wisdom.

Invoking and initiation do not require supplication, but rather surrender. Supplication refers to bowing down to the Goddesses to beg for favors. It places you in a position of fear, in which you try to avoid upsetting the spirits because you don't trust yourself to solve your own problems. Surrender, on the other hand, occurs when you willingly begin to seek your truth and ask the spirits for their assistance in doing so. You reject what is false to you. You experience the spiritual dismemberment of releasing all that no longer serves. You are reborn into who you are meant to be—a sovereign witch who walks the crooked path of the pharmaka.

The Triple Goddesses Ritual

At times while writing this book, the Goddesses insisted that I include certain things that I felt were beyond what I could deliver in written form. This was the case for this ritual of initiation. The version I'm sharing here is similar to the one we do in my coven, with adaptations for doing it on your own. Circe and Medea were strident in their direction that this was the only ritual suited to end your journey into Hekate's Garden. When we perform this ritual, it is common for the presence of the Goddesses to be incredibly visceral. Merging typically occurs, as does spontaneous aspecting. It is profoundly beautiful. May your journey with it be so.

Only you can know when you are ready to claim your rightful place as one of Hekate's chosen. The ideal time for performing this initiation ritual is during Hekate's sacred month of November, but do it whenever the time is right for you.

PREPARATION

⚜ *Timing:* The Dark Moon

⚜ *Purification:* Khernips ritual. I also recommend that you burn an incense of your own design that will become your personal power blend.

⚜ *Location:* If you're doing this outside (which I recommend), find a spot that permits you to connect to the Under World aspects of the Goddesses, like a small cave or marsh that is a natural opening to the deeper world, representing the Cave of Initiation. If doing the ritual indoors, construct a chthonic altar (low to the ground), placing a symbolic crossroads on it to represent your transition from novice to initiate.

⚜ *Adornment:* Create a key of initiation to adorn yourself with during the ritual.

⚜ *Proclamation:* Initiation is an intimate process between you and the Goddesses. Writing your own proclamation of initiation to read during the ritual deepens the experience.

THE
MYSTERY

264

- ⚜ *Altar:* Use iconography of the Goddesses and your favored pharmakoi, and your tools (blade, bowl, censor).

- ⚜ *Offerings:* Chose botanicals to present as your token of affection, commitment, and gratitude.

- ⚜ *Supplies:* Three candles, three images or icons of the Goddesses, anointing oil, and your chosen incense.

- ⚜ *Oracle:* During the ritual, do a divinatory reading seeking the wisdom of these Goddesses. Construct a coterie if you haven't already, or bring your cards into the ritual space.

- ⚜ *Blessing:* All tools of witchcraft can be blessed by the Goddesses during this ritual.

RITUAL

Perform the khernips ritual using your chosen botanicals. Take the time to connect with your breath prior to beginning the ritual, using the Three-Selves Meditation (see page 250). Keep in mind that these are mighty Goddesses, so prior to evocation establish how comfortable you are with merging your energies with theirs. If you're not comfortable letting them in, stand in their presence and let them speak with you.

- ⚜ Kneeling in front of your altar, say:
  I claim this space sacred to myself,
  Protected from all unwanted and unwelcome attention from spirits and
      all other beings.
  I enter into this ritual of my own free will, of sound mind and strong
      spirit.
  I proclaim that I am a practitioner of witchcraft,
  Chosen by Hekate,
  And descended from Circe and Medea.
  I open my Lower Self, seat of emotions and magick, to this ritual and to
      the Triple Goddesses of witchcraft.
  I open my Middle Self, home of action and interaction with the material
      world, to this ritual and to the Triple Goddesses of witchcraft.
  I open my Higher Self, realm of intellect and gateway to the mysteries
      of the Starry Road, to this ritual and to the Triple Goddesses of
      witchcraft.

May my emotions be true,
My actions just,
And my thoughts pure
In this ritual and for all time.

❁ Pause here to let the energies of the Three Selves mingle throughout your being, connecting and activating their correspondences within your soul, until you feel unified within.

❁ Focus on the altar, connecting your own unified energy to the symbols and correspondences upon it, creating an enclosed, merged, energetic space from which you can welcome in the Goddesses.

❁ Make the following petition while presenting your chosen offerings:
Now I make these offerings to you, Mighty Sovereign Queens,
Expressing my gratitude and petitioning your presence.
I make these offerings to Hekate and her Eternal Witches.
To Hekate, Queen of Wisdom, Regina Maleficarum, Keeper of the
    Keys of Witchcraft, I call now, hear my words, accept this humble
    offering, and bless me with your presence.
To Circe, Original Witch, Regina Pharmakeia, Queen of Botanical
    Witchery, I call now, hear my words, accept this humble offering, and
    bless me with your presence.
To Medea, Eternal Witch, Regina Venificarum, Queen of the Poison
    Path, I call now, hear my words, accept this humble offering, and
    bless me with your presence.

❁ Pause here to let them accept the offerings, then stand in front of the altar and, with your hands at your heart center, say:
In this state of grace and position of power,
I now call upon the Goddesses of witchcraft.
- *Hail , Hekate, Regina Maleficarum!*

❁ With your right hand down, say:
Hail, Circe, Regina Pharmakeia!

❁ With your left hand up, say:
Hail, Medea, Regina Venificarum!

❁ Pause, taking three deep, quick breaths, breathing out your energy and breathing in theirs, connecting to their presence. Then, with your hands at your heart center, say:

I welcome you into this place,
Attend me now!

✤ Pause, taking three deep, quick breaths, breathing out your energy and breathing in Hekate's, connecting to her presence. Then, with your right hand down, say:

Hail, Circe, Regina Pharmakeia,
Original Witch,
Sorceress Divine,
Queen of Animals, Plants, and Minerals.
Revealer of Truth,
Spirit Speaker.
I welcome you into this place,
Attend me now!

✤ Pause, taking three deep, quick breaths, breathing out your energy and breathing in Circe's, connecting to her presence. Then, with your left hand down, say:

Hail, Medea, Regina Venificarum,
Mistress of Healing and Pain,
Queen of Fire and Passion,
Goddess of the Shadows,
She Who Commands the Cauldron of Rebirth
And Wields the Dragon's Chariot,
I welcome you into this place,
Attend me now!

✤ Pause, taking three deep, quick breaths, breathing out your energy and breathing in Medea's, connecting to her presence. Then, with your hands at your heart center, say:
Hail, Hekate, Regina Maleficarum!

✤ With your right hand down, say:
Hail, Circe, Regina Pharmakeia!

✤ With your left hand up, say:
Hail, Medea, Regina Venificarum!

✤ Pause, taking three deep, quick breaths, breathing out your energy and breathing in theirs, connecting to their presence. Then, with your hands at your heart center, say:

Hail, Hekate, Regina Maleficarum,
Anima Mundi, Spirit of All.
Queen of Witches.
I claim my place among your witches.
Bless and protect me.

✤ Kiss her image with the index finger of your dominant hand, light the appropriate candle, and anoint your crown with the index finger of your nondominant hand.

✤ Pause here to welcome Hekate's blessing. Then, with your right hand down, say:
Hail, Circe, Regina Pharmakeia,
Original Witch,
Sorceress Divine,
Bless and protect me.

✤ Kiss her image with the index finger of your dominant hand, light the appropriate candle, and anoint your crown with the index finger of your nondominant hand.

✤ Pause here to welcome Circe's blessing. Then, with your left hand up, say:
Hail, Medea, Regina Venificarum,
Mistress of Healing and Pain,
Queen of Fire and Passion.
Bless and protect me.

✤ Kiss her image with the index finger of your dominant hand, light the appropriate candle, and anoint your crown with the index finger of your nondominant hand.

✤ Pause here to welcome Medea's blessing.
Great Goddesses and Witches,
Ancient but new,
I honor myself and each of you.

✤ Now you can make your commitment petition and adorn yourself with your talisman. While in this state of activation and connection, ask each Goddess for guidance by drawing one card/rune/bone/etc. in their name. You may also claim their blessing on all tools of witchcraft at this point.

THE
MYSTERY

- ⚜ When you are finished, stand again, if you have been kneeling or sitting, and say:
  Goddesses of Witchcraft,
  In gratitude for your blessing, accept my affection and fond farewell.

- ⚜ Pause here to begin the process of disconnection. Take three releasing breaths, then say:
  Blessed Hekate, Regina Maleficarum, accept my gratitude and fond
  *   farewell.*

- ⚜ Pause, take three releasing breaths, then say:
  Blessed Circe, Regina Pharmakeia, accept my gratitude and fond
  *   farewell.*

- ⚜ Pause, take three releasing breaths, then say:
  To Medea, Regina Venificarum, accept my gratitude and fond farewell.

- ⚜ Take three releasing breaths.

Hekate, Circe, and Medea keep their own schedule and counsel. Always keep this in mind. If they attended and blessed you during the ritual, they most likely will be close to you, perhaps even remaining constantly by your side. Or they may come to you after the ritual. The Goddesses don't always recognize our need for chronological time. Make a record of your initiation in your Book of Life.

Acknowledgments

I am most thankful to the magick, medicine, and mystery of the Garden of the Goddess. It is within the Green World, both material and etheric, that I found my own true healing. To Hekate, from whom the Garden flows, for inspiring me to take up the keys of plant spirit magick, medicine, and mystery. To Circe, who guides me through the wild woods and along the sea cliffs, and watches over my practice of plant spirit witchcraft. To Medea, the teacher who speaks only truth, no matter how harsh the medicine. To Namiweh and Millie, my spirit teachers, who have shown me the power of the plant spirits.

My corporeal teachers in plant spirit magick are many. In particular, my dear sister-witch, Willow, has shared her own medicine with me, teaching me the power of botanicals. My sister of blood and soul, Anjali, our shared passion for plant medicine has been such a blessing that we now share together with the world. Her passion for healing through herbalism has greatly inspired me. Many thanks for reading the manuscript, too.

To the students of Keeping Her Keys who read sections of the manuscript and tested the preparations, techniques, and rituals in this book, my sincerest thanks. The Keeping Her Keys community is so amazing. Every day, I receive messages saying how my work has led them to the magick, medicine, and mystery of Hekatean witchcraft. I am forever humbled and inspired by your words. To Geoffery, Ivy, Kaycee, Linda and Tania, I am so blessed to have you walk this journey with me. I can't even begin to say how thankful I am.

I also want to express my gratitude to Pinar for her excellent advice on the use of the translations and my modern adaptations of these powerful words. Pinar and I had many conversations regarding the way I took the roots of ancient words and then transformed them into new ones.

Finally, to my sons. I am the trunk that joins your roots and branches. Together we are whole. Thank you for being willing recipients of my plant spirit magick, medicine, and mystery, and my helping hands.

To learn more, visit *keepingherkeys.com*

Sources and Further Reading

Nyssa: The Call

Brannen, Cyndi (2019). *Seeking Hekate and the Deeper World. patheos.com.*

———(2017). *Hekate and Beginnings. patheos.com.*

Origio: The Source

Brannen, Cyndi (2019). "Who Are Hekate's Horde of Spirits." *keepingherkeys.com.*

——— (2019). *Keeping Her Keys: The Rise of Hekate and Her Witches. patheos.com.*

——— (2018). "Circe: Summoning the Original Witch." *keepingherkeys.com.*

——— (2018). *Medea: Her Story, Themes, Correspondences, Rituals, Spells and More. patheos.com.*

d'Este, Sorita (2002). *Circle for Hekate—Volume 1: History and Mythology.*

Harvey, William, J. (2013). "Reflections on the Enigmatic Goddess: The Origins of Hekate and the Development of Her Character to the End of the Fifth Century BC." *ourarchive.otago.ac.nz.*

Miller, Frank Justus, trans. (1960). *Seneca's Tragedies Volume 1: Hercules Furens, Troades, Medea, Hippolytus, Oedipus.*

Ogden, Daniel (2002). *Magic, Witchcraft, and Ghosts in the Greek and Roman Worlds: A Sourcebook.*

Seaton, R. C., trans. (1990). *Apollonius Rhodius: The Argonautica.* Loeb Classical Library.

Smith, William, and Charles Anton (1884). *A New Classical Dictionary of Greek and Roman Biography, Mythology and Geography.*

Spretnak, Charlene (1992). *Lost Goddesses of Early Greece: A Collection of Pre-Hellenic Myths.*

Praeparatio: The Foundation

For wildcrafting, I recommend the two classic books by Euell Gibbons, *Stalking the Wild Asparagus* (1962) and *Stalking the Healthful Herbs* (1966).

The Plant Spirit Familiar by Christopher Penczak is an excellent in-depth exploration of the many types of plant spirits.

Ratio: The System

Denning and Phillips (2011). *Planetary Magick: Invoking and Directing the Powers of the Planets*. My favorite reference for the planets.

Myss, Caroline (1996). *Anatomy of the Spirit: The Seven Stages of Power and Healing*. One of the books that has most influenced my way of thinking about the self.

Penczak, Christopher (2005). *The Temple of Shamanic Witchcraft*. Greatly influenced my approach to the Three Worlds.

Three Initiates (1912). *The Kybalion*. Explains the Hermetic principles that greatly inform the seven sacred laws. You can read it at *sacred-texts.com*.

Practica: The Process

Blackthorn, Amy (2018). *Blackthorn's Botanical Magic: The Green Witch's Guide to Essential Oils for Spellcraft, Ritual and Healing*.

Brannen, Cyndi (2019). *A Practical Guide for Making and Using Poppets in Witchery*. *www.patheos.com*.

Hieros Pyr: The Fire

Blackthorn, Amy (2019). *Sacred Smoke: Clear Away Negative Energies and Purify Body, Mind, and Spirit*. Fantastic resource for using smoke in plant spirit witchcraft.

Gnosis: The Knowledge

The information shared in the monographs was based on research from many sources, including the books listed below. The ethnographical information was based partly on the Database of Botanical Medicine of North American Indigenous Peoples, which can be found at *naeb.brit.org*.

Andrews, Ted (2009). *Animal Speak: The Spiritual and Magical Powers of Creatures Great and Small*.

Arber, Agnes. (1938). *Herbals: Their Origin and Evolution*.

Betz, Hans Dieter, ed. (1992). *The Greek Magical Papyri in Translation*.

Beyerl, Paul (1984). *The Master Book of Herbalism*.

Cech, Richo (2000). *Making Plant Medicine*.

Conway, David (1973). *The Magic of Herbs.*

Culpeper's Complete Herbal Index. *www.complete-herbal.com.*

Cunningham, Scott (1990). *Encyclopedia of Wicca in the Kitchen.*

———— (1985). *Encyclopedia of Magical Herbs.*

Grieve, Margaret (1971). *A Modern Herbal. botanical.com.*

Harrison, Karen (2011). *The Herbal Alchemist's Handbook: A Grimoire of Philtres, Exilirs, Oils, Incense, and Formulas for Ritual Use.*

Heaven, Ross, and Howard G. Charing (2006). *Plant Spirit Shamanism: Traditional Techniques for Healing the Soul.*

Illes, Judika (2014). *Encyclopedia of Witchcraft: The Complete A–Z for the Entire Magical World.*

Kynes, Sandra (2014). *Llewellyn's Complete Book of Correspondences.*

Lawless, Julia (1995). *The Encyclopedia of Essential Oils: The Complete Guide to the Use of Aromatic Oils in Aromatherapy, Herbalism, Health, and Well-Being.*

Müller-Ebeling, Claudia, Christian Ratsch, and Wolf-Dieter Storl (2003). *Witchcraft Medicine: Healing Arts, Shamanic Practices, and Forbidden Plants.*

Pearson, Nicholas (2019). *Stones of the Goddess: Crystals for the Divine Feminine.*

Pendell, Dale (2005). *Pharmako Gnosis: Plant Teachers and the Poison Path.*

Roth, Harold (2017). *The Witching Herbs: 13 Essential Plants and Herbs for Your Magical Garden.*

Simmons, Robert, Naisha Ahsian, and Hazel Ravel (2015). *The Book of Stones.*

Information on specific plants for the monographs came from a variety of sources, including:

American mandrake and mandragora: *keepingherkeys.com.*

Cinnamon: *sacredearth.com.*

Moss: Chandra, Satish, Dinesh Chandra, Anupam Barh, Pankaj, Raj Kumar Pandey, and Ishwar Prakash Sharmaa. *Journal of Traditional Complementary Medicine.* January 2017; 7(1): 94–98. *Bryophytes: Hoard of remedies, an ethno-medicinal review.*

Oak: *offthegridnews.com.*

Pine cones: LiDonnici, Lynn R. (2001). Kernos Revue internationale et pluridisciplinaire de religion grecque antique. *Single-Stemmed Wormwood, Pinecones and Myrrh: Expense and Availability of Recipe Ingredients in the Greek Magical Papyri.*

Roses: *patheos.com.*

Seaweed: Cunningham, Scott (2002). *Earth Power: Techniques of Natural Magic.*

Skullcap: *pennstatehershey.adam.com.*

Vervain: *academia.edu.*

Walnut: *druidgarden.wordpress.com.*

Magikeia: The Spell

Learn more about the psychology of flow at *positivepsychology.com.*

Brannen, Cyndi (2019). *Spellbound: Ways of Using Binding in Witchery. patheos.com.*

———— (2019). *The Truth of "A Witch That Can't Hex, Can't Heal." patheos.com.*

———— (2019). *Reasons Why Spells Fail and Remedies for Avoiding Magickal Disasters. patheos.com.*

Miller, Jason (2017). *The Elements of Spellcrafting: 21 Keys to Successful Sorcery.* A good reference.

Sibylika: The Prophecy

Auryn, Mat (2020). *Psychic Witch.* An extensive compendium of practices for unleashing your predictive powers.

Brannen, Cyndi (2017). *Dark Mother Tarot Ritual: Healing the Shadow and Revealing the Truth through Hekate's Wisdom. patheos.com.*

———— (2019). *Witches Are Soul Collectors. patheos.com.*

Pollack, Rachel (2012). *New Tarot Handbook: Master the Meanings of the Cards* is great for learning the tarot through exercises.

Sharman-Burke, Juliet (2007). *The New Complete Book of Tarot,* a great all-round reference.

Webster, Richard (2017). *Llewellyn's Complete Book of Divination: Your Definitive Source for Learning Predictive and Prophetic Techniques.*

More on the Sibyl of Cumae and her cave is available at *italiangems.wordpress.com* and *classicalwisdom.com.*

Agia: The Sacred

Dominguez Jr., Ivo (2012). *Casting Sacred Space: The Core of All Magickal Work.* An in-depth guide to casting circles and more. Highly recommended.

Sophia: The Wisdom

Brannen, Cyndi (2018). *Hekate and Soul Retrieval. patheos.com.*

———— (2019). *Managing a Spiritual Upgrade. keepingherkeys.com.*

Ingerman, Sharon (2011). *Soul Retrieval: Mending the Fragmented Self*. A classic that is excellent for learning more about reclaiming your missing pieces.

Parma, Gede (2012). *Ecstatic Witchcraft: Magick, Philosophy and Trance in the Shamanic Craft*. A good guide for inspiring you to take your practice deeper.

Initio: The Mystery

Brannen, Cyndi (2018). *Hekate and November: The Underworld, Crossroads, Death Walking & Initiation*. *patheos.com.*

———. Video demonstrating Hekate's Breath Chant. *youtube.com.*

About the Author

Cyndi Brannen, PhD, teaches the keys of magick, medicine, and mystery of the deeper world. The Keys of The Goddess she keeps are those of healer, teacher, and author. The author of the bestselling *Keeping Her Keys: An Introduction to Hekate's Modern Witchcraft*, Cyndi has also written *True Magic: Unleashing Your Inner Witch* that teaches the Sacred Seven Laws of healing, relationships, sovereignty, growth, connection, abundance, and wholeness. Her newest book is *Entering Hekate's Garden: The Magick, Medicine, and Mystery of Plant Spirit Witchcraft*.

Cyndi's extensive repertoire of healing practices include archetypal psychology, counseling, divination, energetic healing, mediumship, plant spirit medicine, psychic development, and shamanic practices. An acclaimed researcher on women's and family health, Dr. Brannen developed her passion for incorporating traditional methods of healing with her expertise on effective psychological interventions over her two decades in academia and healthcare.

Cyndi holds an earned doctorate in applied social psychology. In addition, she has studied various treatments and approaches for improving personal well-being. Her former career in health research and academia brings to her teaching and writing her expertise in evidence-based self-help programs in maternal depression, PTSD, and various childhood vulnerabilities.

Committed to equality, Cyndi is an outspoken ally for marginalized groups and is a recognized expert in gender-based analysis.

Cyndi has been teaching and writing about spiritual development, mindfulness, and meditation for over a decade. She can occasionally be coaxed to throw the bones if you ask very nicely. She lives on the coast of rural Nova Scotia with her two sons in a slightly shabby witches' cottage.

Learn more about her at *keepingherkeys.com*.

To Our Readers